The Papacy
and the Church
in the United States

Bernard Cooke,
editor

PAULIST PRESS
New York ♦ Mahwah

Library of Congress Cataloging-in-Publication Data

The Papacy and the Church in the United States / Bernard Cooke, editor.
    p. cm.
    Includes bibliographies,
    ISBN 0-8091-3070-X : $10.95 (est.)
    1. Catholic Church—United States—Bishops—History. 2. Papacy—History. 3. Catholic Church—United States—History. 4. Popes—Primacy—History of doctrines. 5. United States—Church history.
    I. Cooke, Bernard J.
    BX1407.B57P47   1989
    262'.02—dc20   89-32689
                                            CIP

Published by Paulist Press
997 Macarthur Boulevard
Mahwah, NJ 07430

Printed and bound in the
United States of America

Contents

Introduction *by Bernard Cooke* 1

Pope and Bishops Before Trent: An Historical Survey 11
    Brian Tierney

Church Unity and National Traditions:
The Challenge to the Modern Papacy, 1682–1870 25
    William L. Portier

From the Pope to the Bishops:
Episcopal Authority from Vatican I to Vatican II 55
    James L. Heft, S.M.

Rome and the Origins of the United States Hierarchy 79
    James Hennesey, S.J.

John Ireland, the Vatican, and the French Connection 99
    Marvin R. O'Connell

The Vatican and the American Church Since World War II 119
    Gerald P. Fogarty, S.J.

The Power of the Keys: The Patristic Tradition 141
    Agnes Cunningham, S.S.C.M.

Local, Regional and Universal Church Law 161
    Frederick R. McManus

The Papacy: Power, Authority, Leadership 189
    James H. Provost

Notes on the Contributors 217

Bernard Cooke

Introduction

One of the perennial patterns of the Catholic Church's life during the past millennium has been a tension between the bishop of Rome and the bishops of the rest of the Christian world. At times this has clearly been a power struggle, as in the disagreements of Nicholas I and Hincmar of Reims or in the convening and conduct of the Council of Trent. At other times the clear ascendancy of one side or the other has tended to give a surface appearance of total agreement. This latter situation prevailed in the century following Vatican I, for the council had in many people's view—even many bishops' view—solved the issue once and for all in favor of the papacy. Under the surface, however, the questions remained, found somewhat new formulations as part of the broader twentieth century challenges to social and political power, and finally led to the Second Vatican Council where the relationship between pope and bishops was the primary item on the agenda.

Vatican II's shift away from over-concentration on papal power and to the collegiality of the bishops including the pope has been acknowledged as a major reorientation, at least in theory, of the official structures of the Roman Catholic Church. There is less recognition that the context for discussing power in the church has been drastically changed because of the council's definition of the church as "the people of God" and the consequent emphasis on the active role of the laity. As with the teaching on episcopal collegiality, theory still needs to be translated into practice, but in principle the Catholic Church has turned from its "top down" model and is in the process of regaining primitive Christianity's understanding that the saving power of God is rooted in and flows from the Spirit's presence in the people.

For the moment the two issues, the relations between bishops and Rome and the recovered role of the laity, remain fairly distinct from one another. However, their interrelationship is slowly becoming apparent, and nowhere is discussion of the two questions and their intersection more creative and more important for the future of the church than in the United States. A national tradition of political democracy and relative social equality has given the church in the U.S. an ethos quite different from European Catholicism. This distinctiveness has been accentuated by the working-class immigrant origins of the U.S. church and by the fact that the episcopacy has arisen out of the common people. As early as the late eighteenth century this "democratic" aspect of U.S.

3

Catholicism had colored relations between this country's hierarchy and the Vatican.

In the wake of Vatican I and the papal encyclical "Testem benevolentiae" of 1899 condemning the "phantom heresy" of Americanism, the papacy undertook a systematic Romanization of the church in the U.S. Though for decades this proved successful—U.S. Catholicism and particularly the U.S. hierarchy became and still remains an exceptionally Rome-oriented portion of the Catholic Church—the years following Vatican II have seen a growing uneasiness in the U.S. church with regard to the Vatican's power over and intervention in Catholic life in this country.

For the moment, the felt tensions have not grown into rebellion nor essentially weakened the strong attachment of U.S. Catholics to the person of the pope, despite the somewhat sensationalizing attempts of the secular press to dramatize disputes that have arisen. Perhaps the best description of the changed climate was given by Donna Hanson during the recent visit by Pope John Paul II. Speaking as a representative for Catholic laity she pointed out that U.S. Catholics, and in a special way the laity, have come of age. There has been a major advance in people's level of information about their church and therefore in the sophistication of their understanding of their Catholicism. Exemplifying the active orientation of North Americans, large numbers of Catholics in the U.S. have assumed that Vatican II was "for real" and have started to act on the principles it stated.

This is not to say that the U.S. church as a whole is enthusiastically embracing Vatican II and trying to translate it into action. Catholics in this country are deeply split in their response to the "new" things happening in their church, and probably the majority still cling to the understandings, attitudes and practice of the 1930s, 1940s and 1950s. Not a few consider the council a mistake and expect—or at least hope—that it will gradually prove ineffective of real change. Those on the "conservative" wing of U.S. Catholicism who have had the benefit of a more educated knowledge of Vatican II and of contemporary Catholicism in general appeal to those statements in Vatican II documents which emphasize continuity with the past and, with some justification, accuse "liberals" of selective emphasis on the conciliar statements that point to change. More than a few bishops are in this more conservative group, whether out of personal conviction or out of a sense of loyalty to the present pope.

This allegiance to Pope John Paul II, whether by bishops or by others in the U.S. church, is a major factor in the growing division of American Catholicism because the Vatican has contributed in no small measure to the split. One can point to a number of incidents—the Mary Agnes Mansour case in Detroit, the still unresolved situation of Father Charles Curran and intervention in other tenure cases at Catholic University, the Archbishop Hunthausen affair—but the fundamental issue is the papacy's appointment of bishops. One can attribute to the pope nothing but the best of motives, but the fact remains—and we must acknowledge it honestly—that episcopal appointments in recent years have not increased the collegial unity of the U.S. hierarchy. This has not been accidental.

It has not helped that, despite the traditional Vatican practice of operating in secrecy, the appearances point to behind-the-scenes papal support for some basic Reagan government policies in both domestic and foreign relations, and to some pressure brought on the U.S. bishops as they spoke out on issues of war/peace and the economic order. None of this may actually be true, but belief that it is true contributes to tensions within U.S. Catholicism and between many dedicated and concerned U.S. Catholics and the Vatican. What is needed is a clearing of the air, a frank and honest confrontation of the issues, a conversation that while not elitist will draw from accurate professional knowledge and be carried on amidst genuine respect for one another's views. This must replace the present situation where the issues are being obliquely addressed by those who understandably wish to avoid too open a rupture in U.S. Catholicism or between U.S. Catholics and Rome or where the issues are argued polemically and ideologically by advocates of one position or the other. The U.S. church has reached the level of religious and cultural maturity that makes creative interchange possible; the process that produced the two pastoral documents of the U.S. bishops on war/peace and on the economy illustrated this maturity.

For the time being, U.S./Vatican tensions are focused on the relation between U.S. bishops and the papacy. This is part of the larger worldwide issue of the role to be played in the Catholic Church by national groupings of bishops. Vatican II encouraged such regional episcopal conferences and supported their claim to genuine authority as collegial agencies in the church. However, the special synod of bishops held in 1985 made it clear that important forces in the Vatican, such as Cardinal Ratzinger, view regional groupings of bishops as a threat to papal power. Theological clarification is not only needed, it is underway—for example, the international meeting last summer in Salamanca (papers published in *the Jurist*).

On the level of working out practically the interaction of regional groupings of bishops with the Vatican the U.S. bishops have a special role to play. Because of the present place of the U.S. in world affairs, and the consequent prominence of the U.S. church, the autonomy and role of the USCC is paradigmatic for the development of the post-Vatican II church worldwide.

Obviously, the relationship between bishops and pope is worked out in the day-by-day guidance of the church's life, and much of the resolution of the tensions involved has to do with pragmatic decisions, personalities, and formation of policy in the course of actual experience. However, all this is grounded in certain understandings of the church, i.e. in one or other ecclesiology, and so there is need for accurate and up-to-date ecclesiology that reflects the directions suggested by Vatican II and that takes account of the operation of Christ's Spirit in the Christianity of today's world. Though Vatican II provides valuable orientations, there is a pressing need for a more developed theology of papal jurisdictional authority and power vis-à-vis the authority and power of the people and of their bishops on the local level.

It was to contribute to this endeavor that the conference whose papers are published in this volume was held at the College of the Holy Cross in Worcester, Massachusetts. While the four days of presentations and discussions among bishops, historians, and theologians dealt also with the broader issues of papal/episcopal authority, the conference concentrated on the U.S. context.

Because the more recent history of the papacy developed out of the medieval situation and needs to be understood against that background, the first essay deals with the emergence of papal/hierarchy relations as the medieval world gives way to modern times. In this chapter, Professor Brian Tierney of Cornell University, internationally recognized scholar of late medieval canon law and church institutions, provides a brief sketch of the socio-religious dynamics that led up to and found expression in the Tridentine Catholic Church.

Though the papacy played a key role at Trent and the council strengthened the position of the pope in Catholic life—to some extent at the price of institutionalizing the sixteenth century split of the Christian church—the papacy had not yet reached the full recognition of primacy in both teaching and government. This would come with Vatican I. To describe this development and to assess its claims to irreversibility is the purpose of our volume's second essay. Its author, William Portier, professor of church history at Mount St. Mary's College in Emmitsburg, centers his treatment around the response of ultramontanism to Gallican emphasis on the local church, points to the dilemma this posed for U.S. bishops participating in Vatican I, and fleshes out the historical picture needed to contextualize the council's statements.

Between the two recent Vatican Councils a subtle but critical shift occurred, away from the papal absolutism of Vatican I toward the "collegiality" taught by Vatican II. What needed most to be clarified in the reflection that took place during those decades was the nature and origin of episcopal authority. In the volume's third essay, James Heft, S.M., chair of the religious studies department at the University of Dayton, addresses this issue by examining the manner in which Vatican II deals with Vatican I's teaching on the papacy's relationship to the episcopate.

The next three chapters of the volume focus on the historical development of the U.S./Vatican relationship. James Hennesey's essay describes the manner in which John Carroll, the first U.S. bishop, was elected by the priests of the then infant U.S. church rather than being selected by the pope. But Hennesey, professor of church history at Canisius University, goes on to tell how during Carroll's tenure in office the selection of U.S. bishops already passed into Vatican control.

By the second half of the nineteenth century the church in the U.S. had become a prominent element in American life and in the universal Catholic Church, and American Catholics could point with pride to eminent ecclesiastics like John England, James Cardinal Gibbons, or John Ireland. Such leadership could not, of course, avoid notice by Vatican officials and even arouse some concern in Rome about the independence and growing power of this young church. No prelate of that period was more outspoken about the merits of U.S. Catholicism or more a champion of the "rights" of the U.S. Catholic community than John Ireland. Because Ireland was so much a reflection of his time, the chapter by the University of Notre Dame historian Marvin O'Connell gives us an insight into the decades that closely followed upon Vatican I, and at the same time it introduces us to—or deepens our acquaintance with—one of the great churchmen of U.S. Catholic history.

Picking up the historical narrative, our volume goes on to Gerald Fogarty's description of the interaction of the Vatican and the U.S. hierarchy since World War II. Fogarty, who teaches church history in the religious studies department of the University of Virginia, traces quickly the complex interaction of the Vatican, the U.S. hierarchy and the U.S. government in the years prior to and following the Second Vatican Council and indicates the basic shifts in attitude and activity that occurred as the church in this country increased in size and influence. Inevitably this has led to a changed role of the U.S. bishops within society and within the universal Church.

The final third of the volume considers theologically the questions raised by the historical essays. In her paper on the groundings in tradition for episcopal and papal authority Agnes Cunningham, professor of patristics at the Chicago archdiocesan seminary, reviews the evolution of church order in the first centuries of the church. While historical studies no longer permit the simplistic view that the twelve were the church's first bishops—monoepiscopacy is not a universal pattern until well into the second century—there is an organic development that justifies later application of the notion of *de jure divino* to both episcopacy and papacy. At the same time the early centuries of the church provide no clear resolution of contending episcopal and papal claims to authority.

Since the centuries-long polarity is that between Rome and the local church, the essay by Catholic University canonist Msgr. Fred McManus approaches this issue from the viewpoint of church law, including the most recent revision of the code. What emerges from his analysis is the opening that is possible, even within present church legislation, toward a more autonomous role of the bishop within his diocese and of regional groupings of bishops. However, the present code still has not been freed from the ecclesiology of Vatican I; more thorough revision of church law awaits fuller ecclesiological growth.

In the volume's final chapter, James Provost, also a professor of canon law at Catholic University, examines the interlocked realities of power, authority and leadership as these find expression in the contemporary papacy. While he describes briefly the nature of these three realities, Provost concentrates on the exercise of power and authority by recent popes, examining the four specific issues of liturgy, sexuality, doctrinal truth and social justice, issues that have been of particular concern to Catholics in the United States during recent decades. Without contesting a special role for papal authority in each area, the essay points to a corrosion of Vatican credibility because of the actual exercise of power.

What emerges from the various historical and theological presentations is that the activity of the papacy in dealing with the bishops of the world has not over the centuries followed any unchanging pattern that can be called "the tradition," nor has the pope's claim to ruling authority been consistently stated and unquestioningly accepted by the episcopacy. Much post-Vatican I ecclesiology presented a simplistic view of the pope's primacy, an over-emphasis on papal authority accompanied by a lack of appreciation for the role of the bishop, both in the local church and in collegial cooperation with his fellow bishops.

Consequently, though Vatican II provided the guidelines for probing more deeply the character of ecclesiastical power and authority and for examining the structures in which this power and authority are expressed, there is a crying need for an updated ecclesiology that is capable of dealing with the realities of the church's existence in the world of today. While this is a complicated task, one which ultimately will coincide with creation of a "new" christology and pneumatology, there are certain neuralgic points of current church life which seem to ask for more immediate attention. Our essays draw attention to two of these, papal appointment of bishops and the role and authority of regional groupings of bishops.

In different parts of the world talented historians and theologians are working on these and related questions which are central to the future development of the church. The present volume is, we hope, a small contribution to this effort, one which may have distinctive input by drawing from the experience of U.S. Catholicism as a source of theological insight.

Brian Tierney

Pope and Bishops Before Trent: An Historical Survey

Since it is obviously impossible to cover fifteen hundred years of papal history in one short essay, this paper will present only a few pictures, some models as it were of the papacy. To begin at the beginning: Those first shadowy popes of the liturgy exercised hardly any of the prerogatives of a modern pope. They did not judge and rule and administer the affairs of the whole church. They did not appoint bishops. Bishops were chosen by local communities, and when matters of common concern arose they met together collegially in local councils. But, so far back as we have any record at all, all looked to Rome as a specially faithful guardian of apostolic tradition. The doctrine of a juridical primacy of the pope was overtly formulated in the last century of the western Roman empire. The older doctrine of episcopal collegiality survived, however, and both doctrines have persisted down to the present day. The constitutional history of the church is mainly the story of the interplay between them. Since those early days there have been many kinds of papacy and many kinds of popes. Some were great figures who seemed to carry the whole church—the whole world—on their shoulders; some were nonentities; some were scoundrels.

Let us begin with one of the great ones. I am thinking of Gregory I, called Gregory the Great, around 600. He lived in a ruined world. All the provinces of the Roman empire were invaded by barbarians, and Rome itself had been half-destroyed in the last bouts of fighting. Gregory himself described the scene in one of his sermons as pope:

> What Rome herself, once the Mistress of the world, has become we now see, wasted away with afflictions, the loss of citizens, the assaults of enemies, the frequent fall of ruined buildings. Where is the Senate? Where are the people? All gone . . . all the pomp of the dignities of this world is gone.

So in this fallen world the pope labored away at the daily tasks that pressed in on him. And he conducted himself with such spirit and wisdom and fortitude that he laid the foundation for a whole western Christian culture that he himself could never have foreseen, for he firmly believed that he was living in the last days of the world.

Gregory was the pastor of his people in the most literal sense. He found food for them when the imperial supply system broke down. He provided spiritual food too in many sermons. He took over the civil government of Rome when there was no one else to do so. He even sent a mission to convert the remote far-off heathens of England. Gregory had an unusual sense of cultural pluralism in the church. He told his missionaries not to destroy the heathen temples of the English but to reconsecrate them: "Then the people will come more rapidly to their old familiar places." He said the pagan folk-customs of the English were to be tolerated, but redirected to the glory of God. Papal missionary policy has not always been so accommodating. One thinks of the Chinese rites controversy of the seventeenth century.

As for pope and bishops: Gregory's *Book of Pastoral Care,* a book of practical guidance for bishops, had almost as great an influence in the early church as Benedict's rule for monks. Gregory certainly asserted the primacy of the papacy in word and deed. But he also cared for the honor of his brother bishops. When the bishop of Constantinople styled himself "universal patriarch" Gregory wrote to rebuke him. But when the bishop of Alexandria applied the same title to the pope, Gregory refused to accept it.

> You have addressed me by the proud title of Universal Pope. I beg you not to do this again . . . I do not consider anything an honor to me by which my brother bishops lose the honor that is their due. . . . My honor is the united strength of my brothers.

These words are not just a historical curiosity, a sort of archaeological fragment dug up out of the past by a modern scholar. They have always lived in the life of the church. Gregory's text was incorporated for instance into Gratian's *Decretum,* the foundation of western canon law, in 1140, and it was endlessly drawn into later discussions on the nature of the church. It has been quoted approvingly by Paul VI in the twentieth century.

Gregory was the pontiff who incorporated into the papal titles *servus servorum dei,* servant of the servants of God. He provides a distinctive model of the papacy, one of enormous authority achieved through tireless dedication to pastoral ministry. I like the epitaph a later pope put on his tomb, "In a straitened age, he disdained to be cast down, though the world failed."

It did not last of course. The chaos in western Europe became worse, after a brief rally under Charlemagne. From the eighth century onward the pope became firmly established as temporal ruler of central Italy, a sort of petty Italian duke as well as head of the church, and an immediate, disastrous result was that the local bandit nobility, men with no sense of religious vocation, began struggling for the papacy as they struggled for any other secular lordship. Things reached a nadir in the middle of the tenth century with Pope John XII. Here is another model of the papacy, described by Msgr. Duchesne:

> Rome was soon the witness of truly appalling scandals. . . . The young people took no pleasure in the ceremonies of the church . . . his days and nights were spent with women and young men in hunting and feasting. His sacrilegious love affairs were flaunted unashamedly. . . . No decent woman was safe in Rome. The Lateran was become a bawdy house. Cruelty crowned the debauchery . . . and blasphemy. Men told how, in the feasting at the Lateran, the pope used to drink the health of the devil.

It is a bit highly colored. And the medieval account comes from an adversary of the pope. But no one has ever supposed that John XII was a model of Christian virtue. A pope like this exercised no significant control over the western episcopate as a whole. Everywhere the appointment of bishops fell under the control of local kings and dukes. And yet—this is an odd phenomenon to reflect on perhaps—while the church seemed to be going dead at the center, there was a good deal of vitality on the periphery. Missionaries from northern Germany and England began the conversion of Scandinavia. Missions from eastern Germany worked among the northern Slavs. The beginning of the Polish church dates from this era. As for John XII himself, he was eventually deposed for rape, sodomy, simony, incest, arson, blasphemy, murder . . . and anything else you can think of.

Well, of course, that did not last either. Toward 1100 there began a great movement of renewal initiated by Pope Gregory VII. It was a decisive turning point, perhaps the decisive turning point in the whole history of western institutions. The papacy first reformed itself, then undertook the reform of the whole church. Gregory's war cry was *libertas ecclesiae,* liberty of the church, by which he meant liberty of the clergy from control by lay rulers. Above all he demanded that kings abandon their long-established right to appoint bishops. When the kings refused, Gregory embarked on the first great conflict of church and state, to use the language of a later age. (I would like to add a word in parentheses here. I do not intend to go on and on about church and state, but will get back to my proper theme of pope and bishops. However, the relation of pope and bishops has never been just a bilateral one. It has always been a three-cornered relationship—pope, bishop, and secular government. So it was in Gregory VII's dealings with Germany in 1075; so it is now in John Paul's dealings with the Polish church. The whole Vatican outlook has been shaped by such relationships over the course of the centuries. But America has a unique tradition in this area of church-state relations. That is one reason, I think, why people in the Vatican so often fail to understand what is going on in the American church.)

But to return to Gregory VII about 1100. The language of Gregory VII about papal authority was strikingly different from that of Gregory I.

Here are some propositions from the register of the later pope: "The Roman pontiff alone is rightly to be called universal." "He can be judged by no one." "He alone can depose and reinstate bishops." "The pope is the only one whose feet are to be kissed by all princes." "He can depose emperors." Gregory wanted liberty for the church but he could only conceive of liberty as dominance, dominance of clergy over laity, dominance of pope over both bishops and kings. Another model of the papacy.

Around this time, about 1140, an alternative model was propounded by the great St. Bernard of Clairvaux in a work intended as a book of advice for a newly elected pope. Bernard described the dignity of the papal office in glowing terms, but he worried about the growing accumulation of worldly business at the curia. If this continued, he wrote, "When will you find time for prayer? When will you teach the people? When will you edify the church? When will you meditate?" Bernard was especially anxious that the pope should not usurp the rights of other bishops. "You err," he wrote, "if you regard your apostolic authority as not only the highest but the only one instituted by God." "Remember above all things that the holy Roman church is the mother, not the mistress, of the other churches and that you are not the lord and master of other bishops but one of them."

Bernard's ideal remained only an ideal. The popes of the twelfth and thirteenth centuries did not seek power—I think for the most part power to do good but anyway a real legal sovereignty. The twelfth century was a time when the church expressed its own consciousness of its own nature—more than in any other age perhaps—in terms of law. The canon law of the twelfth century, beginning with Gratian's Decretum in 1140, was more complex than people used to think. It was not just an instrument of papal absolutism. There was always a kind of subtext which preserved the older tradition of the church, like that passage of Gregory the Great that I mentioned—so in later controversies between popes and bishops both sides could appeal to canonistic texts. But at first one major function of canon law was certainly to provide legal techniques for the practical exercise of a papal sovereignty.

The great popes of this age were activists; they were trying to re-shape the whole world, trying to build a sort of City of God on earth. They were Marthas, not Marys. In fact Innocent III, the greatest of them all, around 1200, once wrote to a bishop who wanted to quit and go off to a monastery, "You are not to think that Martha chose a bad part." I find it hard to come to terms with this imperial papacy of the thirteenth century. It helped to inspire a brilliant Catholic Christian culture, the culture of Chartres Cathedral and Thomas Aquinas, which as a medieval-ist I find very appealing. And yet it was only transient. The whole medieval endeavor ended in a breakdown of Christian unity after all.

Innocent III was not just the worldly pontiff of some old-fashioned textbooks. He was also an active reformer, who for instance encouraged the radically new ways of religious life that Francis of Assisi and Do-minic were introducing into the church. To try to build the City of God on earth is indeed no ignoble task, but in undertaking it the popes perhaps forgot that they were vicars of one who said, "My kingdom is not of this world."

At any rate, the mention of Francis and Dominic can lead us to the next phase of papal-episcopal relations, a dispute in which the Francis-can and Dominican Orders were intimately involved. The great growth of papal power I have described so far took place with the general support of the western episcopate. The overt disputes were more with secular kings. But there was an inherent tension between the new, evan-gelical transforming energy of the new orders of friars, accountable only to the pope, and the solid, traditional, historical institutions of dioceses and parishes through which the pastoral work of the church was carried on. The friars, armed with papal privileges, could enter parishes without permission of the local clergy, preach, hear confessions, collect offer-ings . . . The popes were creating a new pastoral structure alongside the old one. Some conservative theologians came to see this as subversive of all right order in the church.

An overt quarrel broke out at the University of Paris in the 1250s. One can hardly exaggerate the importance of this dispute in the history of papal-episcopal relations. For the first time the greatest theological minds of Europe became engaged with this question including Thomas Aquinas and Bonaventure. The debate established the terms in which the issue has been discussed ever since. And yet it began as a petty affair. The masters of theology, jealous of the friars and annoyed with them over a sort of trade union dispute, tried to exclude them from university chairs. Then the dispute broadened into a general attack on

the friars' mission and then finally into an impassioned debate about the
concept of papal power that authorized their mission.

The first great adversary of the friars and defenders of episcopal
rights against them was William of St. Amour. Some of the Franciscans
had suggested that a new era of the church was at hand, when existing
institutions would melt away, and the friars would inaugurate a new
reign of the Holy Spirit. Williams' response was that indeed the last age
of the church was at hand and the friars were indeed evidence of it, but
they were agents of the anti-Christ, not heralds of the Holy Spirit. His
favorite ploy was to take Paul's epistle to Timothy. "In the last days
perilous times shall come. Men shall be lovers of their own selves,
covetous, boasters, proud, blasphemous, disobedient, unthankful, un-
holy . . ." and so on and on and on. Then William would preach a
sermon or write a chapter on each individual word, showing how perfectly it applied to the friars of his own day. Many would err from the
truth in those days, he said. Perhaps even the pope would err. It had
happened in the past, William thought, and it might happen again. It
was something to be on guard against. Especially there was need to
guard against the danger of the pope usurping all the rightful power of
the bishops.

William's substantive argument was devised from both scripture
and canon law. In Matthew 16 we read the famous words of Jesus to
Peter, "I will give you the keys of the kingdom of heaven, and whatever
you bind on earth it shall be bound in heaven." But then in Matthew 18
Jesus repeated these same words to all the apostles, "Whatsoever you
shall bind on earth shall be bound in heaven," so it seemed that they all
shared in the authority first given to Peter. And then in John 20, Jesus
said to all the disciples, "Receive the Holy Spirit. Whose sins you shall
forgive they are forgiven them. . . ." So apparently they too shared in
the power of the keys. And there are other texts scattered through
scripture where Jesus apparently conferred authority on all the apostles
and disciples.

William supplemented these scriptural texts with a canonical passage from the Decretum of Gratian

> The other apostles received honor and power with Peter in equal
> fellowship. . . . When they died bishops succeeded them—and
> 72 disciples were chosen of whom priests are the successors.

William took this to mean that Jesus had not only established a monarchy
in the church; he had established a whole constitutional order. The pope
ruled the church but his power was limited by the divinely ordained

authority of bishops and priests. If the pope sent out floods of friars to usurp the functions of lesser prelates he would be destroying the divine constitution of the church. William therefore constantly contended—or pretended—that the pope could not really have intended to grant such a general privilege. He had a considerable gift for sustained irony. Even Jesus had sent out only individual, carefully selected preachers, William said. It was not likely that the lord pope would abandon the example of Jesus. And St. Paul had declared, "No one should glory in another man's office." It was not likely that the lord pope would intend to go against St. Paul. And Gregory the Great had written "I do injury to myself if I disturb the rights of my brother bishops." It was not likely that the lord pope would intend to differ from St. Gregory. Since the lord pope evidently did intend precisely what William said, he ought not to intend all this with a sort of polite insolence. But the insolence veiled a complex theory of ecclesiastical constitutionalism that persisted at the University of Paris until the Gallicanism of the seventeenth century.

The greatest early champion of the opposing, papalist, point of view was St. Bonaventure, arguing for the Franciscans. One of the modern experts on Bonaventure's ecclesiology incidentally was a young German professor called Joseph Ratzinger who has since gone on to higher things. Ratzinger insisted that Bonaventure's theology of the papacy was the real foundation of counter-reformation papal absolutism. Bonaventure maintained that the pope held a *plenitudo potestatis,* plenitude of power, and this meant not only that he was the supreme judge and head of the church, which everyone acknowledged, but that all ruling authority in the church was derived from him just as, Bonaventure wrote, "In heaven all the glory of the saints flows from Jesus Christ." To meet the argument that every bishop and priest had the power of the keys, Bonaventure distinguished sharply between the power of holy orders and power of jurisdiction. (The distinction was well known to the canonists but it had not been used in quite this way before.) The power of the keys that all bishops and priests held was merely the power of orders; only the pope received the powers of jurisdiction—the actual power to rule—and from him it descended to all inferior prelates. The distinguishing characteristic of the papacy was this pure absolute power. In Bonaventure's words, bishops were simply vicars of the pope.

This argument was carried to its ultimate extreme a little later by the Dominican, Herveus Natalis. Herveus went through all the New Testament texts in which Jesus seemed to confer power on the apostles and disciples and explained that they always referred to some duty or mission but never to a grant of actual jurisdiction. The apostles received no ruling power from Christ. And anyway, even if they did—this was a sort of second line of defense—later bishops did not inherit such powers. They were mere delegates of an all-powerful pope. Herveus was at pains to point out that bishops did not stand to the pope like feudal princes to a king. The princes after all had some intrinsic right to their position. But bishops were just servants—like stewards or bailiffs.

Those are the two positions then. All power is in the pope, or there is an ordered constitution of the church set out once and for all in the New Testament. Neither position is wholly satisfactory. The bishops were seeking to defend the divinely ordained structure of the church as they understand it but they were sometimes motivated by jealousy of the friars or even mere financial self-interest. Also there was very little trace of what we should now call collegiality in the episcopalist argument; each bishop was rather defending his own individual autonomy like a feudal lord in his own fief.

As for the friars: they were resolved that no fossilized institutions should impede them in their evangelical work. But because they depended on papal support they were led to define the very essence of the papal office as sheer naked power. They introduced a possibility of total fluidity in the future shape of church institutions. And this is a dangerous game even from a papal point of view. If one is to call everything into question it's only one more little step to call into question papal powers also—and the step was soon taken by medieval anti-papalists, some of them Franciscans. If one is going to attack bishops in general, why stop at the bishop of Rome?

To return to the Paris dispute of the 1250s—in the end the popes won the contest, at least on the administrative level. The Franciscans and Dominicans got their university chairs back. The friars continued to receive papal privileges. William was driven into exile and compelled to live out his life in his native village of St. Amour. But on a theological level the issue was never settled. The episcopalist position continued to be upheld at Paris by a series of great theologians into the seventeenth century. The whole issue was debated at the Council of Trent, with the Jesuits now taking the place of the friars as partisans of the pope against the bishops, but it was not settled there. It was not settled at Vatican Council I either. Perhaps it was settled once and for all at Vatican Council II—or perhaps we shall have to wait and see.

After 1300 there ensued another model of the papacy which I shall call the Avignon model. The popes settled in Avignon, partly because of the turmoil in central Italy, built themselves the great fortress-palace that still stands there, and proceeded to organize the greatest machine of bureaucratic administration that the middle ages had ever seen. Now more than ever before, papal influence was felt in the detailed life of the local churches through a vast patronage system. Innumerable benefices throughout Europe were "reserved" for papal appointment down to the parish priest level. And people had to pay for the appointments. The whole operation has been described as systematized simony. In 1305 Pope Clement V reserved the appointment of all bishops to the pope, but again it was a revenue raising measure. The pope didn't actually choose bishops in the modern fashion, supposedly for pastoral reasons. Bishops continued to be chosen by local powers, often kings, sometimes cathedral clergy; but to enter into their office they now had to have papal approval, and they had to pay very heavily for it. In this model of papacy, bishoprics were seen largely as accounting units or, as they say nowadays, profit centers.

The popes of Avignon were not bad men on the whole. They were hard-headed administrators who knew how to run a bureaucracy. They would have done very well in the Pentagon. But I sometimes think they really believed that Jesus Christ had come down to earth to establish a curial bureaucracy and that the rest of the church was a sort of after-thought intended to provide a source of revenue to keep the bureau-cracy running. It's a constant Vatican temptation. One has been getting whiffs of it again recently.

In some ways it was an efficient system. The community of the church was given discipline and government. Individuals could usually be kept happy by a constant stream of papal privileges, indulgences, and dispensations. But men and women of truly deep religious experience were becoming alienated. The poet Petrarch called Avignon "the impi-ous Babylon, the hell on earth, the sink of vice, the sewer of the world," and the great St. Catherine of Siena said with greater brevity but equal force that "it stank like Hell."

This pattern of papal government collapsed in 1378 in the crisis of the great schism. The popes returned to Rome but almost at once there was a disputed papal election. For forty years, first two and then three lines of would-be pontiffs struggled for the papal throne. After a genera-tion of futile bickering it became widely accepted that only a general council, exercising authority over all the claimants, could bring the schism to an end. And in these desperate circumstances another model of papal-episcopal relationships grew up, the last I shall consider, which I will call the conciliar model. The conciliarists of this age were not content to give the church a new head; they wanted to give it a new constitution as well, or rather, in their own minds, a return to the old constitution. They regarded the recent highly-centralized papalism as a temporary aberration. They wanted to reform the whole church in head and members.

I will take as a representative of model the greatest theologian of the age perhaps, Jean Gerson. He was incidentally greatly influenced by Bernard of Clairvaux in his view of the papacy and he often quoted Gregory the Great. He insisted that the papacy was a ministry of service, not an office of dominance. He didn't like the definition of the papacy as pure naked jurisdiction. If that were true, he said, a lay person could be pope—why, even a woman could be—the ultimate absurdity of course. Gerson wanted the future pope to be a true pastoral bishop who would guide the church in cooperation with his brother bishops.

From our point of view the interesting thing about Gerson is that he combined the old view of each bishop's autonomous role as a successor of the apostles with an emphasis on the corporate authority of all the bishops together—what we should nowadays call collegiality. In a declaration made at Paris in 1409 Gerson insisted that bishops and priests were not just delegates of the pope. Each had an individual right (a *ius*) in his office. There is a new note in this emphasis on rights. To make sure everyone had gotten the point Gerson preached a sermon in French in Notre Dame cathedral with a reiterated insistence on the word *droit*. But Gerson did not think of the bishops only as isolated individuals with rights. He held rather that the full authority that Christ had initially bestowed on the church could be exercised in its plenitude only when all the bishops were gathered together in a corporate collegiate assembly. For Gerson no bishop was an "island entire of itself." He was a "piece of the continent, a part of the main." Sometimes Gerson expressed this thought in Aristotelian language. The full authority of the church, he said, existed only potentially in the scattered bishops and priests. It could be exercised in act, in actuality, when they were gathered together in a council. More often, Gerson preferred the scriptural imagery of the mystical body. In a sermon of 1407 he declared: "No one doubts that the church abhors its own division since it is one mystical body as the Apostle says." And then he spoke of "the life-giving power by which the mystical body of the church can unify and write itself." For Gerson a general council, if one could ever meet, would be a visible representation of the mystical body, able to exercise all its inherent virtue.

Well, in the end a council did meet at Constance in 1414 and in 1415 it enacted the decree *Haec sancta,* one of the most controversial documents in the history of the church. *Haec sancta* declared:

This holy synod of Constance, representing the church militant, holds its power immediately from Christ, and anyone of whatsoever state or dignity—even the papal—is bound to obey it in matters relating to the faith, the rooting out of the schism and the general reform of the church in head and members.

And it went on to say that this applied also to future councils. I myself think that the text has a more moderate sense than appears at first glance. I think the fathers of the council were claiming authority for themselves in an emergency situation when there was no certain pope. And they were also looking forward to a future reform of the church by general councils. And they expected the pope to adhere to the decrees of those councils. But the councils they envisaged would not be, like the existing emergency assembly, a body of bishops and clergy without the pope but rather pope and bishops meeting together collegially. One can argue this because we know a great deal now about the ecclesiology of the council fathers who were actually there at Constance, hacking out *Haec sancta* clause by clause, and they all accepted the role of the pope as divinely ordained head of the church. Gerson himself wrote that there could not be a real general council without the authority of a pope, when a pope actually existed to lead it.

In the past thirty years a huge new literature of hundreds of books and articles has grown up about the decrees of Constance, especially *Haec sancta*. It used to be regarded as a cul-de-sac, a dead end of history. Catholic historians treated it as a revolutionary break with the medieval tradition of papal government. Catholic theologians saw it as an heretical aberration from the true doctrine of the papacy. Then historians began to argue that *Haec sancta* was not revolutionary at all but a reasoned application of the old constitutional law of the church to a novel and difficult situation. And theologians began to ask whether the decree, in its difficult awkward way, perhaps expressed some permanent truth about the nature of the church. The theological interest stimulated more historical inquiries. And the historians' results interested the theologians. And so a fruitful dialogue grew up. It has still not reached any agreed conclusion.

William L. Portier

Church Unity and National Traditions: The Challenge to the Modern Papacy, 1682–1870

Gallicanism's central role in the background of Vatican I and its decrees is commonly assumed.[1] The relationship between pope and bishops as explained in the dogmatic constitution *Pastor Aeternus,* for example, is to be interpreted against this background. But theologians, especially those whose notion of their art has been shaped by a positive experience of separation of church and state, tend to treat Gallicanism as an abstract set of positions about the limits of papal power. Such an approach tends to miss the significance of the political, cultural, and especially legal dimensions of Gallicanism, and hence of ultramontanism and Vatican I.[2]

Most Catholics in the United States, for example, remain unaware of the extensive legal restrictions which the various governments of modern France placed on the French church and its relations with the papacy. This legal dimension of Gallicanism helps to explain the heavily juridical cast of *Pastor Aeternus,* much lamented by contemporary theologians. This essay, therefore, will draw attention to the significant impact of the interaction between the church and the modern state on Vatican I's treatment of the relationship between papacy and episcopacy.

The essay has four parts. It begins with brief surveys (Sections I and II) of the Gallican Articles of 1682, and of the trend to subordinate church to state in modern Europe. Section III focuses on the rise of ultramontanism in France. Finally, in an attempt to stimulate specifically U.S. Catholic reflection, Vatican I is treated from the perspective of two U.S. bishops whose ideas on papacy and episcopacy had been shaped in interaction with a different set of political institutions and a different experience of modernity.

Two clarifications on this form of organization are necessary. First, the essay begins with the modern period instead of with the Council of Trent. This is due to considerations of both space and substance. Although Trent renewed the episcopacy and counted on the bishops to implement its reforms, the present shape of papal-episcopal relations owes more to nineteenth century developments than to Trent. Second, the essay emphasizes Gallicanism, the modern French version of subordination of church to state, as the background for ultramontanism and Vatican I. This is not to deny the significance of such subordination in other states, e.g. the Italian question, but to recognize both limits of space and the near paradigmatic stature of France as a modern state.

I. Gallicanism and the Gallican Articles of 1682

Gallicanism in general has been described as "the tendency, while accepting the Papacy as of divine institution, to oppose or minimize papal claims as they have been made in history."[3] But if we agree with Rahner in his treatment of human consciousness as "spirit in the world," and with Lonergan in his shift to "historical-mindedness," we have to take French scholars seriously when they pronounce Gallicanism "a purely French phenomenon."[4] Yves Congar points out that before it was a system, Gallicanism was a "temperament," a "practical attitude linked to the situation of France under the authority of her kings."[5] The term *Gallicanism* first appears in the polemical context of the nineteenth century.[6] Gallicanism's chief historian, Victor Martin, rightly insists that broad definitions such as the one above would make Gallicans of a host of people such as Cyprian and the third century African bishops.[7] He traces its origins to the beginning of the fifteenth century (ca. 1408) at which time what he calls the three "fundamental ideas" were in place and had coalesced in the Pragmatic Sanction of Bourges (1438).[8] Martin identifies the three ideas as: (1) The "most Christian King" (le roi Très Chrétien) is sovereign in the government of his state. This affirmation resulted from the struggle with the German emperors as well as those with the popes. (2) General councils are above the pope. (3) The pope's powers in France are limited by the canons of the ancient councils and by the "Decrees of the holy Fathers."[9] As the French scholars have insisted, this complex of ideas makes little sense in abstraction from the political experience of France under the *ancien régime*.

This royal or political Gallicanism included a genuine sense on the king's part of his responsibility to protect the faith of the French church. Charlemagne and St. Louis IX achieved symbolic stature in this regard, and even a king such as Philip IV (Philippe le bel) was concerned to honor his religious obligations.[10] In the fourteenth and fifteenth centuries, the so-called "Gallican liberties," implied in Martin's third idea but always extremely vague, came to be viewed as means to reform the Church.[11] The center of this ecclesiastical Gallicanism was the Faculty of Theology at the University of Paris usually supported by the episcopacy.[12] Church reform was seen as the role of the clergy in union with the king. In spite of tensions and a seeming tendency to a national church, the bishops and theologians of the *ecclesia gallicana* wished to remain in communion of faith and discipline with the Church of Rome. We find the most eloquent expression of this sentiment in the writings of Jacques B. Bossuet (1627–1704), archbishop of Meaux, e.g. his 1682 "Sermon on Church Unity."

As France evolved into a modern nation state, it began to develop its own legal tradition distinct from the Latin one. The French language replaced Latin and the complex of ideas described above took a more secular turn. The Parlement of Paris—"not a representative body . . . but a corporation of lawyers with the power of registering acts so that they had the force of law"[13]—began to codify and gradually define the vague sense of "Gallican liberties." Thus developed "parliamentary" or "administrative" Gallicanism. It was the province of legal historians and jurists such as Pierre Pithou whose classic work on *The Liberties of the Gallican Church* appeared in 1549. Their main concern was to preserve royal prerogatives vis-à-vis the pope and the French clergy.[14]

These three—royal, ecclesiastical, and parliamentary—are usually listed as the forms of Gallicanism. In reality of course they were related. Beneath the apparent unity of Martin's three ideas lies a plurality of Gallicanisms. Each group—the king, the bishops, the Parisian Faculty of Theology, the parliamentary jurists—professed their devotion to the Gallican liberties, but interpreted them and formed appropriate alliances according to their respective interests. This is clear from the variety of positions on issues such as the conflict between Jesuits and Jansenists, the question of tolerance for French Protestants or of a Protestant king for France, questions about papal taxation and the control of the economic resources involved with church offices and properties.

At the "apogee of Gallicanism," Congar has set the Gallican Articles of 1682.[15] The articles find their political context in a conflict between the French king, Louis XIV, and the pope, Innocent XI. As was usually the case, the conflict had to do with the benefices attached to ecclesiastical offices. The Pragmatic Sanction of Bourges had restored ecclesiastical elections and placed limits on the pope's ability to levy taxes in France. The Concordat of Bologna of 1516 had given the king more influence in clerical nominations.[16] At the end of the seventeenth century, Louis sought to expand this influence by extending to conquered territories his right "to fill the benefices of a bishop while the bishopric was vacant . . . to gain possession of the income of vacant bishoprics."[17] A conciliatory preamble affirmed the primacy of the pope and the majesty of the apostolic see which teaches the true faith and safeguards the unity of the church.[18] The four articles which follow the preamble are based on six propositions published in 1663 by the Faculty of Theology at Paris. These state the Gallican case in quite modest form and therefore provide an interesting contrast and touchstone for interpreting the articles.[19]

The first article affirms the sovereignty of the king of France in temporals and denies to "Saint Peter and his successors, vicars of Jesus

Christ" any direct or indirect temporal power over the sovereign. The pope's plenitude of power is limited to things spiritual. The propositions of 1663 had presented this position as a statement of fact about France. The first article of 1682 presents it as an abstract "doctrine" about church and state. Further it claims that this doctrine "conforms to the word of God, to the tradition of the holy Fathers and to the example of the saints."[20] Bellarmine's doctrine of the "indirect temporal power" is rejected. The abstract form of the first article would facilitate use of the French legal tradition by political theorists and enlightened monarchs in other states.

The second article declares that the pope's plenitude of power in spirituals is such that the decrees of the

> holy ecumenical Council of Constance on the authority of general councils, contained in Sessions IV and V [*Haec Sancta Synodus* and *Frequens*], approved by the apostolic Holy See, confirmed by the practice of the Roman pontiffs and the whole Church, and observed religiously in all times in the Gallican Church, remain in full force.[21]

The article goes on to reject other interpretations of these decrees which either cast doubt on their authority or hold that they were extraordinary measures limited to the time of the Great Western Schism of the fourteenth and fifteenth centuries.

Having ruled out interpretations of *Haec Sancta Synodus* as invalid or as an *in extremis* emergency measure, the second article, therefore, implicitly interprets it as an abstract or general teaching about the superiority of council over pope.[22] In this it goes beyond the propositions of 1663 which had simply denied that it was the teaching of the Faculty of Theology that the pope is above an ecumenical council.[23]

The third article deals with the limitations on papal power and ascribes them to two sources. First it declares that the exercise of the Holy See's apostolic power must be limited by adherence to the canons "established by the Spirit of God and consecrated by universal respect."[24] This latter formula is taken from Pope Leo the Great and seems well within the limits of orthodoxy in any period.[25]

The second part of the third article deals specifically with national traditions and with the limitations on papal power in France. It extends these limitations not only to the canons, but also to the laws and customs of the Gallican church, and most significantly to the laws and customs accepted in the kingdom. The Gallican liberties are presented here in quite ambiguous form. The ongoing tradition of parliamentary Gallicanism would continue to specify them.

Crucial for the interpretation of *Pastor Aeternus,* Chapter III, these liberties would eventually include among others the notion that the pope's judgments on matters of faith had to be formally and canonically accepted in freedom by the French bishops (this often meant the king) before they could be published in France. Thus the king was able to delay publication of the decrees of Trent in France and some bishops never published various Roman censures of Jansenism.[26] Also included among the Gallican liberties were the denial of jurisdiction to the Index and other Roman Congregations, the multiplicity of Gallican liturgies, and restrictions on the pope's communication with the bishops and other clergy. These and more were included in the "organic articles" attached by Napoleon to the Concordat of 1801 and only came to an end when they were swept away in the waves of "veuillotisme" which preceded Vatican I and their formal condemnation.

The fourth article is perhaps the most innovative and controversial. It received much attention at Vatican I and was explicitly condemned in *Pastor Aeternus,* Chapter IV. While acknowledging in a patristic-sounding phrase the pope's "principal part" in matters of faith, and that his decrees pertain "to all churches and each church in particular"— terminology reminiscent of an earlier ecclesiology—it nevertheless asserts that his decrees are not "irreformable, unless the consent of the church be given" (*nisi Ecclesiae consensus accesserit*).[27]

Conspicuously absent from the fourth article is any mention of the indefectibility of the Holy See (rather than its bishop) as held by Bossuet based on the ancient distinction between the *sedes* and the *sedens.*[28] In 1663 the Faculty of Theology had stated for the first time its objection to the thesis of papal infallibility. Without condemnation it had simply stated that papal infallibility was neither a teaching nor a doctrine of the Faculty, unless the consent of the church were given.[29] In 1682 by contrast the Assembly erected into a formal teaching of the French episcopate that the *consensus ecclesiae* is the sole definitive authority in matters of faith. Other opinions, Bellarmine's conspicuous among them, which might be held by other churches, were thereby excluded.[30] At Vatican I, in his *Relatio* on Chapter IV of *Pastor Aeternus,* Vincenz Gasser, bishop of Brixen, would speak at length, using the term *consensio* instead of *consensus,* on the sense in which the "consent of the churches" could be taken as the rule of faith.[31]

As a set of abstract concepts, Gallicanism can be summarized as (1) the temporal sovereignty of the state; (2) the superiority of council over pope; (3) the limitation of papal power by church canons and local laws and traditions; (4) the *consensus ecclesiae* as the rule of faith. Doubtless there is much of Louis XIV's absolutism in the way in which the Articles inflate the cautious statements of the Faculty of Theology from 1663. The Articles claim doctrinal status for theological opinions and make false claims to antiquity, much as papal absolutists have been accused of doing. Nor can it be denied that assertions of Gallican liberties during the eighteenth and nineteenth centuries went far beyond legitimate diversity and subsidiarity in church life to subordinate the church to the state and call forth a massive reassertion of the church's unity and independence.

Nevertheless, underneath all the politics and legalism of Gallicanism and the Articles of 1682 is still discernible a set of venerable theological instincts. They are related to what might now be called an "ecclesiology of communion" and are embodied in what Yves Congar identifies as the tendency "to put first the unity of the *ecclesia,* the body of the faithful; then, and in its full force, the hierarchical service to the body," and the resistance to the absorption of the "pole *ecclesia*" by the "pole *papatus.*"[32]

II. Political Enlightenment: The Subordination of the Church to the Modern European State (1648–1800)

The Peace of Westphalia of 1648 fixed the political map of Europe in a configuration of confessional states. With this multiplicity of sovereignties came the tendency to established churches or state religions which viewed the church as a department of state and bishops as its functionaries. The pattern of subordination had already begun to emerge in papal dealings with Louis XIV of France (1638–1715). As was the case with Louis and Innocent XI, it was often related to the incipient capitalist economy and its need to free the concentrations of wealth which were held in the dead hand of ecclesiastical endowments and property. Less often, as was the case with Austria's Emperor Joseph II, the enlightened monarchs were also motivated by a genuine desire to reform the church.[33]

Domination of the church by the state varied with the political and cultural conditions which accompanied the rise of modern nationalism in the European states. We have seen something of Gallicanism. Although the French legal tradition exercised undeniable influence outside of France, Josephism (Austria), Febronianism (Germany), Pombalism (Portugal), the situation in Ireland, and even Anglicanism are best interpreted on their own terms than as various species in the genus Gallicanism.[34] Whatever their differences, each of these state church movements effectively diminished the influence of Rome. In addition Protestant states were understandably unwilling to allow the papacy to function in its traditional role as arbiter in international disputes.[35]

The net result was a loss of prestige and influence for the eighteenth century popes. Procedures for papal elections made a pope such as Alexander VI highly unlikely. At the same time, the enlightened rulers of Europe would hardly have been satisfied with a Hildebrand or an Innocent III. The governments of Spain, France and Austria used their "veto" power to prevent anyone too formidable from occupying the chair of St. Peter. The popes who won election were usually safe, usually very old, not likely to surprise, and, if they did, not likely to live long. They have been described as "good men," usually not heroic: "humane, comfortable, paternal, considerate. . . . In a good-humoured age, then, mostly good-humoured men led the Roman Catholic Church."[36]

Widespread nomination of bishops by increasingly secular states put the episcopacy in a difficult position. If in a high papalist theology bishops might be viewed as the pope's legates, in the "episcopalist" theology characteristic of the state churches they tended to be viewed as legates of the sovereign monarch. Bishops such as Bossuet could find themselves pulled in both directions simultaneously.

While Voltaireans regarded the Vatican as a bastion of obscurantism, enlightened rulers mocked its political pretensions. When in 1768 Pope Clement XIII claimed to nullify an edict of the Duke of Parma— Parma was an Italian duchy claimed by the papal states—Frederick of Prussia summed up their reaction in this remark: "The Grand Lama of the Vatican is like a tight-rope walker who has grown old and in the sickness of old age wants to repeat the triumphs of his youth, and so falls and breaks his neck."[37] The ultimate testimony to the papacy's weakness in the eighteenth century occurred on July 21, 1773. Succumbing to mounting pressure from various European governments, Pope Clement XIV (Ganganelli, 1769–74) suppressed the Society of Jesus.[38]

III. Romanticism and the Rise of Ultramontane Movement (1800–1870)

The twilight of the eighteenth century saw a widespread and dramatic rejection of its norms in politics, literature, architecture, and religion. In France, where the church's bondage to the state was most pathetic, the revival of religion which had characterized the lower classes in the eighteenth century now spread to the various elites. Chateaubriand, confessing no particular spiritual illumination, simply wept and believed. So much for the previous one hundred and fifty years of critical reason. The pope emerged as the symbolic center of the Catholic revival known as ultramontanism. This look "beyond the mountains" originated in a certain post-revolutionary nostalgia for the old order, but it also included a true sympathy and respect for the persecuted "martyr popes," Pius VI and Pius VII, who had suffered grievously under the Directory and Napoleon.

The religious, social and political movement of ultramontanism came in two waves. The first is best represented by the twin figures of Joseph de Maistre (d. 1821) and Felicité de Lammenais (d. 1854). Maistre himself has been called "a human preface" to the First Vatican Council and his book *Du Pape* (1819) is a basic document of ultramontanism. Recently it has been argued that Maistre's notion of political sovereignty underlies the legal interpretation of papal primacy and infallibility in *Pastor Aeternus*.[39] Ironically Maistre's book enjoyed more popularity between 1850 and 1870 than at the time of its publication. During the nineteenth century, it would go through some forty editions.[40] But it was Lammenais whose vision and rhetoric captured the imaginations of the younger clergy during the Bourbon restoration and the beginnings of the July monarchy. It has been claimed—by a French historian of course— that Karl Marx in the social field and Lammenais in the religious were "the two great visionaries of the nineteenth century."[41]

Ultramontanism's second wave, or neo-ultramontanism as it came to be called, carried it to triumph at Vatican I. Its momentum was generated in part by the charismatic figure of Pio Nono, himself a "martyr pope," whose symbolic *mana* far exceeded his political clout. It was organized and sustained among the French clergy by nineteenth century French religious journalism's answer to A.J. Matt, Louis Veuillot, known to one of his detractors as "His Holiness Mgr Veuillot, most illustrious Patriarch and Coadjutor to the Holy Father, and Vicar of Jesus Christ." The layman Veuillot edited the newspaper *L'Univers,* "the most powerful organ of the ultramontane movement." Indeed, Veuillot was quite literally a *coadjutor* to the pope in facilitating his free communication with the French church often denied in the application of the organic articles. The French government's suppression of *L'Univers* in 1860 testifies to the importance of this role.[42]

By the time of the Concordat of 1801 between Napoleon and Pope Pius VII, only the pretensions of royal and ecclesiastical Gallicanism remained. The Civil Constitution of the Clergy had left the episcopate in shambles. By the Concordat Napoleon inherited the right of the French kings to nominate bishops.[43] Gallican theology, which would enjoy a brief revival in the years before the council, had lost its heart and soul with the dissolution of the Faculty of Theology at Paris. Only parliamentary Gallicanism remained. The Gallican liberties were now in the hands of imperial bureaucrats. All were lawyers, well versed in the French legal tradition. Some were religiously informed and sensitive, but were nevertheless committed to carry out Bonaparte's policy of turning the church into the state's religious arm and the clergy into its *gendarmes* for public order and morality.

In this context, Gallicanism came to signify what we might call base culture capitulation. To embrace ultramontanism in this milieu was to stand up for the rightful independence of the church from the state, and to see the pope as the heroic guardian and guarantee of the church's independence and unity, a beleaguered bulwark against its slipping into a collection of state churches. The term connoted the same kind of "National Apostasy" that so offended the Tractarians and sent them in a Romeward direction.[44]

The Latin language, the Roman liturgy and Gregorian chant, and devotion to our Lady and the Sacred Heart all became symbolic bearers of the universality of the Church and France's need to repent of its apostasy.[45] But it was the figure of the pope, epitomized in the blasphemous apotheosis of Pius IX, which became the church's chief totem and symbol of its supranational status.[46] Yet even in this counter-revolutionary cult of the pope, ultramontanism was in its beginnings a movement of the voiceless and powerless—lay people and younger clergy in the French church.

As far as the episcopate was concerned, a commonly used French legal text defined it as "a function of the Church exercised in the name and under the control of the State."[47] Lammenais advocated nomination of bishops by the pope and denounced the French bishops as "tonsured lackeys." For him Gallicanism was "a system which consists in believing as little as possible without being a heretic, in order to obey as little as possible without being a rebel."[48] According to one of the Ministers of Religion under the July Monarchy:

> The payment which ministers receive from the public purse constitutes a bilateral contract between the religious society and the political society, according to which the one promises its protection to the other and receives in return submission. . . .[49]

To this cultural captivity of the church and clergy, Lammenais responded with an impassioned ultramontanism:

> Without the pope, there can be no Church, without the Church no Christianity, and without Christianity no religion and no society, which implies that the life of the European nations is solely dependent on the power of the papacy.[50]

By the end of the restoration in the late 1820's, Lammenais' opposition to the Gallicanism which he associated with the *ancien régime* led him in a republican direction. Along with papal supremacy and infallibility, the pages of *L'Avenir* also advocated the end of the temporal power, the separation of church and state, religious liberty and the general reconciliation of the church with democracy. The perspicacity of these views, uniquely joined with his high view of the papacy, justly entitles Lammenais to visionary or prophetic stature. He was harassed and arrested by the state, and all of his ultramontanism was not enough to prevent the condemnation of his liberal views by *Mirari vos* in 1832.[51]

By mid-century, despite the continued opposition of Lammenais' former associates such as Montalembert and Lacordaire, Maistre's monarchist form of ultramontanism had won the day. Maistre's view of the papacy is little concerned with theology. He was a diplomat, whose book was written while he was attached to the Russian court at St. Petersburg, and a lawyer with many years of experience in the Parliament of Savoy. He accepted the world of the *ancien régime* of which Gallicanism was a part and developed his arguments accordingly. They are set in a world of lawyers and kings which had little place for people who understand theology as it has developed under the separation of church and state.

Maistre's concept of sovereignty is a practical way of dealing with the social upheaval arising from the French revolution interpreted as Satanic. It simply means that in politics and religion there must be a court of last appeal. Obviously the pope will be guided by the canons, but sovereignty and infallibility mean precisely that there is no other to tell us that he has so judged or who can force him (legally) to do so. The strictly theological claims Maistre makes for papal infalliblity are relatively modest. He limits its scope to "matters of faith," and dismisses complaints about the "formidable jurisdiction of the pope over the human mind" by confining it "within the limits of the Apostles' Creed."[52]

Maistre's political ideology would be taken up into the social and cultural movement of ultramontanism at mid-century. Crucial to its rise was the support of the lower French clergy. They had little advantages under the French state church system and often preferred to see themselves as directly responsible to Rome rather than to their bishops. Lammenais' earlier ill-fated pilgrimage to Rome illustrates this tendency. Their oracle was Louis Veuillot whose *L'Univers* had 12,000 subscribers at the time of its suppression in 1860. The unraveling of what was left of the *ecclesia Gallicana* would come swiftly:

In a rapid and energetic ultramontane campaign between 1848 and 1853 the French dioceses had been compelled to give up their local liturgies and adopt the *rit romain,* the Roman Index had swept through French ecclesiastical libraries with devastating effect, and the Roman Curia, suddenly stirred into life, had begun handing down judgments, opinions, rescripts, interfering, encouraging appeals, and generally undermining episcopal authority. An ultramontane opposition, with Roman support, had appeared at every level of Catholic affairs; and the campaign had culminated in the encyclical *Inter Multiplices* of 1853 condemning Sulpicianism and the entire concept of 'the liberties of the Gallican Church'.[53]

Despite a brief revival of Gallican theology in the 1860s, the French church had been converted from a Gallican to an ultramontane organization.[54] The aging and frustrated champion of liberal Catholicism, Montalembert, described this shift as the "rapid and complete transformation of Catholic France into a backyard of the antechamber of the Vatican." The pope now appeared as "a papal Louis XIV" and an "idol set up for themselves in the Vatican by the lay theologians of Catholicism."[55]

IV. Vatican I as a Crossroads for the U.S. Tradition of Episcopal Autonomy and Collegiality

Ultramontanism drew its strength and support from widespread Catholic opposition to the abuses of the previous century's state church system. Simultaneously in the United States, Catholicism was developing in interaction with its culture and the political institutions peculiar to it. The experience of these political institutions would imply for Catholics in the U.S. a posture toward modernity quite at odds with that of a majority of their French counterparts. In the process Catholicism in the U.S. developed what James Hennesey has called a sense of episcopal autonomy and "the strongest nineteenth-century conciliar tradition in the Western Church."[56] Since Vatican II, in a long series of articles which deserve to be gathered and published in a book, he has painstakingly established the existence and traced the initial gropings of a tradition of theological reflection based on the experience of the church under the American form of government. This line of thought has been taken up, nuanced and developed in varied directions by other scholars. I want to give a brief summary of this "inchoate" tradition, and conclude by showing how Vatican I represented something of a crossroads, if not a crisis, for it.

1. The revolution of 1776 and the experience of living under its Constitution differed sharply from the European Catholic experience.

While European ultramontanes demonized the French revolution, Catholics in the U.S. tended to regard their earlier one as providential. They tended to develop a positive view of separation of church and state, on historical or providential grounds rather than on theoretical grounds. They consistently interpreted nineteenth century Roman condemnations of liberalism as directed at the European scene.

2. Far removed from Rome and European politics, Catholic bishops governed the church by means of councils. Thirty-four such gatherings took place during the century. Most conspicuous among them were the three plenary Councils of Baltimore. The theological writings of the bishops reflected their shared sense of responsibility for the church in this country, rooted in their sense of being a part of the larger body of bishops.

3. Even after their division into liberal and conservative ranks after 1884, U.S. bishops continued their characteristic resistance to Roman centralization of administration. Their high view of the episcopacy unwittingly contributed to this trend. They had resisted the formation of cathedral chapters for the nomination of bishops, and their often cavalier treatment of the clergy and laity occasioned recourse to Rome and eventual intervention.

4. Adherence to the pope is one of the essential characteristics distinguishing Catholics in the U.S. from their fellow Christians. At the same time as they developed a theological apologetics for papal primacy, we should not be surprised that they also developed an intense loyalty and personal devotion to the pope.[57] To the extent that this aspect of "devotional Catholicism" participated in the growing nineteenth century cult of the pope, we might speak of ultramontanism, but it would have to be the republican ultramontanism of a church that had never been subordinated to an enlightened state. To the U.S. Congress episcopal nominations were a matter of indifference.

If the term *Gallicanism* is to be understood with reference to the context of French politics and history, what could it possibly mean to call the convictions of U.S. bishops about episcopal autonomy and collegiality Gallicanism? The differing political contexts between France and the United States, and the resulting lack of comparable experiences of modernity, render the terms *Gallicanism* and *ultramontanism* suspect and of limited value for interpreting U.S. Catholic life and thought—regardless of where John England and Peter Kenrick went to school.[58]

Yet when the bishops of the United States arrived in Rome for the council, the lines of debate had already been drawn around the old political and cultural question about how to respond to the French revolution. Their sense of episcopal autonomy and collegiality, based on their experience rather than on any set of Gallican principles retained from seminary days, was on collision course with their genuine loyalty to the pope. In this sense, Vatican I appears as a crisis for the incipient U.S. theological tradition.

Vatican I's dogmatic constitution *Pastor Aeternus* is most often remembered for its definition of the infallibility of the papal magisterium, which appears only in its closing paragraph. The definition is just a part of the fourth of four chapters. The first deals with the institution of the Petrine primacy, a "primacy of jurisdiction over the universal Church of God," to be distinguished from a mere primacy of honor.[59]

Most significant is the third chapter devoted to the nature and powers of the papal primacy. It is addressed to the situation of the Church's bondage to the state during the eighteenth and nineteenth centuries, and appears to have been written with a careful eye to the Gallican articles of 1682, especially the second and third. In this context, Chapter III can be read as a declaration of independence from the strictures of parliamentary Gallicanism under the Concordat. It declares:

> the Roman Church possesses preeminence of ordinary power above all other churches; and that this power of jurisdiction of the Roman Pontiff, which is truly episcopal, is immediate.[60]

The rest of the chapter is replete with statements that reflect the nineteenth century European political situation. In a clear allusion to parliamentary Gallicanism under the Concordat, Chapter III further claims the pope's "right, in the exercise of his office, to communicate freely with the shepherds and flocks of the entire Church." It condemns the opinion that decisions of the Holy See "do not have force and value unless confirmed by the *placet* of the secular power," and denies that any authority could "examine juridically its [the Holy See's] decisions."[61]

Each of these claims denies a corresponding right alleged by the French sovereigns or bishops in the name of the Gallican liberties. Similar claims were common in other states during the modern period. Chapter III of *Pastor Aeternus* represents a clear rejection by the church of the kinds of practices common under parliamentary Gallicanism. That it should be framed in legal terms is hardly surprising. Parliamentary Gallicanism was a legal tradition. But at what theological price, in terms of the episcopacy, did this legal declaration of independence come?

To many among the minority bishops, the description of papal ordinary jurisdiction as "episcopal" and "immediate" seemed to render local ordinaries superfluous, and to strengthen a tendency whereby the pope eventually replaces the bishops and becomes in effect the only bishop.

This would make of the universal church a vast diocese of which the pope was ordinary. If the fourth chapter on papal teaching authority offended the collegial sense of many bishops from the U.S., the third chapter on papal ordinary jurisdiction as episcopal and immediate offended their sense of episcopal autonomy almost as much. We will briefly consider the responses of Martin Spalding and Peter Kenrick to these two key issues.

In the jurisdiction question, Spalding's May 30, 1870 proposal led to the addition of an explanatory paragraph to the final text:

> This power of the Supreme Pontiff is far from obstructing the ordinary and immediate power of episcopal jurisdiction by which individual bishops, placed by the Holy Spirit and successors of the apostles, feed and rule as true shepherds the individual flocks assigned to them. Rather, the power of the bishops is protected, strengthened, and upheld by the supreme and universal shepherd, as St. Gregory the Great writes: "My honor is the honor of the whole Church. My honor is the solid strength of my brethren. I am truly honored when the honor due to every single one is not denied."[62]

While acknowledging the value of this addition as opening the way for a solution, commentators agree that the present text, as amended according to Spalding's intervention, remains little more than an assertion.[63] Kenrick shared Spalding's concern for legitimate episcopal autonomy. In his "Concio," dated June 8, 1870, Kenrick put the matter in his usual "pull no punches" style:

> In the *Schema, de Romano Pontifice* it is said that he has ordinary and immediate jurisdiction in the Universal Church. Since this is said without making any distinction between ordinary or episcopal power and ordinary patriarchal or primatial power, it would seem to follow that the Pope is actually ordinary or bishop of each of several dioceses of the Christian world. . . . After the *Concordats* have been done away with, which will not be long after the Infallibility of the Pope is established, all episcopal sees will be at the disposal of the Pope alone, *ad nutum;* and thenceforth all bishops will be vicars of the Pope, liable to be removed at his nod, *ad nutum ejus.* Thus the Church, from which the civil society borrowed the form of representative government, to which it owes the rights it has

acquired, will exhibit an example of absolutism, both in doctrine and administration, carried to the highest pitch.[64]

In his recent book on the theology of the papacy, J.M.R. Tillard mines the columns of Mansi to reconstruct the debate on this question. He wishes to draw from it the resources for a theological solution to objections such as Kenrick's. Just as Bishop Gasser's July 11 *Relatio* on Chapter IV, given on behalf of the deputation on faith, became the context in which the minority bishops accepted the definition and in which it has been understood ever since, so, Tillard argues, should the July 5 *Relatio* of Federico Zinelli, bishop of Treviso, on behalf of the same deputation, be used to interpret Chapter III. From Zinelli's *Relatio,* Tillard draws four points:

1. Papal primacy is to be understood without prejudice to, or within the limits of, what is of divine right in the church.

2. In response to a question from Dupanloup, Zinelli interpreted *ordinary* to mean a power which is not delegated, but which the pope possesses by virtue of his office. It is not intended to refer to the day to day exercise of episcopal office by diocesan bishops.[65]

3. Zinelli interpreted immediate in a vague way to mean "without having to pass through an intermediary." The best reading of this term would seem to place it in the context of French obstruction of the pope's communication with bishops, mentioned later in the chapter, and other practices of the state churches. With reference back to the first point, Zinelli insisted that this power could only be used for the building up rather than for the destruction of the church. He urged confidence in the moderation of the Holy See.

4. With regard to the term *episcopal,* replying again to Dupanloup, Zinelli admitted that "the power of the sovereign pontiff is in reality of the same type as that of the bishops." Therefore the same word is appropriate for both. Tillard interprets this as setting the pope "in his proper place within the company of bishops."[66] Peter Kenrick who thought the Roman pontiff had "no other grace of ordination than his brethren who share the same episcopal office" would have found this interpretation congenial.[67]

From his analysis of the speeches of Kenrick and the other bishops of the minority, Tillard concludes that "the minority is anxious to safeguard not prerogatives it fears to be cheated of, but a traditional vision of the Church in which the recognized place of the episcopate is central."[68] Whether *Pastor Aeternus'* rejection of Gallicanism is bought at the price of this vision depends on how the principles drawn from Zinelli's *Relatio* are put into practice in the day to day life of the church.

Finally to the question of infallibility. The "great question" divided the U.S. bishops. The forty-nine "Americans," forty-eight bishops and one abbot, represented the third largest national contingent at the council. By the time of the final vote on July 18, 1870, twenty-two had left Rome. The rest, with the exception of Edward Fitzgerald, bishop of Little Rock, voted for the definition. One can find the chronicle of their participation in James Hennesey's ground-breaking book on the subject. Some, Kenrick and Augustin Vérot among them, spoke against the proposed definition. Others, Spalding chief among them, supported it.

The terms *minority* and *majority* by which their positions are designated are misleading. They conceal, as in the case of the U.S. bishops, the varying shades of sentiment for or against the proposed definition. The view that most of the minority bishops thought a definition "inopportune" simply does not stand up to the evidence. But most importantly it begs the crucial questions about the meaning of papal infallibility and the form of the definition.

The bishops' dilemma is well summed up in this statement of Bernard McQuaid, bishop of Rochester, upon his return from the council: "I have now no difficulty in accepting the dogma, although to the last I opposed it, because somehow or other it was in my head that the bishops ought to be consulted."[69] McQuaid was referring to a common teaching of the U.S. bishops which we can trace from John England's *Diocesan Constitution* to Francis Kenrick's Latin tracts on dogmatic theology and his *Primacy of the Apostolic See Vindicated* (1845) to Martin Spalding's apologetic works, namely that the infallible teaching office of the church resides in the body of bishops, either gathered in council or dispersed in their sees, united with their head. Put in another way, the pope is infallible in conjunction with the bishops. Whether the pope teaching without consulting the bishops was infallible was an open question. But all agreed that the body of bishops united with the pope could teach infallibly. This is part of the American tradition of episcopal collegiality.[70]

The dilemma which the campaign to define the infallibility of the papal magisterium at Vatican I presented to the bishops of the U.S. is well illustrated in the public controversy between Spalding and Kenrick. As his "Concio" shows, Kenrick maintained that doctrinal definitions were to be made by the pope in union with the bishops. Since he thought it dangerous to assume tacit approval, he held that a general council was the only proper place for doctrinal definitions. A council provided the opportunity to debate the issues involved and for the bishops to exercise their office by "witnessing to" and "defining" what is of faith. These latter two notions were essential to Kenrick's understanding of the episcopal office. In his opinion that infallible doctrinal definitions could only be made in a council, Kenrick went beyond what I have called the common teaching.[71]

As a result of Dupanloup's use of Francis Kenrick's writings as part of his case that there was not a majority of theological opinion in favor of papal infallibility, Spalding and Peter Kenrick argued about how the elder Kenrick, brother to Peter Kenrick and mentor to Martin Spalding, ought to be interpreted. In fact they argued about the direction which the American tradition of episcopal collegiality would take. The cross-roads appears in this text from Francis Kenrick's *Primacy,* cited in Peter Kenrick's "Concio":

The personal fallibility of the Pope in his private capacity, writing or speaking, is freely conceded by the most ardent advocates of papal prerogatives, but his official infallibility *ex cathedra* is strongly affirmed by many. While some, as the French Assembly of 1682, contend that his judgment may admit of amendment, as long as it is not sustained by the assent and adhesion of the great body of bishops. Practically there is no room for difficulty, since all solemn judgments hitherto pronounced by the Pontiff have received the assent of his colleagues; and in the contingency of a new definition it should be presumed by the faithful at large that it is correct, as long as the body of Bishops do not remonstrate or oppose it.[72]

In 1819 Maistre had written that "every dogmatical decision of the Holy Father ought to be law until the Church makes opposition to it." "When this phenomenon occurs," he added, "we shall see what must be done."[73] In 1870 the "phenomenon" had occurred. Pius IX clearly wanted a definition of papal infallibility. A significant minority among the body of bishops were remonstrating and opposing such a definition. This involves two interrelated questions: (1) If there is a definition, shouldn't it include reference to the body of bishops? (2) Who would make this definition? How could the council do it, even united to the pope, if the definition made no reference to their power to do so? How could the pope do it alone knowing that a sizable minority opposed it? Isaac Hecker captured this dilemma in a stark series of questions recorded in his diary shortly after his arrival in Rome. The last question in the series reads as follows:

How can the Bishops define on infallibility, unless they be by Divine right, judges of what is of faith? And if so, how can the Pope be declared to be alone unerring?[74]

In contrast to most of the other Americans, Martin Spalding had come to Rome with advance knowledge that there would be a definition of some kind. He therefore set to work on what he regarded as a moderate definition which would avoid the terms *infallibility* and *ex cathedra*. The petition he wrote proposing a compromise definition clearly presupposed unanimous episcopal consent for the definition of a doctrine, even paradoxically, one of papal infallibility.[75] This led to the dilemma expressed so clearly by Hecker.

By the spring, the French bishops had rejected his compromise and he became convinced that there were real Gallicans at the council. He now thought that public opposition to the papacy required a definition, even one that made no reference to the episcopate.[76] His final position is stated in his "Pastoral Letter . . ." of July 19, 1870. He cited "Gallicanism revived" as the main reason why a definition was needed. He provided a very clear explanation of what he meant by Gallicanism. Since he was a member of the deputation on faith, this explanation adds weight to the case that theologians, especially in the United States, need to become more aware of Gallicanism in the strict sense, specifically parliamentary Gallicanism as practiced under the Concordat, as a significant part of the context for interpreting *Pastor Aeternus*. Most significant is Spalding's translation of the offending conclusion of the fourth Gallican article in strictly legal terms: "his [the pope's] judgment is not irreformable unless *ratified* [my italics] by the consent of the Church."[77] Kenrick for his part argued in his "Concio" that Spalding had abandoned his own previously published positions.[78]

We can conclude that if *Pastor Aeternus* is read and interpreted in the light of Gasser's *Relatio* and the documents of Vatican II, especially *Lumen Gentium*, 25, the difficulty of the U.S. bishops is mitigated and they are somewhat vindicated, but not completely.[79] The matter of the relationship between pope and bishops, as it stands with the two Vatican Councils, is framed in entirely non-conflictual, but heavily legal terms. In such a juridical framework, seemingly addressed to a long-ceased situation in France and elsewhere, there is no explicit constitutional recourse for Maistre's "phenomenon." Instead we are admonished to loyalty and trust. In my judgment, this situation discourages bishops from acting like teachers and judges of the faith by divine right.

It is not clear to me that the following opinion, cited by Cuthbert Butler as a representative example of Gallicanism is entirely excluded by *Pastor Aeternus* read in the twofold context mentioned above.

To propose to the faithful a bull of a Pope as having by itself and of its own nature the force to subject to it all minds; or, to propose it as conformable to the doctrine of the Church, are two very different things. In the first case it is to profess openly the dogma of the infallibility of the Popes, unknown to the ancient Fathers, and to destroy the rights of the epis-copate, reducing the bishops to the simple role of executors of the decrees of Rome. In the second case it is to recognize that one does not owe to the Pope's judgments a submission entire and without reserve, save in so far as they are in the analogy of faith; and this can be proved only by the acquiescence of the bishops scattered throughout the Christian world. It is in this latter sense that the Church of France exacts from the faithful submission to the constitutions of the Sovereign Pontiffs.[80]

What is of lasting theological value in this opinion and what is not? Is it compatible with Gasser's *Relatio?* What if Maistre's "phenomenon" should occur and bishops, significant numbers of them perhaps, feel bound in conscience to "remonstrate," as Francis Kenrick put it back in 1845? Must we be bound in conflictual situations by a legal framework designed to free the papacy from enlightened states? In response to needs arising from nineteenth century political conditions, the ul-tramontane Catholics who created "modern Roman Catholicism" con-ceived and practiced the unity of the Church in a highly centralized legal framework that has been called a modern anti-modernism. In a global or post-modern situation of a "world Church," can we reenvision its unity in a way that is compatible with those national traditions which now have nothing to do with eighteenth and nineteenth century subordina-tion of the church to the state in Europe? Our situation is complicated by the fact that in some states outside the west such threats are still quite real. This is the present challenge to the post-modern papacy and to the rest of the church. The modern papacy met its challenge with consider-able success. May we do as well. In our efforts, the old theological instincts of the Gallican Articles, tangled as they are with legal and political threats to the pastoral functioning of the church, might prove useful. In the twentieth century, the chief guardian and repository of those instincts is the venerable Yves Congar. We also find them in the nineteenth century United States, unencumbered by legal and political threats, and suggesting a posture toward modernity that was closed to most Europeans at that time.

The author is grateful to the librarians at the Hugh J. Phillips Li-brary, Mount Saint Mary's College, especially to Ms. Joy Toal, for their help in assembling the resources needed for this paper.

Notes

1. Cuthbert Butler cautions that Gallicanism is "a thing often misunderstood" and that "a right understanding of it is necessary for any just estimation of the Vatican Council." *The Vatican Council, The Story Told From Inside in Bishop Ullathorne's Letters,* 2 vols. (London: Longmans, Green and Co., 1930), I, 33.

2. I am here drawing upon the insight of Joseph Komonchak that "it was the social and political consequences of the Enlightenment that principally engaged the Church's attention during the modern era and that it was to combat these that the Church chose to deal with the intellectual issues as it did. The larger issue was cultural, political and social." See Komonchak's "The Enlightenment and the Construction of Roman Catholicism," *Annual of the Catholic Commission on Intellectual and Cultural Affairs* (CCICA), 1985, 31–59, 34. The terms *seminal* and *groundbreaking* come to mind in describing this essay. The categories it introduces, e.g. "Modern Roman Catholicism," and the literature from European authors which he surveys, provide resources for transforming the present U.S. Catholic standoff between "liberals" and "conservatives." Historical consciousness requires the extension of this line of thought explicitly into the context of the United States. This Komonchak has begun to do in his articles contrasting theology as it would be conceived under "modern Roman Catholicism" and theology as it appears to those who live under the separation of church and state. See "The Ecclesial and Cultural Roles of Theology," in *CTSA Proceedings,* 40 (1985), 15–32 and "The Church and Modernity: From Defensiveness to Engagement," *Commonweal,* Jan. 30, 1987, 43–47.

3. Butler, *Vatican Council I,* I, 23.

4. Victor Martin, *Les origines du Gallicanisme,* 2 tomes (Paris: Bloud & Gay, 1939), II, 325. Aimé-Georges Martimort designates it as "essentiellement un phénomène de l'*Ancien Régime*" in *Le Gallicanisme* (Paris: Presses Universitaires de France, 1973), 5.

5. Yves Congar, "Gallicanisme" in G. Jacquemet, ed., *Catholicisme,* IV (Paris: Letouzey et Ané, 1956), col. 1731. This is the best brief treatment of Gallicanism.

6. On the origin of the term, see Aimé-Georges Martimort, *Le Gallicanisme de Bossuet* (Paris: Les Éditions du Cerf, 1953), 13–14.

7. Martin, *Les origines du Gallicanisme,* I, 30.

8. On the Pragmatic Sanction of Bourges, see *ibid.,* II, 293–324 and Martimort, *Le Gallicanisme,* Ch. III.

9. Martin, *Les origines du Gallicanisme,* II, 325.

10. See Elizabeth M. Hallam, "Philip the Fair and the Cult of Saint

Louis," in Stuart Mews, ed., *Religion and National Identity* (*Studies in Church History,* vol. 18) (Oxford: Basil Blackwell, 1982), 201–214. While not entirely convinced of the depth of Philip's religious devotion, Hallam recognizes it as an important factor.

11. Martimort, *Le Gallicanisme,* Ch. III.

12. See Congar's sympathetic description of the tendencies of Gallican ecclesiology in "Gallicanisme," col. 1736.

13. Owen Chadwick, *The Popes and European Revolution* (Oxford: Clarendon Press, 1981), 280.

14. On these developments, see Claude Sutto, "Tradition et innovation, réalisme et utopie: l'idée Gallicane à la fin du XVIᵉ et au debut du XVIIᵉ siecles," *Renaissance and Reformation,* n.s. 8 (Nov. 1984), 278–97 and Jonathan Powis, "Gallican Liberties and the Politics of Later Sixteenth Century France," *The Historical Journal,* 26/3 (1983), 515–30.

15. Congar, "Gallicanisme," col. 1734.

16. On the concordat, see R.J. Knecht, "The Concordat of 1516: A Reassessment," in Henry J. Cohn, ed., *Government in Reformation Europe 1520–1560* (New York: Harper & Row, 1971), 91–112. On the economic impact of church holdings on the developing modern economy, see *Church and Society in Catholic Europe of the Eighteenth Century* (New York: Cambridge University Press, 1979), especially the Introduction.

17. See Louis Cognet's section on "The Gallicanism of Louis XIV" in *The Church in the Age of Absolutism and Enlightenment,* trans. by Gunther J. Holst (Hubert Jedin and John Dolan, eds., *History of the Church,* vol. VI) (New York: Crossroad, 1981), 65–70.

18. Martimort concludes that the Declaration is less faithful to Bossuet's thought than the "Sermon on Church Unity" and acknowledges the decisive role of Louis' minister, Colbert. See Martimort, *Le Gallicanisme,* 92 and the citations in Congar, "Gallicanisme," col. 1737. Cognet claims in *The Church in the Age of Absolutism and Enlightenment,* 68 that at the Assembly Bossuet "was an instrument in the hands of the Archbishop of Paris," while Martimort emphasizes that the affirmations of the papacy in the Preamble were made against the archbishop's wishes.

19. Martimort gives the text of the propositions of 1663 as well as that of the Gallican Articles of 1682 in French. Congar gives the original Latin text of the articles compared with selections from the 1594 edition of Pierre Pithou's *Traité des libertez de l'église gallicane.* See "Gallicanisme," cols. 1737–38. For an English translation, see Colman Barry, ed., *Readings in Church History,* vol. II (Westminster, MD: Newman Press, 1965), 241–42.

20. Martimort, Le *Gallicanisme,* 93.

21. ". . . simul valeant atque immota consistant" and ". . . demeurent dans leur force et vertu." Martimort, *ibid.,* 94.

22. The solution which reconciles the tension between the Holy See's "plenitude of power" and the authority of a general council by defining a council necessarily to include the pope can only interpret Constance as some sort of emergency measure. On the history of the interpretation of *Haec Sancta Synodus,* see Thomas M. Izbicki, "Papalist Reaction to the Council of Constance: Juan de Torquemada to the Present," *Church History,* 55 (March 1986), 7–20. Since Vatican II, the results of Brian Tierney's research on the origins of conciliar theory have stimulated recent scholars to think of Constance as based in the very constitution of the church and to look for ways to state positively what it teaches about the church. "A Catholic theologian . . . might well maintain that *Haec Sancta* was an attempt—a premature, imperfect attempt, perhaps—to formulate a constitutional law for the Church that would be in keeping with the ancient and never forgotten doctrine of 'collegiality,' the doctrine that eventually found a formal definition at Vatican Council II." Thus Tierney in an important article on the interpretation of *Haec Sancta,* "Hermeneutics and History: The Problem of *Haec Sancta,*" in T.A. Sandquist and M.R. Powicke, eds., *Essays in Medieval History,* presented to Bertie Wilkinson (Toronto: University of Toronto Press, 1969), 369.

23. Martimort, *Le Gallicanisme,* 81.

24. *Ibid.,* 95; "Hinc apostolicae potestatis usum moderandum per canones Spiritu Dei conditos et totius mundi reverentia consecratos"; ". . . faits par l'Esprit de Dieu et consacrées par le respect général de tout le monde."

25. Even Maistre grants this as quite compatible with his notion of sovereignty: "It follows not, however, that because the authority of the Pope is sovereign, it is above the laws, and can sport with them." Joseph de Maistre, *The Pope: Considered in His Relations with the Church, Temporal Sovereignties, Separated Churches, and the Cause of Civilization,* trans. by Rev. Aeneas McD. Dawson with an Introduction by Richard A. Lebrun (New York: Howard Fertig, 1975), 67.

26. See Victor Martin's historical study on the introduction of the decrees of Trent into France between 1563 and 1615, *Le gallicanisme et la reforme catholique* (Paris: Picard, 1919).

27. Martimort, *Le Gallicanisme,* 96. See the remarks of John T. Ford on the contrast between *consensus ecclesiae,* rejected by *Pastor Aeternus* in the sense of a post-definitional ratification, and the *assensus ecclesiae* which can never be wanting to papal definitions; and on "irreformable"

as a juridical term in "Infallibility: Who Won the Debate?" *CTSA Proceedings*, 31 (1976), 186–87 especially n. 37 and 184–85.

28. On this distinction, see Congar, "Gallicanisme," cols. 1736–37, citing Martimort's *Bossuet* (note 6), 400ff, 458, 546, 556.

29. Martimort, *Le Gallicanisme*, 81.

30. For an excellent summary of Bellarmine's position on infallibility, see Butler, *Vatican Council*, I, 36–37.

31. *Ibid.*, II, 136–38. "Finally, we do not in the least separate the Pope from the consent of the Church, provided that consent be not put as a condition, be it antecedent or consequent consent. We cannot separate the Pope from the consent of the Church because this consent can never be wanting to these definitions; as it is not possible that the body of bishops can be separated from their head, nor can the universal Church fail" (137). The original Latin of Gasser's *Relatio* appears in Mansi, *Sacrorum Conciliorum . . .*, 52. This passage is from col. 1216.

32. "On peut, croyons-nous, le [le sens des communs denominateurs du gallicanisme] caractériser, dans l'ensemble de l'histoire des doctrines ecclésiologiques, par la volonté de ne pas laisser absorber le pôle *Ecclesia* par le pôle *papatus*. Tandis que les ultramontains posaient d'abord le pouvoir papal et tendaient à tout faire découler de lui, la démarche spontanée des gallicans était de poser d'abord l'unité de l'*Ecclesia,* le corps des fidèles; ensuite, et dans toute sa force, le service hiérarchique de ce corps. Cette démarche est très nette des l'époque de Philippe le Bel, puis au XVIIᵉ s., chez un Jean Launoi (son *Epist.* XIII à N. Gatin, dans *Opera*, v-2, 665–696) ou chez Bossuet (Martimort, *op. cit.* [Bossuet] 178sq, 396sq., 561, 667." Congar, "Gallicanisme," col. 1736.

33. On this period I have followed Chadwick's *The Popes and European Revolution* and *The Church in the Age of Absolutism and Enlightenment* (notes 13 and 17 above). Chadwick's sixth chapter deals with the reforms. Although treating later but simliar developments in Germany Leonard Swidler's *Aufklärung Catholicism 1780–1850: Liturgical and Other Reforms in the Catholic Aufklärung* (Missoula: Scholars Press, 1978) is also pertinent. The parallels Swidler draws between the reforms of the German Aufklärung and post-Vatican II reforms in liturgy and other areas is uncanny. One can only hope that Swidler's dire prophecies that Vatican II reforms will be swept away as easily as their Aufklärung predecessors will not come true.

34. On the state church movements, see *The Church in the Age of Absolutism and Enlightenment,* ch. 23. Chapter 2 of Patrick Carey's *People, Priests, and Prelates, Ecclesiastical Democracy and the Tensions of Trusteeism* (Notre Dame: University of Notre Dame Press, 1987)

makes a fascinating application of the national church idea to the American situation and trusteeism in particular. See especially 298, n. 1.

35. Chadwick, *Popes and European Revolution*, 255; Jedin and Dolan, eds., *Church in the Age of Absolutism*, 107.

36. Chadwick, *op. cit.*, 256.

37. *Ibid.*, 366, citing Voltaire's correspondence.

38. *Ibid.*, 354–55 and the entirety of Chapter 5. On the earlier expulsion of Jesuits from France, see D.G. Thompson, "General Ricci and the Suppression of the Jesuit Order in France 1760–4," *Journal of Ecclesiastical History*, 37 (July 1986), 426–41.

39. Hermann Josef Pottmeyer, *Unfehlbarkeit und Souveränität: päpstliche Unfehlbarkeit im System der ultramontanen Ekklesiologie des 19. Jahrhunderts* (Mainz: Matthias-Grünewald-Verlag, 1975). I have only skimmed this book and am here relying on John T. Ford, "Infallibility: A Review of Recent Studies," *Theological Studies*, 40 (1979), 273–305. On Pottmeyer's thesis, see 288–89 and Ford's earlier review of the book in *Theological Studies*, 37 (1976), 161–64. On Maistre's thought, see Richard A. Lebrun, *Throne and Altar, the Political and Religious Thought of Joseph de Maistre* (Ottawa: University of Ottawa Press, 1965).

40. Maistre, *The Pope*, xv (from Lebrun's Introduction to the 1975 edition).

41. Adrien Dansette, *Religious History of Modern France*, 2 vols., trans. by John Dingle (New York: Herder and Herder, 1961), I, 211.

42. Austin Gough, *Paris and Rome, The Gallican Church and the Ultramontane Campaign 1848–1853* (Oxford: Clarendon Press, 1986), 229, 285. Gough's Chapter V is devoted to Veuillot's role in the ultramontane movement.

43. On the Civil Constitution of the Clergy, see Dansette, *Religious History of Modern France*, I, 55ff and on the Concordat and the Organic Articles, see I, 120–38.

44. See the comparison of French ultramontanism with the Oxford Movement in Charles Stanley Phillips, *The Church in France 1789–1848: A Study in Revival* (1st edition 1929; New York: Russell & Russell, 1966), 259–63.

45. On the Latin language, see Maistre, *The Pope*, 114; on the liturgy, Austin Gough, "The Roman Liturgy, Gregorian Plain-chant and the Gallican Church," *Journal of Religious History*, 11/4 (1980–81), 437–57; on the "counter-revolutionary mysticism" of ultramontane devotionalism, see Joseph Komonchak, "The Enlightenment and the Construction of Roman Catholicism, 37–41. On the origin of the term, see n. 5.

46. Even the careful Butler felt the need to note the "almost unbeliev-able exuberance of quite untheological devotion to the Holy Father, sometimes bordering, it seemed to many, on blasphemy." *The Vatican Council,* I, 76. My personal favorite is "Rerum Pius [for Deus] tenax vigor." Dansette mentions Gaspard Mermillod's "three incarnations of the Son of God—in the womb of the blessed Virgin, in the Eucharist and in the old man in the Vatican." *Religious History of Modern France,* I, 303. If these are not enough, A.B. Hasler provides a wearying catalogue of shocking expressions in his chapter on Pius IX in *How the Pope Became Infallible: Pius IX and the Politics of Persuasion,* trans. by Peter Heinegg with an Introduction by Hans Küng (Garden City, N.Y.: Doubleday & Co., 1981).

47. Phillips, *The Church in France, 1789–1848,* 286, citing M. Dupin's *Manuel du droit ecclésiastique.* On the wide influence of Dupin's book, see Gough, *Paris and Rome,* 24. Gough's chapter on "Gallicanism Under the Concordat" provides a clear picture of the legal situation as does Bernard Plongeron, "Régime concordaire et police des cultes en France (1801–1905)," *Studies in Religion/Sciences Religieuses* SR, 14/3 (1985), 293–302. See also Dansette, *Religious History of Modern France,* I, 135–36.

48. Dansette, *Religious History,* I, 214; Phillips, *Church in France,* 224.

49. Dansette, *Religious History,* I, 175.

50. *Ibid.,* 214, citing Lammenais' 1817 *Essay on Indifference.* In 1814 Maistre had advanced a similar chain of reasoning.

51. On the complex of events surrounding the condemnation of Lammenais, see Joseph N. Moody, "The Condemnation of Lammenais: A New Dossier," *Theological Studies,* 44 (1983), 123–130.

52. Maistre, *The Pope,* 97, 102, 77.

53. Gough, *Paris and Rome,* vi.

54. Dansette, *Religious History,* I, 228–29; Richard Costigan, "The Ecclesiological Dialectic," *Thought,* 49 (1974), 134–44; "Tradition and the Beginning of the Ultramontane Movement," *The Irish Theological Quarterly,* 48 (1981), 27–45; Michele Despland, "A Case of Christians Shifting Their Moral Allegiance: France 1790–1914," *Journal of the American Academy of Religion,* 52 (1984), 671–91.

55. Dansette, *Religious History,* I, 305.

56. James Hennesey, "The Baltimore Council of 1866: An American Syllabus," *Records of the American Catholic Historical Society of Philadelphia,* 76 (1965), 157–72, 165. See also "Papacy and Episcopacy in Eighteenth and Nineteenth Century American Catholic Thought," *Records . . .* 77 (1966), 175–89. Hennesey's claim is further substantiated

by the detailed study of Eugenio Corecco, *La Formazione della Chiesa Cattolica negli Stati Uniti d'America attraverso l'attività sinodale* (Brescia: Morcelliana, 1970).

57. See Sandra Yocum Mize, "The Papacy in Mid-Nineteenth Century American Catholic Imagination" (Unpublished Ph.D. Dissertation, Theology, Marquette University, 1987).

58. For Hennesey's rejection of the "Gallican syndrome" as a principle for interpreting American Catholicism as well as the resistance of various national hierarchies outside of France to nineteenth century Roman centralization, see "National Traditions and the First Vatican Council," *Archivum Historiae Pontificae*, 7 (1969), 491–512, 498. For arguments against the adequacy of Gallicanism as an explanation for Peter Kenrick's conduct at Vatican I, see his review of S.J. Miller's 1973 study of Peter Kenrick in *Catholic Historical Review*, 62 (1976) 496–98. Michael Gannon argues in a similar vein on behalf of Augustin Vérot, bishop of St. Augustine, Fla. See *Rebel Bishop* (Milwaukee: Bruce Publishing Co., 1964), ch. VIII. On Gallicanism at Maynooth, the Irish seminary where Kenrick studied for the priesthood, see Ambrose Macauley, *Dr. Russell of Maynooth* (London: Darton, Longman & Todd, Ltd, 1983), 136–39. Macauley cites an article which I have been unable to obtain: Patrick J. Corish, "Gallicanism at Maynooth: Archbishop Cullen and the Royal Visitation of 1853," in *Essays Presented to R.D. Edwards* (Dublin, 1978), 176–89. The desire of many Irish Catholics to resist the involvement of the English crown in episcopal nominations seems more important than Gallicanism as a factor favoring episcopal independence.

59. John F. Broderick, ed. *Documents of Vatican Council I, 1869–1870* (Collegeville, Minn.: Liturgical Press, 1971), 54.

60. *Ibid.*, 58.

61. *Ibid.*, 58–59.

62. *Ibid.*, 58.

63. For Spalding's intervention, see Mansi, 53, col. 246, and the commentary cited in James Hennesey, *The First Council of the Vatican: The American Experience* (New York: Herder & Herder, 1963), 222–23. In 1979 Tillard found Spalding's clarifying paragraph "an explanation of capital importance." "The Jurisdiction of the Bishop of Rome," *Theological Studies*, 40 (1979), 5. Three years later, in *The Bishop of Rome*, he thought its assurances read "like a mere dream," 129.

64. "The 'Concio' of Archbishop Kenrick," Appendix V in Raymond J. Clancy, "American Prelates in the Vatican Council," *Historical Records and Studies*, 28 (1937), 93–131, 106. As Paul Hennessy has suggested, it would seem that Kenrick "did not follow in detail the refinements made in the various editions of the schema as a result of the

debate." "Infallibility in the Ecclesiology of Peter Richard Kenrick," *Theological Studies,* 45 (1984), 702–714, 713. On the issue of the three-fold primacy perceptively raised by Kenrick in this passage, see Tillard, *Bishop of Rome,* 49–50.

65. Tillard, "The Jurisdiction of the Bishop of Rome," 9 and *Bishop of Rome,* 139.

66. Tillard, *Bishop of Rome,* 143.

67. Kenrick, "Concio," 128.

68. Tillard, "The Jurisdiction of the Bishop of Rome," 6.

69. Gerald Fogarty begins *The Vatican and the American Hierarchy From 1870–1965* (1982; Wilmington: Michael Glazier, Inc., 1985) with this quotation and describes it as expressing the "American tradition of episcopal collegiality."

70. On John England, see Patrick Carey, *American Catholic Religious Thought* (New York: Paulist Press, 1987), 26, 81; on F.P. Kenrick, see the citations in William L. Portier, "Catholic Theology in the United States, 1840–1907: Recovering a Forgotten Tradition," *Horizons,* 10/2 (1983), 317–333, 319–320; on M.J. Spalding, see the collection of texts assembled by Peter Kenrick in his "Concio," 112–113, 118–119. For a good summary of the issues under discussion here, see Carey, *American Catholic Religious Thought,* 24–30. Nevertheless, the contrast between the enlightened/episcopal and romantic/neo-ultramontane schools should not lead one to doubt the unity of the tradition of episcopal collegiality. While it is true that Francis Kenrick and Martin Spalding were personally inclined to believe in papal infallibility and Peter Kenrick and John England were not, they all accepted the infallibility of the body of bishops united with the pope as a sure and certain position.

71. On Peter Kenrick's position, in addition to the Concio, see his March 22 speech in Mansi, 51, cols. 62–63 and summarized in Hennesey, *First Council of the Vatican,* 143–44; Gerald Fogarty, "Archbishop Peter Kenrick's Submission to Papal Infallibility," *Archivum Historiae Pontificae,* 16 (1978), 205–22; Fogarty's treatment of the same issue in *Vatican and the American Hierarchy,* 2–9, and the article by Paul Hennessy cited in note 64 above. For comparisons of the positions of Spalding and Kenrick, see Barbara Schlaud, "Peter Richard Kenrick and Martin John Spalding: A Study of Their Positions on Papal Infallibility" (unpublished M.A. thesis, University of St. Michael's College, Toronto, 1979) and Paul Hennessy, "Episcopal Collegiality and Papal Primacy in the Pre-Vatican I American Church," *Theological Studies,* 44 (June 1983) 288–97.

72. Francis P. Kenrick, *Primacy of the Apostolic See Vindicated* as cited from p. 537 of the 1845 edition in "Concio," 108–109.

73. Maistre, *The Pope,* 108.

74. Isaac Hecker, "Notes in Italy, 1869–70," Appendix I in William L. Portier, *Isaac Hecker and the First Vatican Council* (Lewiston, N.Y. and Queenston, Ontario: Edwin Mellen Press, 1985), 185–86.

75. For a discussion of this petition, see *ibid.,* 76–80.

76. *Ibid.,* 108–113.

77. For the text of Spalding's pastoral letter, see Carey, *American Catholic Religious Thought,* 152–73, 160.

78. The texts Peter Kenrick produced make a good case. See note 70 above; see also Thomas W. Spalding, *Martin J. Spalding: American Churchman* (Washington, D.C.: Catholic University of America Press, 1973), 290, 391; Portier, *Isaac Hecker and the First Vatican Council,* 74–76.

79. See the discussion of the interpretation of the definition of infallibility in the twofold context of Gasser's *Relatio* and Vatican II in Portier, *Isaac Hecker and the First Vatican Council,* 173–81.

80. Butler, *The Vatican Council,* I, 32, citing a widely used eighteenth century French text.

James L. Heft, S.M.

From the Pope to the Bishops: Episcopal Authority from Vatican I to Vatican II

A bishop with a doctorate in ecclesiology recently gave a presentation on the nature of the church to an ecumenical group. He explained to the group the difference between the church as a worldwide corporation with a central headquarters in Rome and the church as a communion of dioceses. The next day a local paper misquoted him as saying that "The Pope is the Pope of Rome, not the Pope of the World." Catholics who read the newspaper had a variety of reactions: the theologically informed thought it was a misquote, ordinary Catholics were confused, and militant conservatives were indignant. The bishop wrote a correction which the newspaper published. It read: "The Pope is the Bishop of Rome, not the bishop of the world as though the world were all one diocese." Catholics who read the correction had, according to the bishop, a variety of reactions: "Those familiar with theology had their puzzle solved, average Catholics remained confused, and militant conservatives remained indignant." The bishop then drew the conclusion that "for most Catholics the correct statement was as much of a problem as the incorrect one."[1]

Even though the bishop's explanation was solidly grounded in Catholic tradition, most Catholics were unable to recognize it as orthodox. The main reasons for this common misunderstanding can be traced to the relatively recent development of a highly centralized organization of authority in the Roman Catholic Church which was rapidly intensified by social upheaval in Europe in the late eighteenth and nineteenth centuries, and by the success of the ultramontanist movement which achieved dogmatic expression at the First Vatican Council and dominated most church polity until the Second Vatican Council when a more ancient tradition in the church, that of the collegiality of all bishops with the bishop of Rome, received official expression.

In an article such as this, which attempts to delineate the relationship between the pope and the bishops as it developed from Vatican I to Vatican II, it will be necessary to deal only briefly with many topics, all of which deserve more extensive treatment. Choices have therefore been made. I have decided to describe, first, the ultramontanist movement which triumphed at Vatican I in the definition of papal primacy and infallibility. Second, I will look at how the Marian movements and dogmas strengthened papal centralism. Third, I will sketch the extraordinarily rapid and radical change in the manner of appointing bishops in the church. Fourth, I will look at the condemnation of modernism and its consequences and shall consider further examples of centralization and "Romanification." Fifth, I shall indicate various currents that began to flow during the pontificate of Pius XI which deepened during that of Pius XII whose teachings played a special role in preparing for the Second Vatican Council. This will take us to our sixth and final topic, the Second Vatican Council and its teaching on the role of bishops and their collegiality.

1. Ultramontanism and Vatican I

Church historians point out that the early church operated as a loosely organized federation. There was unity in faith but considerable external diversity. "Each bishop exercised full responsibility for his own diocese, while remaining in communion with the college of bishops, particularly through communion with the Bishop of Rome."[2] The movement toward centralization of authority acquired great force during the Gregorian reform in the eleventh century and the reformation in the sixteenth, and reached a peak in the nineteenth century with the ultramontanist movement which extended its influence to the eve of the Second Vatican Council.

This drive toward centralization affected the way in which the idea of tradition was understood. Congar has frequently explained that in the early church a distinction was made between the tradition, that is, the content of the faith received by the church at its origin, and the ministry of the hierarchy. The hierarchy understood its role in witnessing to the doctrine that had always been held. The *quod,* the content of the faith, took precedence over the *quis,* those persons with the authority to guard that tradition. By the time of the reformation, however, formal authority regularly was more emphasized than material authority. At the end of the eighteenth century the tension between these emphases played itself out through on the one hand bishops, especially in France and Germany, who emphasized their rights and the authority of the tradition, at least as they read it, and, on the other hand, the popes, who increasingly stressed their rights to govern and teach the whole church.

Especially during the nineteenth century, events in Europe supported the rapid rise of the ultramontanist movement. Revolutions in France and Germany had destroyed many of the universities and faculties of theology. Before 1789, for example, there existed in Germany eighteen Catholic university centers; by 1815 no more than five faculties of theology functioning remained.[3] Matters were even worse in France.

The end of clerical education in France meant the end of a means to support Gallican ecclesiology.[4] To fill the vacuum, the Roman College reopened in 1824. More national seminaries were opened in Rome and the number of seminarians studying there rose dramatically.

A decisive turning point in the papal response to these turbulent times came with the pontificate of Gregory XVI (1831–1846), who started a tradition of papal initiative that remains strong to this day: the frequent exercise of the ordinary magisterium through the publication of encyclicals on issues of doctrine and discipline directed to Catholics throughout the world.

After a brief two-year courtship with liberal ideas, Pius IX, sobered by the revolution of 1848, directed for the next thirty years all his energies against liberalism in all its forms. With his strong encouragement, the Jesuits founded *Civiltà cattolica* in 1849 to disseminate the pope's ideas throughout Italy and beyond. Again in 1860, the pope supported the establishment of *Osservatore Romano* to disseminate ultramontanist ideas.[5] Modern means of transportation made it possible for Pius IX to require regular *ad limina* visits of bishops and for growing numbers of lay people to make pilgrimages to Rome where they were deeply moved by the wit, warmth and personal charm of this pope, whose pontificate was the longest in the history of the church.

When evaluated in terms of its impact on the episcopacy, the essence of the ultramontanist movement, according to Jean-Marie Tillard, can be stated simply: the bishops are relegated to a subordinate level while everything centers on the pope.[6] The minority bishops of the First Vatican Council voiced over and over again their fear that the strong movement toward centralization of authority would reduce the episcopacy to mere executants of the papal will. Bishop Bernard McQuaid of Rochester and Archbishop Peter Kenrick of St. Louis both had opposed the idea of papal infallibility precisely because, as they understood it, it diminished the role of the bishops. The First Vatican Council itself was mainly a European event with mainly Europeans in attendance. As James Hennesey explains:

> Its plans, debates, and documents reflected preoccupation with Europe's 19th-century problems: the impact of Enlightenment and French Revolution, the influence of Kant and Hegel, 19th-century continental liberalism. The Italian *Risorgimento* was quite literally at the gates of Rome. A thousand years of papal sovereign rule in central Italy were in their final twelve months. Since Pius VII's time, a succession of popes had set official

Catholicism's face squarely against the political, social, and intellectual temper of the times. The Vatican Council was designed by Pius IX to set the seal on that opposition.[7]

Not only was the membership of the council predominantly European, but the European membership was predominantly Latin. When the council opened, two-thirds of those qualified to attend, about seven hundred bishops, were in attendance. However, French and Italian bishops constituted between them fifty-two percent of the assembly (seventeen percent French and thirty-five percent Italian), and almost one hundred more bishops came from Spain and Latin America.[8] In terms of representation, "Central and Eastern Europe had, in 1870, approximately 70 million Catholics; the rest of Europe had about 110 million. Outside Europe, and apart from Latin America, there were perhaps another 21 million. Latin America probably had a civil population of over 70 million, but how many of these could be counted as Catholic is difficult to say. Italy had some 336 bishops for a nominal Catholic population of about 30 millions."[9]

In Latin countries, where Catholics were a majority, support for papal primacy and infallibility was the strongest. Characteristic of some of the formidable number of Italians at the council was the belief in the inerrancy of the pope in matters of discipline, in the "personal" primacy and infallibility of the pope, in the preservation of the temporal power of the pope, and in a rejection of the idea of the *sensus fidelium* or consultation of the laity.[10] Concerning the importance of public opinion, the secretary of state, Cardinal Antonelli, said on the eve of the council that "newspapers should limit themselves to announcing the functions in the Papal chapels and giving interesting news of Chinese insurrections."[11] The Latin and especially the Italian representation was numerous and vocal enough to dominate the council.[12]

It was only at the insistence of the minority bishops including Spalding, many of whom came from countries where Catholics were in the minority or where there were strong currents of episcopalism, that on May 9 an addition was made to the revised schema which stated that the jurisdiction of the papacy did not conflict with that of the episcopate. In the final text, the added paragraph reads as follows:

This power of the Supreme Pontiff is far from obstructing the ordinary and immediate power of episcopal jurisdiction by which individual bishops, placed by the Holy Spirit and successors of the apostles, feed and rule as true shepherds the individual flocks assigned to them. Rather the power of the bishops is protected, strengthened, and upheld by the supreme and uni-versal shepherd, as St. Gregory the Great writes: "My honor is the honor of the whole Church. My honor is the solid strength of my brethren. I am truly honored when the honor due to every single one is not denied."[13]

Despite this assertion of the abiding importance of episcopal author-ity, the clear emphasis at Vatican I, whether the topic was infallibility or primacy, is upon the papal focus and centralization, not upon collegial-ity and the importance of the local church. A careful reading of the texts of the definitions, especially in the context of the conciliar discussions and interventions, reveals in fact that the council finally adopted moder-ate positions. Nevertheless, the absence of any clear delineation of the rights and responsibilities of the episcopate, to balance those claimed for the pope, constituted a serious limitation.[14] Once the council was over, misunderstanding was widespread. Most people understood it to have defined not the irreformability of papal definitions but papal infallibility, not the infallibility of the church as the basis of papal teaching authority, but papal teaching authority as the source of infallibility, and not the right and responsibility of the bishops to govern and teach their dio-ceses, but the power of the pope to teach and direct everyone, starting with the bishops.

Shortly after the publication of the council documents, Otto von Bismarck, the chancellor of the German empire, concluded that the bishops had been reduced to papal functionaries. He sent a directive (dated May 14, 1872) to his diplomatic representatives ordering them to bypass the local bishops and deal directly with the pope. When Bis-marck's directive became public in late 1874, the German bishops drew up and published in February 1875 a remarkably forceful and clear statement of the powers of bishops. They listed eight errors in Bis-marck's understanding of their role:

1. As a result of these conciliar decrees the pope can now take into his own hand the rights of the bishops in each and every diocese and can now substitute his own papal power for that of the residential bishops.
2. Episcopal jurisdiction has been absorbed by papal jurisdiction.
3. The pope no longer exercises, as he did in the past, merely a few determined rights reserved to himself, but now he is the depository of the totality of episcopal rights.
4. He has, in principle, taken the place of each individual bishop.
5. At any time the pope, at his own good pleasure, can in practical affairs take the place of the bishop in his relations with the government.

6. The bishops are now nothing more than his instruments and functionaries with no personal responsibility.
7. The bishops have become, in their relations with their governments,
   the functionaries of a foreign sovereign.
8. The pope, by virtue of his infallibility, is truly a perfectly absolute
   sovereign, more absolute than any absolute secular monarch.

At the end of this list, the German bishops stated: "All of these
statements are without foundation." They then presented the true teaching of the church: "According to this teaching of the Catholic Church,
the Pope is Bishop of Rome, not bishop of any other city or diocese, not
bishop of Cologne or of Breslau. . . . According to the constant teaching of the Catholic Church . . . the bishops are not mere instruments of
the pope, nor papal functionaries with no personal responsibility, but
rather they have been appointed by the Holy Spirit to take the place of
the apostles in order to nurture and rule, as befits good shepherds, the
flock committed to them." What is even more striking than this strong
endorsement of episcopal rights is the response of Pius IX, released less
than a month later. He wrote: "Your statement is indeed so clear and
sound that, since it leaves nothing to be desired, We ought to content
Ourselves by merely giving you Our fullest congratulations."[15]

Despite the clarity and forcefulness of the German bishops' statement and Pius IX's strong endorsement, motivated perhaps in part by
the seriousness of the political situation in Germany and by his desire to
keep the support of the German bishops, most people both inside and
outside the church continued to think about the role of the bishops
pretty much in the way Bismarck did.

2. The Marian Dimension and Papal Authority

Ultramontanists in general, and Louis Veuillot in particular, often
linked their desire to advance the power of the pope with the apparitions
of Mary and the doctrine of the immaculate conception. In fact, the
definition of the immaculate conception in 1854 was an important stage
in the development of ultramontanism. When, for example, the woman
who appeared to Bernadette Soubirous told her on March 25, 1858, "I
am the Immaculate Conception," many saw in these words a persuasive
confirmation of the dogmatic definition of 1854.[16] One of the first historians of Lourdes commented:

No one could have guessed that Mary would step from her
throne, place her feet on the earth and say to all Christians in

the person of Bernadette: This word of the Roman Pope is the oracle of divine truth. I am indeed exactly as the Pope as defined, the Immaculate Conception, and till the end of time, here, in this place where I speak, countless miracles will bear witness alike to the actuality of my appearances, to my Immaculate Conception and to the Infallibility of the Pope.

This point was repeated when Bernadette was canonized in 1933:

That which the Pope by virtue of his infallible teaching office defined, the Immaculate Virgin desired to confirm openly, through her own mouth, when soon after she proclaimed her identity in a famous appearance at the grotto of Massabielle.

In the centenary encyclical of 1958, Pope Pius XII remarked:

Certainly the infallible word of the Pope, the authentic interpreter of revealed truth, required no endorsement from heaven to be valid for the faithful; but with what emotion did Christian people and their shepherds receive from the lips of Bernadette this answer which came from heaven.[17]

The concern to enhance the position of the pope was also clear in the way in which the definition of the immaculate conception was worded. In the weeks immediately preceding the definition, representative bishops from each country were invited to Rome to discuss the final formulation of the dogma. There was some disagreement over whether the proposed bull should state explicitly that the bishops had given their consent to the definition, a consent that had already been ascertained by Pius IX who had consulted 603 bishops in 1849.[18] Bishop O'Connor of Pittsburgh, among others, urged that it be made clear that the definition had been made with the consent of the bishops. Archbishop Andrea Charvaz of Genoa opposed the idea, claiming that to speak of the consent of the bishops where an infallible papal decree was concerned sounded like Protestantism. The bishops supported the Italian prelate.

Even though the pope had consulted the bishops, he promulgated the dogma of the immaculate conception on his own authority. No general council was held. In 1854, Pius IX acted "by virtue of the authority of the holy Apostles Peter and Paul and of Our own authority" and appeared to exercise an infallible teaching authority apart from the faith of the whole church sixteen years before the First Vatican Council met. (This practice was followed closely nearly one hundred years later by

Pius XII, who also without a council pronounced the dogma of the assumption.)

What no one would have predicted, of course, is that through the work of theologians such as John Henry Newman, Matthias Scheeben, Maurice Blondel and especially Yves Congar, the importance of consulting the faith of the people, as Pius IX and Pius XII did before defining the Marian dogmas, would become an essential part of a renewed ecclesiology that, in turn, would make clear that papal infallibility is grounded in the infallibility of the whole church. The importance of the faith of the whole church is especially clear in Pius XII's allocution to the consistory on October 30, 1950: "We have addressed letters to all the bishops asking them to reveal to Us not only their own opinions but also the opinions and the wishes of their clergy and people. In splendid and almost unanimous chorus, the voices of pastors and faithful throughout the entire world reached Us, professing the same faith and requesting the same thing as sovereignly desired by all." A little later the pope speaks of "this remarkable agreement of bishops and the Catholic faithful."[19] In just a few more years, the bishops at the Second Vatican Council would vote to place what they wished to say about Mary in the midst of the document on the church, just as they would vote to speak of papal primacy in the midst of the collegiality of the bishops, and papal infallibility in the midst of ecclesial infallibility which takes the word of God as its norm.

3. Who Appoints the Bishops?

Canon 329 of the 1917 Code of Canon Law states that the bishops of the church are freely appointed by the Roman pontiff. A famous canonist, F. X. Wernz, consulted as an authority right up to Vatican II (though he died in 1914), wrote: "The right to institute bishops belongs properly and by nature (*proprio et nativo jure*) to the Roman pontiff. If bishops of the ecclesiastical Province, or chapters, or even civil authorities, laymen and clergy have come to have some say in the nomination of bishops, it is because of a concession, tacit or explicit, of the Roman pontiff."[20] An examination of the historical record, however, will show that for the greater part of the church's history, the process of nominating bishops was not claimed by the papacy, either personally or as a right. Canon 329, echoed in large part by canon 377 of the new 1983 Code ("The Supreme Pontiff freely appoints Bishops or confirms those lawfully elected," a statement which leaves the door open to an elective system which is not specified), actually represents a very recent development, beginning only in the latter part of the nineteenth century.

During the first thousand years of the church's history, bishops were elected without any formal intervention on the part of the pope. When in the eleventh century princes and kings exercised too much authority in this process, the church responded by requiring, according to canon 28 of the Second Lateran Council which met in the year 1139, that bishops be elected by cathedral chapters. There was still no expectation that the pope should appoint the bishops. From that time until the nineteenth century, two systems operated for the election of the vast majority of the bishops: either by a cathedral chapter or through some royal or imperial patronage. In 1829, for example, the power of the pope to appoint bishops applied to only twenty-four dioceses outside the papal states. In the course of the last one hundred years, the situation has been exactly reversed. And "by 1980, out of the 2,456 dioceses of the Catholic Church, only 24 still had chapter elections. They were mostly in Central Europe, and the Bishop of Basel in Switzerland is the best-known example. There were also 175 surviving examples of state patronage—but they were increasingly an anachronism and were fading tranquilly away."[21] All other bishops, a total of some 2,250 bishops, are Vatican appointments.

What accounts for this dramatic change? The reasons, of course, are complex. It would be far too simple, however, to say that the main reasons the popes acquired this power was for personal advantage and greater control, though it would be hard to rule that out as one factor. I would submit that the main reasons for the shift were for two, often related, reasons: first, the existing methods of selecting bishops no longer worked well; second, the political and social conditions favored the intervention of Rome. Let us examine briefly two examples.

First, consider the situation in Bolivia during the pontificate of Pius IX. There, Catholicism was the "religion of the republic" where by concordat the Church controlled the educational institutions and specific endowments of the Church, and in exchange for these benefits permitted the president of the country what was then called "the patronage or privilege of presenting."[22] In the one hundred and fifty years that followed that country's independence, however, there were two hundred and fifty revolutions. At the time of the First Vatican Council, Bolivia was ruled by a man who was commonly known as "cruel, crude and ignorant—a drunkard, womanizer and public concubinary." Sweeney explains that "this was the man to whom the selection of his country's hierarchy had been entrusted. . . . The bankruptcy of the system (of state patronage) should have been evident."[23]

The change from zealously guarding episcopal independence to enthusiastically embracing papal centralization is perhaps nowhere more striking than in the case of France. The aggressive anti-clericalism of the government of France, which penalized those in schools, fragmented religious congregations, and finally appropriated church property, caused in French Catholics, who just a few years before identified themselves as Gallicans, a stunning switch to ultramontanism. Again, in the words of Sweeney, "Leadership was lacking, they were deeply divided among themselves, and in their distress they turned to Rome. Strong leadership could hardly have been expected of bishops who were paid officials of the State. . . . The pre-1870 situation was exactly reversed: it was not now the Pope who was relying on the French to preserve Temporal Power—it was French Catholicism which was relying on the Pope in its struggle for survival."[24]

One final irony. It seems as though the United States played a key role in the development of the policy of reserving episcopal appointments to the pope. The situation of the church in the United States was unprecedented. There were no cathedral chapters, though, presumably, the twenty-six priests who elected John Carroll in 1789 as the first bishop of the new republic believed that they had followed as closely as possible the spirit of the legislation of Lateran II. Moreover, there was no possibility of lay patronage, as for example in Latin America, given the separation of church and state. In 1808, the five United States bishops wrote to Rome asking that the right of nomination be given to the archbishop of Baltimore and his suffragans. Eleven years later (the pope had been in captivity from 1809–1814) they received a negative response, for such an arrangement seemed to violate the legislation of Lateran II. To avoid a situation in which the hierarchy would be exclusively self-perpetuating, the Vatican agreed in 1822 that the American bishops could have the right to recommend to vacant sees. "Thus was introduced into the Church the combination of local recommendation and papal appointment which, owing to the phenomenal growth in numbers and importance of the American hierarchy, was ultimately to become a pattern for the Universal Church and obliterate the combination of local nomination and papal institution decreed in 1139 by Lateran II."[25]

A more historically aware theology makes it clear today that there are numerous ways in which bishops can be appointed: election by all the people of the diocese, by the priests in the diocese, by the cathedral chapter, or by a priests' senate. They can be elected by neighboring bishops, through a bishops' conference, or by the Roman pontiff. "Thus," stated Karl Rahner in a 1982 interview, "from a dogmatic standpoint as well as the very nature of the Church, a direct appointment by the pope is not the only method of election."[26] Given the situation of the church throughout the world in the early nineteenth century, the transfer of the power of episcopal appointment to the pope was, judges historian Garrett Sweeney, "an immense improvement on the previous situation."[27] The situation today, of course, is different. The entire matter now needs re-examination, especially since we have, with the Second Vatican Council, reaffirmed the importance of the local church and the episcopacy.

4. Modernism and Romanization

The church of the nineteenth century saw itself deeply opposed to the intellectual, social and political consequences of the enlightenment. If politically and socially this required opposition to liberalism and the independence of the state from the church, intellectually it called for opposition to the disregard of authority and tradition. This stance, commonly called ultramontanism, is described by Joseph Komonchak as an "unparalleled insistence on the principle of authority not only in society but also in theology and in philosophy."[28] We have already noted that the destruction of many of the Catholic intellectual centers in Europe in the late eighteenth and early nineteenth centuries left a vacuum that Rome attempted to fill through founding its own institutions of learning and increasing dramatically the number of papal encyclicals, a practice which began with Gregory XVI.

Historians of the nineteenth century often contrast the pontificates of Pius IX and Leo XIII, stressing Leo's greater spirit of openness. Several of Leo's practices would confirm this portrait. For example, he encouraged bishops' conferences, which his predecessor suspected of Gallicanism; he gave the red hat to Newman; he opened the Vatican archives to scholars of every confession and reminded Catholics of the historians' obligation always to tell the truth. It was Leo who told Bishop d'Hulst in 1892 that "the troubled and perplexed would like the Roman Congregations to pronounce on questions still under debate. I am against it and put them off, for scholars must not be prevented from doing their job. They must be allowed time to grope their way and even to err. Religious truth can only be the gainer."[29] Instead of simply condemning the errors of modern society, Leo XIII attempted a more positive response for example by calling in 1879 for a revitalization of the thought of St. Thomas.

Leo placed great hope in the thought of Aquinas. The possible benefits of a Thomistic renewal were thought to be extensive. Komonchak describes Leo's hope in these terms: "Here, in the greatest mind of the Middle Ages, that never again equalled realization of Christendom, were to be found the intellectual principles by which alone could be overcome the fatal disjunctions of reason from faith and of society from religion. In a common dependence on Thomist foundations Catholic thinkers would overcome those divisions into schools which prevented them from making common cause against the enemy. The warfare was on the level of ideas, and the Thomist synthesis would provide Catholics with their most powerful weapons."[30] The neo-Thomism that the encyclical promoted, however, was ahistorical. In its emphasis on universal and objective truth and not on difference in time, historical outlook and cultural expression, it lent itself nicely to the program of a very active ordinary magisterium which wanted to teach authoritatively and uniformly for the universal church. One of its significant weaknesses, in the judgment of Gerald McCool, was that "it was unaffected by the personality and the cultural milieu of individual thinkers. Differences in time, historical outlook, and cultural expression were accidental."[31]

When at the end of Leo's reign the modernist crisis arose, the church was not intellectually prepared to meet it. The very ahistorical character of Thomism was unable to cope with the principal tension in modernism: that between dogma and history. Despite Leo's personal openness and intellectual interests, his lengthy doctrinal encyclicals established more and more uniformity in the intellectual life of Catholics. The number and frequently the length of papal encyclicals increased, addressing not only particular problems but also setting forth official positions on complex intellectual, political and cultural problems. "Catholics gradually assumed the habit," Komonchak concludes, "of looking to the Popes for regular and authoritative guidance in the construction of their mental world, and the following decades were to see the increasing subordination to Roman authority of all other instances of teaching in the Church, whether episcopal or theological."[32]

Another way to describe the impact of these developments on the bishops of the church is to speak of their "Romanization." It is possible to distinguish between the condemnation of Americanism in the United States and of modernism in Europe. Even if both were part of the same effort—"to establish a contemporary identity for an ancient church"— few of the participants or their concerns were the same. "Some Americanists," explains James Hennesey, "knew some Modernists and they shared occasional sympathies, but the movements, which followed one another chronologically, were contiguous rather than continuous. American preoccupations did not run to immanentist philosophy and historico-biblical criticism."[33] Moreover, there was a considerably stronger intellectual life in Europe than in America at the turn of the century. Nevertheless, on both continents, one of the main consequences of the condemnations, at least when we consider its impact on bishops, was the "Romanization" of the hierarchy.

Romanization was achieved principally through two means: first, the process of the appointment of bishops, and, second, the centralization of the very process of the appointment of bishops, both of which we have already described. A Roman education, along with the faithful implementation of papal encyclicals, became the best assurance for advancement in the hierarchy.

5. Fine-Tuning Centralization

I mentioned earlier that Leo XIII from one angle appeared as a liberalizing influence when compared to Pius IX. From another angle, that of the centralization of authority, Pius IX and Leo XIII were the same: they both sought to increase it as much as possible. If Leo XIII supported episcopal conferences, it was because he saw in them means through which to ensure uniform teaching and practice throughout the Church. The plans, for example, of the Third Plenary Council of Baltimore (1884) were drawn up in Rome, and although no Roman prelate was sent to preside, it was clear that Archbishop Gibbons was to act as the delegate of the pope. "The first assembly of the South American episcopate was held in the Vatican, and the pope himself presided. Leo XIII was in any case lavish with his directives to national episcopates and he did not shrink from direct intervention in the conflicts involving religion and politics which were raging in several countries, his intention being to fix the line to be followed by faithful and clergy."[34] Papal nuncios began to assume roles of papal representatives at the local level. The pope appeared more and more as the universal pastor. The authority of the local bishops became, in practice, often less than that of the nuncio.

Pius X enhanced the role of the nuncio precisely in order to maintain a tighter control over every diocese in the world. Aubert tells us:

His policy was to replace career diplomats by bishops or former heads of a religious order and he made it their prime duty to report to the Holy See on the state of the dioceses, to supervise the teaching given in the seminaries, to visit religious houses, and so on. As part of the same pattern, the visits of bishops *ad limina,* obligatory (as we have already noted) since the time of Pius IX, now had to be made on dates strictly laid down, and the bishops were required in addition to submit regular and very detailed reports to the Consistorial Congregation, as indeed were the superiors of religious houses. The choice of

superiors was increasingly controlled from Rome, and the policy inaugurated under Leo XIII of encouraging the transfer of
mother houses to Rome was taken up with renewed vigor,
being spurred to greater success by government hostility to the
religious congregations in France, where many had hitherto
had their headquarters. The reform of the curia . . . by concen-
trating the government of the Church in a few hands, added
particular weight to the interventions of the Roman congregations in the affairs of the Catholic world as a whole. . . . The
new code of canon law was soon explicitly to affirm that by the
expression 'Holy See' should be understood not just the pope
but equally the Roman congregations (Canon 7).[35]

From the time of Leo XIII it became customary for the popes to
encourage, and in some cases even prescribe, the regular meeting of
episcopal conferences. The 1917 Code of Canon Law (Canon 292) required that bishops of every ecclesiastical province met once every five
years. The popes viewed these conferences as excellent vehicles through
which they could pass on their ideas for the renewal of the church. They
were concerned, however, about conferences which appeared to them to
have the potential to exercise independent power.

This was the case with the United States where in 1919 the National
Catholic Welfare Council, originally formed in 1917 and named then the
National Catholic War Council, posed problems for the Vatican, which,
according to the then superior general of the Jesuits Vladimir Ledochow-
ski, tended to find traces of modernism everywhere. Members of the
curia wanted to dissolve the council, but, in the face of great support by
the American hierarchy for its continuation, they then asked that it not
meet every year, that attendance be voluntary, that the decisions of the
meetings not be binding, and that the name "Council" in the title of the
organization be changed to something like "Committee."[36] Such suggestions were made by Rome to limit carefully the organization's scope and
to stress its non-conciliar and non-legislative character.[37]

It was only with vigorous support of the missions and the need for
indigenous clergy, beginning with the pontificate of Benedict XV, that
such meetings began to make clearer the need for a certain degree of
pluralism in church discipline and the importance of the local church.
Uniformity in liturgy and discipline throughout the entire church, clearly
the goal of Pius IX, Leo XIII and Pius X, was no longer sought by Pius
XII, who, in 1944, could say to missionaries gathered in Rome: "The
missionary is the apostle of Jesus Christ. His mission is not to transplant
European civilization to missionary countries but rather to persuade

their populations, some of whom enjoy the benefits of an age-old culture, to accept and assimilate the elements of Christian life and conduct, which should harmonize quite naturally and harmoniously with any healthy civilization. . . ."[38] The way toward the Second Vatican Council was being prepared.

6. The Pope with the Bishops: Vatican II

I have concentrated thus far in this paper on the nature and degree of unprecedented centralization that had occurred in the Catholic Church from the rise of the ultramontanist movement in the middle of the nineteenth century through the pontificate of Pius XII. Given the degree of centralization in the church, it is all the more surprising that the Second Vatican Council even took place, much less that it officially expressed a doctrine of collegiality among the bishops that balances the excessive emphasis on the papacy and the centralization of authority put firmly in place by Vatican I.

The forces at work leading up to Vatican II are many, and only a few of the most important will be mentioned here, and then only briefly. One important change has been the revolution in means of travel. No United States bishop during the nineteenth century ever participated in the election of a pope. The slowness of transatlantic travel made such participation impossible. Improvements in travel made possible the internationalization of a cardinalate that could get to Rome at short notice. Moreover, after 1870 it was no longer important that the pope be an expert in Italian politics; the papacy itself became more of an international position. In the conclave of 1878, for example, the foreign cardinals, who at this time made up nearly forty percent of the Sacred College, were nearly all able to attend thanks to the development of railways. At the 1903 conclave, thirty-eight Italian and twenty-four foreign cardinals were in attendance. Pius XII created an unprecedented number of cardinals, thirty-two in 1946 and twenty-four in 1953, drawing them from many countries and reducing the Italian representation to one-third. At his first consistory, John XXIII abolished the rule, dating from Sixtus V, fixing seventy as the maximum number of cardinals, and by 1962 he increased the college to eighty-seven, making it larger and more international than ever before. Even though almost all of these cardinals were trained in Rome, still other factors were at work in the twentieth century to set the stage for Vatican II.

The condemnation of modernism played its own role in opening up the church, for as a result there was a return by scholars to the sources of the Catholic tradition, the study of the scriptures, greatly facilitated by

Pius XII's 1943 encyclical, *Divino afflante Spiritu*. The renewal of biblical and patristic studies deepened the church's awareness of its historical
character and provided rich and multiple images for thinking about the
nature of the church and the Christian life. Liturgical renewal, encouraged by Pius X, advanced under the vigorous leadership of Pius XI and
Pius XII (who with his 1947 encyclical *Mediator Dei* called for more
intelligent participation in the eucharist, and in the 1950s reformed the
entire Holy Week liturgy). Still another important encyclical, *Mystici
corporis,* also published in 1943, proved to be a decisive step in ecclesiology:[39] it moved the entire church away from an excessively juridical way of thinking about the church. Pius XII was more willing than his
predecessors to see positive elements in the ecumenical movement. In
December 1949, shortly after the formation of the World Council of
Churches, he formally recognized the ecumenical movement and permitted Catholic scholars to dialogue with non-Catholics on matters of faith.

It was especially under Pius XI (1922–1939) that the active involvement of the laity was first sought. I have already mentioned his commitment to the missions and his openness to indigenization of liturgy and
theology. He took the view that Christianity should be active in and not
insulated in society. The laity was being called in the 1920s to a co-
responsibility, a call that was given further delineation in 1931 with the
important encyclical, *Quadragesimo anno.* Pius XI was the pope of
"Catholic Action."

The Franco-Prussian War interrupted the First Vatican Council before it was able to take up the second part of its agenda: a document on the
nature of the church. Thus, only one side of the "papal-episcopal dialectic" was articulated. Members of the minority constantly stated that the
other side—that is, episcopal rights and duties—needed to be articulated
at the same time, only to be reassured just as often by the council's
theological commission that the episcopacy would be discussed later.[40]
"Later" turned out to be more than a ninety year wait; but by then, in
what hardly could have been anticipated by any of the participants of
Vatican I, the minority became the majority. When we turn to Vatican II
we discover that Vatican I's minority became Vatican II's majority.

We should not think that Vatican II reversed Vatican I. What Vatican I stated about papal infallibility and primacy, Vatican II, with very
few adjustments, repeated. What Vatican II did do was receive Vatican I
in a way that restored to the episcopacy its proper place in the more
ancient tradition of the church. "What *Lumen Gentium* has done," writes
Tillard, "is to set this repeat of Vatican I (on papal primacy) within a new
perspective. The vision which controls its teaching on the Church is no
longer that of the ultramontane majority of 1870, but that of the more

balanced and lucid elements in the minority of Vatican I. . . . We may therefore say that at Vatican II *Pastor Aeternus* was 'received' in the dogmatic sense by the minority of Vatican I after nearly a century of deepening study and fresh thought. The importance of this new reception in a new climate is too little recognized: Vatican I and Vatican II together form a dialectical unity in which one should be interpreted by the other."[41]

I shall quote at some length Tillard's excellent summary of Vatican II's teaching on the episcopacy and its relationship to the bishop of Rome. "Where Vatican I sees the Church in its earthly form starting from its 'head,' the bishop of Rome, Vatican II sees its starting from the bishops as 'successors of the apostles' (LG 18, 20, 22, 23, 24, etc.), and who, taken together as a whole, comprise the foundation of the universal Church (LG 19). By divine institution, the bishops are indeed the 'heads' of the Church who 'direct the house of the living God' (LG 18), its shepherds (LG 20), its pontiffs (LG 21), the 'acme of the sacred ministry' (LG 21). All this comes to them through the sacrament of episcopal consecration. At an even deeper level, the bishops are the authentic *vicarii et legati Christi* for the government of the churches (LG 27). Vatican II is thus entirely clear: the fullness of that ministry which builds, guides and leads the whole Church belongs to the body of bishops as such, following in the wake of the mission entrusted to the apostles as a group (LG 20, 21)."[42]

Lumen Gentium repeats the teaching of *Pastor Aeternus* that just as Peter was placed at the head of the other disciples, so the pope, in whom there is a lasting and visible source of unity, ensures the unity of the episcopacy. *Lumen Gentium* adds, however, that the bishops are the successors of the apostles and together with Peter direct the house of the living God (LG 18). Moreover, footnoting the 1875 statement of the German bishops, par. 27 of *Lumen Gentium* explains that the bishops are not to be regarded as vicars of the Roman pontiff, for they exercise an authority which is proper to them, and are quite correctly called prelates, heads of the people whom they govern. Again, Tillard explains, "The scheme no longer has the shape of a pyramid. The line no longer travels from the pope to the bishops, with the weight on the former at the expense of the latter, but from the bishops to the pope. A series of balancing statements, which made the new minority grind their teeth, kept in the forefront of debate the fact that Christ had built his Church not on Peter only but on the apostles with Peter at their head."[43] It is no longer completely accurate, then, to say that only the pope is the vicar of Christ since *Lumen Gentium* par. 27 requires us to say that all the bishops are vicars of Christ.

There was, according to Tillard, an even more profound development in the ecclesiology of Vatican II: "the movement from an ecclesiology starting with the idea of the universal Church divided into
portions called dioceses, to an ecclesiology which understands the Church
as the communion of all the local churches."[44] From this perspective the
universal church is constituted by the communion of the churches. *Lumen
Gentium* also teaches that episcopal authority is founded on a sacrament—the episcopate. "In view of its function, indeed, the power of
hierarchy in the Church can only derive from the sacrament, not from
some distinct *ordo jurisdictionis* with its source in the pope. The episcopate is an essential tool for the construction of the Church."[45]

Vatican II "rereceived" Vatican I's teaching on papal primacy; it
also placed papal infallibility into a new context. The United States
Lutheran/Catholic Dialogue noted seven emphases of Vatican II which
requires that Vatican I's teaching, which Vatican II repeated, be reinter-
preted: (1) its basis in the infallibility of the whole Church, the *sensus
fidelium;* (2) that all defining be done in the context of a renewed collegiality of the bishops; (3) that the prior assent of the church is to be
embodied in the definition; (4) that a pilgrim church will always need to
reform its always inadequate definitions; (5) that the inescapable sinful-
ness of the church will affect even its dogmatic statements and mark
them with limitations; (6) that other churches not in full communion
with the Roman Catholic Church will need to be consulted in some way
in the formulation of teachings; (7) that the hierarchy of truths enhances
ecumenical dialogue and suggests the possibility that authentic faith in
the basic Christian message may exist without explicit belief in all defined dogmas.[46]

Finally, it should be noted that *Lumen Gentium* never made clear
just what limits should be respected in the practical order when it comes
to the exercise of the authority of the pope and that of the other bishops.
Pope Paul VI made an attempt to insert into the document's treatment
of collegiality a phrase that said that the pope is "answerable to God
alone." After considering this, the theological commission of the council
rejected the amendment as an oversimplification inasmuch as "the Roman Pontiff is also bound to revelation itself, to the fundamental structure of the church, to the sacraments, to the definitions of earlier councils and other obligations too numerous to mention."[47]

A second indication of the lack of clarity on this important matter is
provided by the famous *nota praevia,* that is, the preliminary note of
explanation given by the theological commission as a guide for interpreting the council's teaching on collegiality. In essence it said that the pope
was to make his decisions always taking into consideration the good of

the church, or, as Vatican I put it, for the building up of and not the destruction of the Church. Nothing more specific was stated. "Vatican II thus gave no firm juridical norm, no canonically formulated limit which would make it quite clear how far the pope's power extended."[48] This lack of clarity has continued since the council to be a source of confusion and tension.

In 1980 a French church historian remarked that the Catholic Church had in the last decade changed more than it had in the previous century, that the church of Pius XII was closer to that of Pius IX than to that of Paul VI.[49] The ecclesiology of Vatican II is, as we have seen, significantly different from that of Vatican I. That many ordinary Catholics and some prelates and theologians still think that the church is a worldwide corporation with central headquarters in Rome, and that the bishops are only the pope's local representatives, reveals the distance we have yet to go to realize the teaching of the Second Vatican Council.

Notes

1. Kenneth Untener, "Local Church and Universal Church," *America* (October 13, 1984): 201–05.

2. Untener 202.

3. Yves Congar, *Tradition and Traditions* (The Macmillan Co., 1967) 196.

4. Richard Costigan, "Tradition and the Beginning of the Ultramontane Movement," *The Irish Theological Quarterly* 48 (1981) 27–45.

5. Derek Holmes, *The Triumph of the Holy See* (London: Burns and Oates, 1978) 135.

6. J.M.R. Tillard, *The Bishop of Rome* (Michael Glazier, Inc., 1983) 22.

7. James Hennesey, *American Catholics* (Oxford University Press, 1981) 168.

8. Roger Aubert, *The Church in a Secularized Society* Vol. 5: The Christian Centuries (Paulist Press, 1978) 61–62.

9. Aubert 61–62.

10. Garrett Sweeney, "The Primary: The Small Print of Vatican I," *Bishops and Writers,* Adrian Hastings, ed. (Anthony Clarke, 1977) 100–103.

11. Sweeney 103.

12. Sweeney 105.

13. John F. Broderick, *Documents of Vatican Council I* (Collegeville, Minnesota: The Liturgical Press, 1971).

14. Tillard 27.

15. Untener 205–06; see also Tillard 138–41; and F. Donald Logan, "The 1985 Statement of the German Bishops on Episcopal Powers," *The Jurist* 21 (1961); 285–95.

16. Holmes 140.

17. All three quotes from Holmes 140–41.

18. James Heft, "Papal Infallibility and the Marian Dogmas," *Marian Studies* 33 (1982): 47–89.

19. Tillard 230–31.

20. Tillard 182.

21. Peter Hebblethwaite, *In the Vatican* (Bethesda, Maryland: Adler and Adler, 1986) 94.

22. Sweeney 220.

23. Sweeney 220–21.

24. Sweeney 226–27.

25. Sweeney 216–17.

26. Paul Imhof, ed. and Schubert Biallowons, trans., *Karl Rahner in Dialogue* (New York: Crossroad, trans. 1986) 321.

27. Sweeney 208.

28. Joseph Komonchak, "The Enlightenment and the Construction of Roman Catholicism," Catholic Commission of Intellectual and Cultural Affairs (1985) 44.

29. Aubert 179.

30. Komonchak 44–45.

31. Cited by Gerald P. Fogarty, *The Vatican and the American Hierarchy from 1870–1965* (Michael Glazier, 1985).

32. Komonchak 45–46.

33. Hennesey 196–97.

34. Aubert 67–68.

35. Aubert 68–69.

36. Fogarty 225.

37. Hennesey 230.

38. Aubert 430.

39. Yves Congar, *L'Eglise de saint Augustin à l'époque moderne* (Paris: Les Editions du Cerf, 1970) 471.

40. Gustave Thils, "The Theology of Primary," *One in Christ* 10 (1974): 13–30.

41. Tillard 35.

42. Tillard 36.

43. Tillard 36–37.

44. Tillard 37.

45. Tillard 39.

46. P. C. Empie, T. A. Murphy and J. A. Burgess, ed., *Teaching Authority and Infallibility in the Church: Lutherans and Catholics in Dialogue* VI (Minneapolis, Minnesota: Augsburg Publishing House, 1978) 27–28.
47. Untener 203.
48. Tillard 42.
43. Emile Poulat, *Une Eglise Ebranlée: Changement, conflit et continuité de Pie XII a Jean Paul II* (Paris: Casterman, 1980) 41.

Bibliography

Aubert, Roger. *The Church in a Secularized Society.* Vol. 5: The Christian Centuries. Paulist Press, 1978.

Broderick, John F. *Documents of Vatican Council I.* Collegeville, Minnesota: The Liturgical Press, 1971.

Congar, Yves. *Tradition and Traditions.* The Macmillan Company, 1967.

———. *L'Eglise de saint Augustin à l'époque moderne.* Paris: Les Editions du Cerf, 1970.

Costigan, Richard. "Tradition and the Beginning of the Ultramontane Movement." *The Irish Theological Quarterly* 48 (1981): 27–45.

Empie, P.C., T.A. Murphy and J.A. Burgess, eds. *Teaching Authority and Infallibility in the Church: Lutherans and Catholics in Dialogue* VI. Minneapolis: Augsburg Publishing House, 1978.

Fogarty, Gerald P. *The Vatican and the American Hierarchy from 1870–1965.* Michael Glazier, Inc., 1985.

———. *Nova et Vetera: The Theology of Tradition in American Catholicism.* The 1987 Pere Marquette Theology Lecture. Marquette University Press, 1987.

Hebblethwaite, Peter. *In the Vatican.* Bethesda, Maryland: Adler and Adler, 1986.

Heft, James. "Papal Infallibility and the Marian Dogmas." *Marian Studies* 33 (1982): 47–89.

Holmes, Derek. *The Triumph of the Holy See.* London: Burns and Oates, 1978.

Hennesey, James. *American Catholics.* Oxford University Press, 1981.

Imhof, Paul, ed and Schubert Baillowons, trans. *Karl Rahner in Dialogue.* New York: Crossroads, 1986.

Komonchak, Joseph. "The Enlightenment and the Construction of Roman Catholicism." Catholic Commission on Intellectual and Cultural Affairs, 1985.

Logan, F. Donald. "The 1985 Statement of the German Bishops on Episcopal Powers." *The Jurist* 21 (1961): 285–95.

Poulat, Emile. *Une Eglise ebranlée: Changement, conflit et continuité de Pie XII a Jean Paul II.* Paris: Casterman, 1980.

Sweeney, Garrett. "The Forgotten Council." *Bishops and Writers,* Adrian Hastings, ed. Anthony Clarke, 1977.

————. "The Primary: The Small Print of Vatican I." *Bishops and Writers.*

————. "The 'Wound in the Right Foot': Unhealed?" *Bishops and Writers.*

Thils, Gustave. "The Theology of Primary." *One in Christ* 10 (1974): 13–30.

Tillard, J.M.R. *The Bishop of Rome.* Michael Glazier, Inc., 1983.

Untener, Kenneth. "Local Church and Universal Church." *America,* October 13, 1984: 201–05.

James Hennesey, S.J.

Rome and the Origins of
the United States Hierarchy

A ddressing a group of visiting Austrian bishops at the Vatican in the spring of 1987, Pope John Paul II advised them in no uncertain terms:

> You must have no doubt as to the right of the pope to be free to appoint bishops, a right which, in the struggle for freedom, unity and the Catholic character of the Church, has been made clearer in the course of history.

In that statement the pope enunciated clearly his philosophy (or theology?) of history. He has no difficulty in accepting the historical fact that the process of choosing bishops has changed over the centuries. He sees what has happened as a positive development, resulting as it has in an almost universal system of papal selection and appointment of Catholic bishops. This, he informed the Austrian bishops, has nothing to do with "categories of power"; universal papal selection secures appointments motivated only by the needs of the church's spiritual mission, the service of souls and the communal interests of the church.[1]

The question is, of course, whether the tradition must necessarily be read this way. "Latest" is not always "best." Reform in every age of the church has set aside what it judged less worthy or less useful in the practice inherited from previous generations. We do not fault the German reformers and their pupil, St. Gregory VII, for reversing the thrust given the church by the popes of the tenth century. Episcopal selection is a process that has varied greatly. From the dimmest mists of history until the latter part of the last century, local selection was the norm. Papal selection (as opposed to "confirmation," or "institution," or "granting of communion") was a sign that a local ecclesial community was considered to be in a missionary status. The means of local selection was a further question. Since the twelfth century it was the prerogative of the priests of a diocese, usually exercised through the cathedral chapter. But, as debates at the Council of Trent suggested, this had proven to be a weak reed. Election by neighboring bishops was never the vogue. Civil governments filled the void, and it was their role that was challenged and has been well-nigh eliminated by the nineteenth century papal pre-emption of the selection as well as the confirmation process.[2]

Papal selection of bishops is today accepted as standard in the western church. The London *Tablet* has spoken of the "undisputed papal prerogative" in the matter.[3] Explaining why an auxiliary bishop from an alien tribe had been named for the diocese of Gulu, Archbishop Karl-Josef Rauber, papal pro-nuncio in Uganda, referred to the "long, careful and impartial consultation" that had been carried on, but he was categorical in stating that "the responsibility for appointing a bishop" was "exclusively that of the pope."[4]

The pope's remarks to the Austrian bishops were occasioned by protests at the naming of an obscure Benedictine monk to succeed Cardinal Franziskus König as archbishop of Vienna, an appointment followed by that of a controversial auxiliary bishop to the same see. The Ugandan case addressed by Archbishop Rauber included accusations of insensitivity to local tribal interrelationships. Even more complex is the situation in the People's Republic of China, where two Catholic churches function side by side, one suffering for the church-political modalities of its linkage with Rome, the other publicly rejecting such ties. China's rulers have insisted that ecclesiastical polity include the "three selfs" approach: that churches be self-governing, self-propagating, and self-financing. The rhetoric, if not necessarily the reality, is startlingly like that found in the thought and writing of John Carroll, the fifty-four year old former Jesuit who two hundred years ago became the first Roman Catholic bishop in the United States.[5] The story of his selection and institution as first bishop in an independent nation emerging from the worldwide colonial expansion of Europe has a contribution to make to the historical development of which Pope John Paul spoke to the Austrian bishops, the development which, in the pope's understanding, has made his *as right* the naming of bishops throughout Latin Catholicism.

Both Spanish and French colonial enterprises played a significant role in the myth-history of American Catholicism. In consequence of changing migration patterns, the Spanish heritage in particular has taken on a new importance in the latter part of the twentieth century. The "people's history" of much of the present-day United States church is resolutely Spanish or French. But, except for Louisiana, the structured institutional church in this country did not grow from these roots, but from the Maryland colony, founded in 1634 under the patronage of the second Lord Baltimore by a band of English Catholic gentry and their more numerous, and largely Protestant, servants.

Maryland Catholics reached out to Virginia's Northern Neck and to Quaker Pennsylvania, where missionaries worked among the Pennsylvania Dutch and in the cosmopolitan town parish of Philadelphia. There were mission stations in New Jersey and for a time a school in King James II's New York. For its first century and a half, from 1634 to 1784, the Catholic Church in England's seaboard colonies was a very "presbyterian" Catholic Church. The only priests were Jesuits attached to the English province of the order; they reported to their own superiors in England. These reported to Jesuit headquarters in Rome, which maintained contact with the Congregation for Propagation of the Faith.[6]

The American church had no episcopal oversight, although in 1722 Bishop Bonaventure Giffard, vicar-apostolic of the London District, approved holy-day regulations and granted some marriage dispensations.[7] Writing to Rome in 1756, Bishop Richard Challoner, coadjutor vicar-apostolic of the London District, asserted that the Maryland mission had been subject to London for "time out of mind," but no substantiation for this was found in Roman archives. Propaganda gave the London vicar-apostolic, Bishop Benjamin Petre, jurisdiction in 1757 and renewed it for Challoner, who succeeded to the vicariate on Petre's death in 1758. Challoner's several reports to Rome over the next few years noted the impossibility of government *a longe*. He admitted that the Jesuits did their work "in a very laudable manner," but complained of their "unspeakable reluctance to receive within their midst a bishop." His solution was to recommend that the bishop of Quebec be delegated for episcopal functions in the seaboard colonies.[8]

The Maryland Catholic laity got wind of plans to send them a bishop, and in 1765 two hundred and fifty-six of them, led by the formidable Charles Carroll II "of Annapolis," petitioned the English Jesuit provincial to cooperate with Challoner in blocking the scheme. It would make their religious practice public, thus upsetting the arrangement that allowed Catholic practice so long as it was kept private; even the established Anglican Church had not appointed a colonial bishop, and a Catholic nominee was sure to invite persecution. Ignorant that the plan was Challoner's own, Carroll wrote him his fears that "peace and harmony would soon be banished" were it put into effect. Challoner was convinced that the Jesuits were behind the lay petition, but the plan was dropped.[9] Bishop Briand of Quebec was commissioned by Rome to visit the colonies, but inquiry made on his behalf elicited a negative reply in 1773 from the German Jesuit pastor in Philadelphia, Ferdinand Farmer, who wrote: "It is incredible how hateful to non-Catholics in all parts of America is the very name of Bishop, even to such as should be members of the Church which is called Anglican."[10]

The suppression in the summer of 1773 of the Society of Jesus, to which all the priests working in the colonies belonged, and the series of events leading to the Declaration of Independence in 1776 caused a hiatus in organizational planning. Maryland Jesuit John Mattingly, caught by the suppression at his post as dean of Rome's English College, was ordered to prepare for Propaganda a report on the American mission.[11] But no contact was made with the actual missioners, whose last religious superior, John Lewis, continued to function, but now as delegate of the London vicar apostolic. The ex-Jesuits, Europeans and Americans alike, stayed at their posts and were joined by Marylanders who had been stationed in Europe, among them John Carroll. Organization was minimal, and little provision was made for new recruits. As the revolution came to an end in 1783, Bishop James Talbot of London cut the colonial church adrift: he declined to give priestly faculties to a pair of American ex-Jesuits returning to ministry in their homeland.[12]

Prodded by Carroll, the priests in Maryland hammered out a "Constitution of the Clergy," which included both a rule of life and arrangements for the ownership and management of ex-Jesuit properties.[13] A novel feature was the provision that the "spiritual superior" of the clergy should have no control over their physical and financial assets. They also authorized a letter to Pope Pius VI which explained that they were "no longer able as formerly to have recourse for our spiritual jurisdiction to bishops or vicars apostolic who live under different and foreign government."[14] Foreign jurisdiction was a major issue. Concretely it came to mean two things: (1) subordination of the American church to a European bishop, English or French, or (2) a status of dependence on the Roman Congregation for Propagation of the Faith. Such status signaled that a given church community was not considered fully established and organized, that it was a "mission" and not a "local church."

The American priests' petition asked confirmation of John Lewis as their ecclesiastical superior. It was forwarded through the English ex-Jesuit John Thorpe, who became the Americans' Roman agent. John Carroll, one of the signers, addressed a covering letter to Vitaliano Borromeo, a curial official soon to become a cardinal.

"You are not ignorant," he wrote, "that in these United States our Religious system has undergone a revolution, if possible, more extraordinary than our political one." "Free toleration" and "a communication of all Civil rights, without distinction or diminution," were widespread. Catholics must respond to the changed atmosphere by "avoiding to give any jealousies on account of any dependence on foreign jurisdictions, more than that, which is essential to our Religion and acknowledgement of the Pope's spiritual Supremacy over the whole Christian world." Continued dependence on the London vicar-apostolate was impossible. Neither congress, nor the state legislatures, nor "the people at large" would tolerate it. Authority must be given to an American priest, preferably Lewis.[15]

John Thorpe proved to be an able Roman agent. He counseled brevity and clarity in petitions from America and, above all, patience in prosecuting them. "They are at the beginning of a new system," he wrote Charles Plowden, a mutual friend of his and Carroll's, "which if begun with a mistake may long suffer the influence of it." The Americans must make sure of "perfect harmony" among themselves, and realize how matters looked from Rome:

> The Propaganda will be tenacious of its authority, & give out its powers in small portions, much less than what the present circumstances of the N. American mission loudly call for.

"But this inconvenience," he advised, "may be redressed by time and importunity."

Thorpe saw as the two initially critical points (1) appointment of an ecclesiastical superior and (2) control of the funds and extensive landholdings in Maryland and Pennsylvania of the defunct Jesuit Order. He advised his American clients to speak with one voice and not to be surprised or intimidated by Roman moves. Carroll could explain matters to them if he had not forgotten "what he has seen of the foul side of Rome." Thorpe was himself convinced that "the very spirit of the government and the laws by which the Americans now are protected & enjoy all the rights of good subjects" demanded that their church be temporally independent.[16]

While the American ex-Jesuits were considering their future, officials at the *Propaganda Fide* were not idle. Eleven months before the priests' petition and Carroll's covering letter to Borromeo, the papal nuncio at Paris was directed to solicit the influence of the French government to secure in the peace treaty ending the American revolution a clause ensuring the free exercise and maintenance of the Catholic religion in the new republic, "all the more, since the Catholic religion may have made some progress in that country, on account of the stay of the French troops there." What Rome had in mind at this juncture was royal French patronage and possible financial support. They understood that it was doubtful that subsidy would come from the American government and were ready to assign an allowance from Propaganda funds to maintain a bishop or other ecclesiastical superior.[17]

Negotiations continued during 1783, involving the foreign minister, Count de Vergennes, Bishop de Talleyrand, minister for church benefices, and Benjamin Franklin, United States commissioner at the French court. One scheme called for dispatch of eight or ten French priests headed by a diocesan bishop or vicar-apostolic who would be a Frenchman. Franklin proposed that the bishop live in France and have an auxiliary in the United States. He advised the nuncio at Paris that Rome might, on its own initiative, take whatever measures seemed necessary. Congress would give tacit approval to whatever decision Rome, in concert with himself, made. He advised the nuncio that there was no hope of government subsidy, but suggested that a college to train priests for America might be endowed by seizing English monastic establishments in France and selling them to realize some fifty to sixty thousand *livres.* "These monks are few. The want of subjects makes those who remain useless, at least," was his comment.[18]

The monasteries were not seized nor was a French bishop named. Consideration was given to having the Paris nuncio supervise the American church, as the nuncio of Brussels supervised Holland. Inquiry made of the Continental Congress elicited the reply that the business was none of theirs. They did suggest it might be the business of individual states, but that was too complicated a dose of American federalism for the Romans to digest, and matters proceeded without further attempts to enlist state intervention.[19]

The planning was done in a vacuum, so far as knowledge of the actual situation of Roman Catholics in the United States went. Propaganda advised the Paris nuncio that "if in time any native should be found available for the sacred ministry, there is no doubt that the vicar or bishop would be free to ordain him and to employ him in the missions."[20] In fact, there were in Maryland and Pennsylvania at that point over two dozen ex-Jesuits, half of them American-born, and other priests were arriving regularly.[21] Once more Benjamin Franklin leaped into the breach. He recommended that John Carroll be named to head the American church. They had met on a diplomatic mission to Quebec in the spring of 1776. The French minister in America helped out by warning that the natives would disapprove a foreign appointment and "could very well choose the worthiest of their own priests and present him to His Holiness for consecration if he judges him qualified."[22]

While Roman attention focused on John Carroll, the American priests' petition arrived. The request for John Lewis as superior was turned down. At sixty-four he was in Roman eyes past "the age of activity." Carroll was presumed to be younger, since his name came last among the petitioners. That positioning also suggested to curial officials that he was not cooperating with "the earnest sollicitations of Mr. Franklin on his behalf."[23] The decision was made with no further consultation to name him ecclesiastical superior of the mission, the lowest rank in the hierarchical pecking order. Promotion to vicar-apostolic or diocesan bishop was deferred until Carroll had demonstrated how he handled authority and an assessment could be made of Congress' reaction to the initial appointment.

The Rome-Paris approach did not coincide with the understanding of how a bishop was chosen held by John Carroll and his closest English correspondent, Charles Plowden. In an April 1784 letter, the latter wrote that "the Missioners in North America constitute the Catholic clergy of the country." Since no concordat made other arrangements, he felt it was up to the clergy, "agreeably to the ancient canons" to make provision for themselves and choose a bishop. Conscious of his own situation under England's penal laws, and of the almost universal practice of some form of government involvement, he recommended that the process be carried out "with the allowance of the civil power," but he was sure that "the Pope would not dare refuse ordinary powers to such a Bishop elect."[24] Carroll agreed. The nub of the question was that, outside the bailiwick of the papal states, Rome chose bishops only in mission countries. To accept a Roman appointment was to acknowledge mission status, which Carroll resisted doing. "To govern the spiritual concerns of this country as a mission is absurd," he wrote. The United States had "a regular clergy belonging to it; and with God's assistance there will be in time, a succession of ministry to supply their places, as they drop off." Carroll saw the effort at Roman choice and appointment as a power play by the Congregation of Propaganda: "The Propaganda hope, by appointing a Bishop now, to establish the precedent of appointing one hereafter." "Little do they know," he continued in unfulfilled prophecy, "of the jealousy entertained here of foreign jurisdictions."[25] Even as he was writing those words, in September 1784, his appointment by Propaganda as superior of the mission was on its way to America.

Propaganda notified Carroll of his new post in a letter dated June 9, 1784, which he received the following November.[26] On June 19 Bishop James Talbot of London was formally relieved of the American responsibilities he had long since rejected.[27] Benjamin Franklin confided to his diary that "the Pope's Nuncio called, and acquainted me that the Pope had, on my Recommendation, appointed Mr. John Carroll Superior of the Catholic Clergy in America."[28]

Carroll was unhappy about the origin of his appointment in a "foreign congregation" and about the limited powers it conveyed. Both Thorpe and Plowden sympathized. Thorpe warned him not to be complacent, lest he find himself a cipher. He needed to be a bishop directly under the Holy See, not a vicar-apostolic under Propaganda, and he must keep control of funds and property.[29] Plowden fastened on the office of vicar-apostolic, writing that many English priests thought "apostolical vicars the ruin of Catholicity in England, and that bishops properly established, would be the fit instruments of building a solid edifice, both here and in America."[30]

The question had long agitated English Catholics. The issues had been put squarely to King James II by the "Old Chapter":

> By a Bishop who is an Ordinary is meant one who hath power in Himselfe to govern the flock over which he is sett, according to the common received Rules or Canons of the Church, and is not revocable at pleasure. On the contrary a Vicar is one who hath no power in himselfe, but only the Use or Exercise of the power of the Person whose substitute he is. . . . He is not properly bishop of the flock to which he is sent, but Officer or Delegate of the person who sends him.[31]

John Carroll shared these views. Two months before being named superior he wrote to Plowden:

> But this you may be assured of; that no authority derived from Propaganda will ever be admitted here; that the Catholick Clergy & Laity here know that the only connexion they ought to have with Rome is to acknowledge the Pope as Spiritual head of the Church; that no Congregation existing in his States shall be allowed to exercise any share of his spiritual authority here; that no Bishop Vicar Apostolical shall be admitted; and if we are to have a Bishop he shall not be *in partibus* (a refined Roman political contrivance), but an ordinary national Bishop, in whose appointment Rome shall have no share.[32]

The language sounds strong until we remember that Carroll's Catholic Church was one in which since the Second Lateran Council in 1139 choice of bishops had been a local matter. Ideally it was confided to the canons of the cathedral chapter of the diocese in question. In practice, governments of the "Catholic" states had usurped the canons' rights, sometimes in concordatory agreement with Rome. But, despite the monarchizing and centralizing movement of the nineteenth century, it was not until as late as 1884 that the Holy See claimed the universal right of episcopal appointment now echoed in the canon law codes of 1918 and 1983.[33] In Carroll's day the pope claimed direct right of appointment only in the papal states and in mission territories, regions where normal church structures were not yet in place.

Carroll resisted under two headings, one civil, the other ecclesiastical. He believed that the kind of operational control envisaged by Rome constituted impermissible foreign interference in American affairs, and from an ecclesiological point of view he denied the inference that the American church did not possess

> . . . a permanent body of national Clergy, with sufficient powers to form our own system of internal government, and . . . to chuse our own Superior, & a very just claim to have all the necessary Spiritual authority communicated to him, on his being presented as regularly and canonically chosen by us.[34]

He also rejected Roman control of the American church assets as "the expression of those claims which Rome has always kept up, tho universally disregarded . . . that the pope is the universal administrator, some have even said *Dominus* of all ecclesiastical property."[35]

The pope's spiritual authority, on the other hand, was an essential Catholic tenet. Rome was "mother and mistress," the pope's spiritual supremacy the bond of Catholic unity. Rome's bishop was head of the universal church, his see the center of ecclesiastical unity. But the "extent and boundaries" of papal spiritual authority—there was the nub. How in practice were universal headship and central role spelled out in the church's life and functioning? For John Carroll this was, along with the use of Latin in public liturgy, one of the "greatest obstacles" to Christian unity as well as to the spread of Catholicism in the United States.[36]

"The religion of Jesus Christ," Carroll wrote ex-Constitutional bishop Henri Gregoire, "will be best preserved in its unity and integrity, by the intimate union and correspondence between its visible head, and the bishops and pastors diffused over the Christian world." But he was cautious. He would work to "inspire veneration for the independent power of the Holy See and the episcopacy," but he added: "confining however that jurisdiction within the limits of the bestower of it, beyond which it ought never to have been extended, I mean things purely spiritual."[37]

Roman response to the American situation was part of a larger reorientation taking place within world Catholicism. Richard Costigan has long since pointed to "all the evidence that the Church in the early centuries had a rather decentralized and more collegial form of polity." Applying this to nineteenth century developments, he continued:

> If the Bishop of Rome was not actually an all-powerful supreme ruler and teacher in the early centuries, then one may be more reluctant to apply the term 'traditional' to the highly monarchial form of papal primacy, which is perceived as having emerged gradually some centuries later than the era of early Christianity.

Costigan, whose earlier work was a favorable study of ultramontane currents in the nineteenth century French church, concluded:

> This in turn would tend to place Ultramontanism in a less favourable light in terms of tradition than such less monarchial, non-papalist ideologies as Gallicanism or Febronianism.[38]

John Carroll and his correspondents were eighteenth century people. They antedated the nineteenth century ecclesiological revolution within Catholicism. Their views were shaped in another understanding of what was the great tradition. Rome on the other hand was moving to a position which considered the whole rest of the church as "in mission."

Traditional episcopal arrangements dating from the misty past were in force in Europe's Catholic countries and their colonies. "Cramping clauses" about which Carroll complained in his own letter of appointment were, Thorpe told him, copied from "an old unmeaning formulary" devised for an African mission and might be ignored.[39] Individual plans were being crafted for religiously plural nations. Agreement between Rome and the king of Sweden (1783) yielded a vicariate-apostolic in Stockholm complete with state subsidy.[40] Pope Pius VI accepted in 1784 the creation the previous year by Czarina Catherine II of a metropolitan see at Mohylew governed by an archbishop and a coadjutor whom she had named.[41] Carroll and his correspondents kept tabs on these developments as they refined their ideas about what suited the American scene.

There would be neither subsidy on the Swedish model nor state control on the Russian. But, in a pattern that would become familiar in twentieth century emerging nations, great care had to be taken to avoid all appearance of dependence on foreign control. The United States, John Thorpe wrote, was not a mission, but "a dominion wherein the Catholic Religion is by Law established, & in which a Bishop in Ordinary is most suitable to the system of civil government."[42] John Carroll agreed, telling Joseph Berington it would help greatly if the English vicars-apostolic bestirred themselves to obtain "a more independent Appointment and Jurisdiction."[43] And if there were to be a bishop, he must be locally chosen: "If the Clergy here are not allowed to chuse and present for approbation the person whom in their judgment they approve as best qualified, the consequences to Religion may be fatal."[44]

By 1786 Carroll had persuaded Propaganda that the American priests might present two candidates for Roman choice, but he was not satisfied that this addressed the basic question, which was: Who in the final analysis picks bishops? In an arrangement that laid the groundwork for basic Roman appointment, the Americans were told they might ask, for the first time only, to present only a single candidate. This they did in 1788, and the "privilege" was granted to exercise the basic right of a local church. John Carroll was chosen by twenty-four votes out of twenty-six. The voters were the priests exercising the care of souls in the new diocese of Baltimore. In the papal brief *Ex Hac Apostolicae* (November 6, 1789) the diocese was "erected" by the Holy See; its bishop was "appointed."[45]

A sharply worded demur from John Ashton, procurator of the clergy estates, provoked John Carroll's last fulminations on the subject of the relationship of Rome and local churches. Ashton objected that the brief claimed for Rome the right to name future bishops and to commission the new bishop "to administer clergy incomes." In reply, Carroll said Thorpe had advised him that the clause on future episcopal appointments was *pro forma* and negotiable. He reiterated his own position:

> The pope, according to the pretensions, which the see of Rome has always supported, says, he will nominate hereafter. But I conceive that the Clergy will have as good a right to say, that the election shall be held by members of their own body, & that they never can, with safety, or will admit any Bishop, who is not so constituted.

As for finances, Carroll's comment was brief: "Rome cannot give what it never possessed, administration of our estates." Soon thereafter he signed a memorandum disclaiming "any right of interference" in the management of the clergy estates.[46]

The letter to Ashton in 1790 was the last such sally of Bishop Carroll's life, which still had a quarter-century to run. More importantly, he failed completely to get into place a workable system for local choice of bishops. He noted to Ashton the "great inconveniencies" of having all the clergy vote. The matter was remitted to a future diocesan synod. When that met in 1791, it recommended an electoral college of the ten priests senior in service, plus five episcopal nominees. Rome would have the "right to reject candidates until someone is chosen who meets the full approval of the Pope." This last provision was intended to emphasize Carroll's "sollicitude to provide for a close & intimate union with the Holy See."[47]

The electoral committee was never created. Carroll nominated Lorenz Graessl for coadjutor bishop after seeking "the counsel of the older and more worthy workers in the vineyard of the Lord."[48] He asked

Roman permission to set up an advisory chapter of ten or twelve priests headed by a dean who would administer the diocese during a vacancy, but nothing came of it. When Graessl died before hearing of his Roman appointment, Carroll recommended Leonard Neale for the coadjutorship "on the advise [*sic*] of men of exceptional prudence who labor in this vineyard of the Lord."[49] No ordered system was established. There was no more talk of impertinent foreign jurisdictions. Papal selection of bishops, although it was not at all the pattern in the universal or even the western church, came to be taken for granted in the United States. The French revolution was on, and John Carroll was dismayed by its "furious democracy." He was also, as he wrote to Charles Plowden, preoccupied with the dangers of "disunion with the Holy See."

In 1804 Bishop Carroll refused to take a hand in the ecclesiastical affairs of the diocese of Louisiana and the two Floridas, based at New Orleans and now largely United States territory as a result of the Louisiana Purchase. He reported to Rome that he had advised the Louisiana petitioners:

> . . . that I had no authority over them, that their episcopal see established by the Apostolic See still functioned, that if it was now vacant no doubt a successor would be named by the Holy Father, and that the person chosen and confirmed would shortly receive notification.[50]

A more ultramontane statement of the case would be difficult to write.

In June 1807, Carroll recommended to Propaganda the division of the diocese of Baltimore. With what consultation or lack of it, we do not know, he proposed candidates for Boston, Philadelphia and Bardstown. He asked that he be made administrator of Louisiana and that a new diocese at New York be temporarily administered from Boston. His nominees were appointed to the first three dioceses, but his recommendation for Louisiana was set aside and an Irish Dominican who had spent the past forty years in Rome was appointed to New York. Archbishop Carroll acquiesced when he got word of the new arrangements from the archbishop of Dublin, five months after his new suffragan was consecrated at Rome for New York. "His Holiness wished to provide at once for all the places," he explained to Plowden. In almost the same words used by Cardinal O'Connor of New York in welcoming an unanticipated new auxiliary bishop nearly two hundred years later, Carroll added that he "always had a favourable account" of the appointee, Richard Luke Concanen, O.P.[51]

Minus Bishop Concanen, who never got past Naples on his way to

New York, the new American hierarchy met at Baltimore in 1810. Resolution four adopted at the meeting read:

> In case the Holy See will graciously permit the nomination to vacant Bishopricks to be made in the United States, it is humbly & respectfully suggested to the Supreme Pastor of the Church to allow the nomination for the vacant Dioceses to proceed solely from the Archbishop & Bishops of this Ecclesiastical Province.[52]

The tones of the 1780s are definitely missing. In their place a novelty has been suggested: nomination of bishops by a provincial hierarchy. In his magisterial study of episcopal appointments, Canon Garrett Sweeney exploded:

> The claim of a hierarchy to be exclusively self-perpetuating bore no resemblance whatever, was without precedent in the canon law of the Church, and had obvious dangers: the development of a closed shop of inbred bishops, chosen by croneyism.[53]

No immediate answer came to the 1810 suggestion. Pius VII was Napoleon's prisoner and would be for another four years. When the bishop of Philadelphia died in 1814, Carroll asked the surviving suffragans and administrators of vacant sees to advise him on selection of "one, two or three persons, best esteemed by us," whose names he would send to Rome "with our respective nominations." He also asked their approval to consult "the most discreet and experienced" priests in the Philadelphia diocese for their advice.[54]

The final round of John Carroll's time had to do with Irish interference in American affairs. He had not objected to the Concanen appointment. Nor when the Irish Dominican died in Naples in 1810 did he move to pick a successor. The diocese lay vacant, with Jesuit Anthony Kohlmann as administrator. Carroll explained in 1814 that he understood the pope intended to name the Suplician Ambrose Marechal bishop. "So," he continued, "when we heard of the Pope's intentions, we refrained entirely from giving any kind of advice regarding the vacant see."[55] He was similarly restrained when he learned sometime in the late spring of 1815 that another Irish Dominican resident in Rome, John Connolly, had been named to New York the previous October and consecrated in November. But he did react strongly to rumors that still one more Irish friar, William Harold, O.P., was under consideration for the see of Philadelphia. The reason was, however, personal, not ecclesiological. Harold had been in the diocese and involved in conflict there during Bishop Egan's time.

By the time Archbishop John Carroll died in 1815, final say in naming American bishops was firmly in the hands of the Congregation for Propagation of the Faith. Some bishops were dispatched with little or no consultation in the United States; others were picked in Rome from a *terna* submitted by United States bishops. Priests were either excluded from the process or allowed a minor role in its preliminary stages. Lay people did not get a look-in. The "closed shop" of which Canon Sweeney wrote was established. Jo Ann Manfra has seen the bishops as seeking to forge a cohesive governing elite in a church exposed to the dangers of a turbulent young America. In the process they sought monarchical-style rule, not only at Roman expense, but at the expense of priests and people.[56] Two bishops sent as papal inspectors, Gaetano Bedini in 1853 and George Conroy in 1878, provide an interesting coda. Conroy in particular was acutely aware of the mediocrity engendered by a system so exclusively dependent on episcopal patronage.[57]

Writing of the demand by the Americans in the 1780s that they be recognized as a church, not a mission, Giuseppe Alberigo sees in those events "a decision of considerable doctrinal importance, even if it was not followed by the desired effects. . . ." It marked, Alberigo thinks, "a particularly significant precedent in the de-Europeanization of ecclesiology," which he clearly approves, although he admits that "a contrary tendency would be increasingly associated with the excesses of pseudo-universalism."[58] The fact remains that the American assertion of the traditional rights of a local church was largely over as soon as it began. Garrett Sweeney has more soberly pointed out that it was the combination of local recommendation (*by the hierarchy*—an innovation) and papal appointment that historically was the American contribution, "ultimately to become a pattern for the Universal [Latin-rite] Church and obliterate the combination of local nomination and papal institution decreed in 1139 by Lateran II."[59]

Notes

1. *The Tablet* (London), July 4, 1987.

2. Robert Trisco, "The Debate on the Election of Bishops in the Council of Trent," *The Jurist* 34 (1974) 257–291.

3. *The Tablet*'s concession of papal "undisputed prerogative" occurred in a September 5, 1987 report on delay in filling the see of Dublin. After the announcement on January 21, 1988 of Monsignor Desmond Connell's appointment to the vacant see, the *Irish Times* com-

mented: "Procedures for consultation have been shown to be virtually meaningless, and it is clear that neither Rome nor its representative in the person of the papal nuncio, Dr. Alibrandi, are prepared to place any great premium on wishes locally expressed" (quoted in the *National Catholic Register,* February 7, 1988, p. 8). See the thoughtful piece by Louis McRedmond, "Dublin's New Archbishop," *The Tablet,* January 30, 1988, p. 130. Objection in Ireland was not so much to the individual chosen as it was to the procedure followed. "Nobody," he wrote, "challenges the papal authority to make the ultimate decision in such appointments," but ignoring local recommendations has led to bad morale among the priests, "apathy" among most lay people, and "deep depression for some of the most concerned."

4. *The Tablet,* April 4, 1987.

5. James Hennesey, S.J., lecture at the University of San Francisco, November 21, 1986, "Maryknoll and Twentieth-Century Catholicism," reported in *National Jesuit News* (January 1987).

6. James Hennesey, S.J., *American Catholics: A History of the Roman Catholic Community in the United States* (New York/Oxford 1981) 36–54.

7. Edwin H. Burton, *The Life and Times of Bishop Challoner 1691–1780* (2 vols.; London 1909) 2:124.

8. *Ibid.* 125–148.

9. Thomas Hughes, S.J., *The History of the Society of Jesus in North America, Colonial and Federal* (4 vols.; New York 1907–1917) Text 2:591.

10. John Tracy Ellis, *Documents of American Catholic History* (3 vols.; Wilmington 1987) 1:125–128.

11. Archives of the Congregation for Propagation of the Faith (APF), Rome, Scritture riguardanti l'esecuzione del breve di soppressione, 1774, missioni, miscellan. V, fol. 22; Congressi, America Centrale, I, fols. 557 r–v and 558 r.

12. Edward I. Devitt, S.J., "The Suppression and Restoration of the Society of Jesus in Maryland," *Woodstock Letters* 33 (1904) 381.

13. Thomas O'Brien Hanley, S.J., ed., *The John Carroll Papers* (3 vols.; Notre Dame 1976) (*JCP*) 1:71–77.

14. John Lewis *et al.* to Pope Pius VI, n.p., November 10, 1783, *ibid.* 68. See Finbar Kenneally, O.F.M., ed., *United States Documents in the Propaganda Fide Archives* (Washington DC 1966) 1:10, n. 42.

15. Carroll to Vitaliano Borromeo, Maryland, November 10, 1783, *JCP* 1:80–81.

16. Archives of the English Jesuit Province, London (AEP), Thorpe to Plowden, March 3, 1784.

17. Jules A. Baisnée, S. S., *France and the Establishment of the Ameri-*

can Hierarchy: The Myth of French Interference 1782–1784 (Baltimore 1934) 45–48.

18. *Ibid.* 54–56.

19. Worthington C. Hunt *et al.*, eds., *Journals of the Continental Congress 1774–1789* (33 vols.; Washington DC 1904–1936) 27:368.

20. Baisnée 54–56.

21. James Hennesey, S.J., "Several Youth Sent from Here: Native-Born Priests and Religious of English America 1634–1776," in *Studies in Catholic History in Honor of John Tracy Ellis* (Nelson H. Minnich *et al.*, eds., Wilmington 1985) 1–26.

22. Baisnée 80.

23. *Ibid.* 114–117.

24. Allan Nelson, "An Anglo-American Catholic Correspondence: The Letters of John Carroll and Charles Plowden 1778–1816," *Records of the American Catholic Historical Society of Philadelphia* 97 (1986) 11.

25. *JCP* 1:151.

26. Baisnée, pp. 117–118.

27. *Ibid.*, pp. 118–119.

28. Albert Henry Smyth, ed., *The Writings of Benjamin Franklin* (10 vols., New York 1905–1907) 1:349.

29. AEP, Thorpe to Plowden, Rome, August 7, 1784.

30. Archives of the Archdiocese of Baltimore, Plowden to Carroll, September 2, 1784.

31. Basil Hemphill, *The Early Vicars Apostolic of England 1685–1750* (London 1954) 7–8.

32. Hughes, Documents, 1, 2:619–620.

33. Garrett Sweeney, "The 'Wound in the Right Foot': Unhealed," in *Bishops and Writers: Aspects of the Evolution of Modern English Catholicism* (ed. Adrian Hastings; Wheathempstead Herts, 1977) 225; 228–231. Sweeney draws upon Antonio Rosmini-Serbati's *Cinque piaghe della santa Chiesa,* the ms. of which was completed in 1832. Published in 1848, it was put on the Index of Forbidden Books the following year.

34. Carroll followed the Paris doctor Alexander Natalis (Noël Alexandre, O.P., 1639–1724, *Selecta Historiae Ecclesiasticae Capita* [24 vols.; 1676–1686], a work on the Index from 1684–1734 because of the author's approach to medieval papal-imperial conflict. See *JCP* 1:156–157.

35. *Ibid.*, 1:437.

36. *Ibid.*, 2:201–203; 1:148–149.

37. *Ibid.*, 3:105.

38. Richard F. Costigan, S.J., "Tradition and the Beginning of the Ultramontane Movement," *Irish Theological Quarterly* 48 (1981) 28.

39. AEP, Thorpe to Plowden, Rome, July 27, 1785.

40. *Ibid.*, May 22, 2784.

41. James J. Zatko, *Descent into Darkness: The Destruction of the Roman Catholic Church in Russia 1917–1923* (Notre Dame 1965) 5–6.

42. AEP, Thorpe to Plowden, July 27, 1785.

43. JCP 1: 218–219.

44. *Ibid.*, 1:166.

45. Ellis, 1:163–167.

46. *JCP* 1:435–437.

47. *JCP* 1:548; 2:32–33; 2:39–40; Nothing in the 1791 synodal decrees (*ibid.*, 526–541) deals with episcopal choice and appointment, and the question is ignored in Peter Guilday's chapter, "The First National Synod," in *A History of the Councils of Baltimore 1791–1884* (New York 1932) 60–61.

48. *JCP* 2:95–96.

49. *Ibid.*, 2:129–130.

50. *Ibid.*, 2:435.

51. *Ibid.*, 3:71–73.

52. Guilday 75.

53. Sweeney 216.

54. *JCP* 3:291–292; Annabelle M. Melville, *Louis William DuBourg, 1766–1833* (2 vols.; Chicago 1986) 1:320–322. For a detailed account of episcopal exchanges on early U.S. appointments, see 2:644–666.

55. *JCP* 3:303.

56. Jo Ann Manfra, "The Catholic Episcopacy in America, 1789–1852," unpublished Ph.D. dissertation, The University of Iowa, 1975.

57. James F. Connelly, *The Visit of Archbishop Gaetano Bedini to the United States 1853–4* (Rome 1960); Robert Trisco, "Bishops and Their Priests in the United States," in *The Catholic Priest in the United States: Historical Investigations* (ed. John Tracy Ellis; Collegeville MN 1971) 197–202.

58. Giuseppe Alberigo, "The Local Church in the West 1500–1945," *The Heythrop Journal* 28 (1987) 137.

59. Sweeney 217.

Marvin R. O'Connell

John Ireland, the Vatican, and the French Connection

T hey had come to Paris only a few days before from Orleans, where the archbishop had scored another of his many oratorical triumphs, this one a panegyric of Joan of Arc, delivered in the florid French he had learned as a seminarian almost a half-century before. Five thousand persons of quality had packed the cathedral to hear him, while a similar number, unable to find even standing room inside, had spilled out through the portico and down the steps into the adjacent square. He had not disappointed them, the eloquent *archeveque americain;* for two hours—the powerful voice rising and falling, the rounded phrases and learned allusions blending into one another—he had eulogized the Maid of Domremy as a statesman, soldier, woman, and saint, as one who "in her whole life . . . was the embodiment of patriotism and religion. Her life and her death spoke love of country and love of Church."[1] It was the archbishop's most familiar theme, one he had expounded from a thousand platforms and pulpits—so much so that it had become identified with him and, through him, with the vibrant Catholic Church in the United States. At Orleans the huge congregation had listened to this Americanist message again, enraptured, most of them, at the preacher's "refined figure, charming and strong, in which sweetness seemed mirrored in intelligence."[2]

Now on this May morning, in the year of our Lord 1899, they walked purposefully out of the Tuileries Gardens, turned right across the corner of the vast Place de la Concorde, and right again into the Rue de Rivoli—the archbishop and his young priest-secretary taking their constitutional, unmistakably American in their suits of somber black broadcloth, with starched white Roman collars at their throats and soft felt hats, the brims turned up, set squarely on their heads. The archbishop, at sixty, was stout and silver-haired, with a Celtic cream and ruddy complexion. He was of medium height, though he looked taller as he strode vigorously along, his thick shoulders thrown back and his massive jaw thrust upward and outward. The younger man had difficulty keeping up with him.

The glitter and symmetrical elegance of the new Paris created by Baron Haussmann crowded in around them, as did the splendid symbols of nineteenth century pride and achievement: behind them, up the broad Champs-lyses, loomed the Arc de Triomphe, and across the river stood Monsieur Eiffel's celebrated tower of iron, erected only ten years before. There were signs as well of present concerns: they passed a news

101

vendor's kiosk and could see that in the headlines of the papers displayed there the most prominent name was that of Alfred Dreyfus.

But the archbishop stared blankly straight ahead and seemed oblivious to his surroundings, as had been so often the case since this European journey had begun the previous January. They had gone first to Rome, and then, with the spring, to Naples and a holiday on the coast. By mid-April they were in Turin, and on May 8 the archbishop had preached his sermon in Orleans. Ahead on the schedule were a series of lectures in Paris, dinner with the king of the Belgians in Brussels, two weeks of receptions and luncheons in London as guests of the duke of Norfolk and finally a visit to the archbishop's native County Kilkenny and a speech to a temperance rally in Cork City. The archbishop had plunged into all the public activities with his accustomed zest, and the secretary did not doubt that he would continue to do so. But in between ceremonial engagements, at odd, unoccupied moments, a cast of weariness came over his eyes and a moody silence enveloped him.

They turned left into the Rue Castiglione and walked past the smart shops and restaurants which, at this early hour, were shut up tight. When they crossed the Rue Saint-Honor and approached the entrance to the Place Vendôme, the archbishop suddenly stopped. The secretary, a few steps behind and slightly out of breath, drew abreast of him and followed his gaze up at the statue of Napoleon I, garbed in a Roman toga, atop the obelisk in the center of the square.

"Did you know," the archbishop said, "that the base of the obelisk was constructed out of cannon captured by Napoleon at the Battle of Austerlitz in 1805?"

"No, Your Grace," the secretary said.

"One of his greatest victories. It is called the battle of the three emperors. French, Austrian, Russian."

The secretary nodded. Accumulating military lore was one of the archbishop's favorite diversions.

The archbishop spoke again, his voice now sharper, almost gravelly in tone. "When we were in Rome," he said, and paused—"do you know what they asked me in Rome? At the Vatican?"

"No, Your Grace."

"They asked me," the archbishop said, his shoulders hunching forward, "they asked me if I believed in the divinity of Christ."

With that John Ireland straightened and set off briskly across the Place Vendôme, the imperious eye of the great Napoleon upon him.[3]

The first notice of John Ireland to be found in the records of the Vatican bureaucracy was this laconic statement entered in 1875 by one of the officials of the Congregation of Propaganda: "Finally, for the Apostolic Vicariate of Nebraska, no name remains save that of the priest Ireland, about whom there is, besides, sufficient satisfactory information."[4] By February that not altogether enthusiastic endorsement had come to the knowledge of the local newspapers in St. Paul. "The Rev. John Ireland," one of them reported, "Rector of the Cathedral Parish and Secretary of the diocese, has been elevated by His Holiness Pope Pius the Ninth . . . to the dignity of Vicar Apostolic of Nebraska, Wyoming, Montana and part of Dakota. . . . He has concluded to accept the new dignity conferred on him, and . . . he will be accompanied to his new field of labor by his father, mother and other members of his family." There was widespread consternation at this news, even among those elements in the community which did not always see eye-to-eye with the aggressive young priest. One editor spoke the mind of all: "While wishing the reverend gentleman every success in his future home, we must say that St. Paul and Minnesota can badly afford to lose his valuable services, and that it may be many years before the void he leaves can be suitably filled."[5] Over the succeeding weeks people waited for some definitive statement, but none was forthcoming. Ireland himself remained smilingly non-committal. Then, in the last days of March, it was announced that the bishop of St. Paul, Thomas Langdon Grace, had departed for Rome, and even the dullest Minnesotan could guess the reason why.

The appointment of Ireland to Nebraska was a part—a relatively insignificant part indeed—of a plan for the canonical reorganization of the church in the middle west. In March 1874 the suffragans of the Province of St. Louis, Grace among them, met in the home of their metropolitan, Archbishop Peter Richard Kenrick. Among the results of that meeting was a petition to Rome to carve out of the enormous province of St. Louis two new ecclesiastical provinces, one to be centered in Milwaukee and the other in Santa Fe. The bishops also recommended that the diocese of Chicago, which then embraced all of the state of Illinois, be divided, with a new see created in Peoria, and—of more direct consequence to Grace—that the northern two-thirds of the diocese of St. Paul be constituted a separate vicariate. All these territorial changes were approved by Propaganda.

Another piece of business on the agenda of the gathering at Kenrick's house was the preparation of a slate of candidates for the vicariate of Nebraska, whose incumbent had recently died. Among the faults often laid at the door of the American bishops—a maddening one to the legalistic officers of Propaganda—was the casual, even haphazard, manner in which they prepared ternae. Such apparently was the case in St. Louis in 1874, at least according to the resume put together by one of Propaganda's clerks. Kenrick and his suffragans duly submitted a terna for the vicariate of Nebraska, but at first (*dapprima*) they nominated the same persons also (*anche*) for the new bishopric of Peoria they were proposing. *Dignissimus* was a Vincentian named Edward Hennessy, *dignior* was Michael Hurley, a pastor in Peoria, and *dignus* was John Ireland.

What this in effect amounted to was the submission of three names for two positions, clearly an unacceptable procedure. So sometime later (*in sequito*) a separate terna for Peoria was sent to Propaganda, and on it were the names Frederick Wayrich, a Redemptorist from New York, John Lancaster Spalding of the diocese of Louisville, and John J. Kain, pastor at Harper's Ferry, West Virginia. Now the prefect of Propaganda and his colleagues had the requisite six nominees, but, sticklers for legal niceties as they professed themselves to be, they nevertheless proceeded to treat the six in a curiously unlegal fashion, lumping them all together as they pondered their decision. Hennessy, Wayrich, and Spalding they dismissed because of unfavorable reports about their fitness for office (*a motivo delle sfavorevoli notizie*). Kain was about to be appointed bishop of Wheeling. Hurley, though strictly speaking his name had not appeared on the terna for Peoria, was deemed, as a resident pastor there, the appropriate choice for the new diocese. That left Ireland for Nebraska.[6]

And that sent Bishop Grace scurrying off to Rome where, in April 1875, he laid seige to the huge black palazzo which housed Propaganda on the edge of the Piazza di Spagna. He explained to the prefect, Cardinal Barnab, that he had allowed Ireland's name to appear on the original terna only after his colleagues in the province assured him that the appointment to Nebraska would never come to pass. Inclusion had been intended to be a compliment to a deserving young priest, nothing more. Grace did not mince words. He expressed his personal displeasure at the turn of events. He warned that Ireland's departure would cause deep resentment in Minnesota and would lead to a host of unspecified troubles. He threatened, finally, to resign.

Barnab, the seasoned bureaucrat, then put his finger on the glaring weakness in Grace's case. Was Father Ireland worthy to be a bishop or was he not? If he was, why did Grace stand in the way of his promotion? If not, why had his name been placed upon the terna, when the bishop of St. Paul could easily have prevented it? Grace replied, rather lamely, that he had always intended to ask that Ireland be appointed his coadjutor. Ireland, he told Barnab on April 30, "knows intimately the state of my diocese, and is eminently qualified for episcopal rank."

Meanwhile, back in St. Paul, the object of these negotiations had his own role to play, a role carefully orchestrated with that of Bishop Grace. On April 22 Ireland wrote a letter addressed directly to Pius IX in which he asked the pontiff to revoke the appointment. He enclosed this letter, together with the papal documents naming him a titular bishop and a vicar apostolic, with another letter to Grace, to whom he wrote: "As you will perceive from reading this letter [to the pope], I enter into no details as to the reasons of my resignation, taking the liberty to refer to your statement of the case. . . . I put Nebraska entirely out of my mind and settle down quietly into my old attachment to Minnesota." Then, with a docility not altogether characteristic of him, he added: "I never by any direct acting or choosing of my own have fashioned my destiny; it has been always apparently fashioned for me. . . . In this whole present affair, it would be a hard task for me were I myself to decide alone what I should do. My consolation is that it is all in your hands, and not in my own."

The packet containing this letter and the accompanying documents never reached the bishop, because the mail-steamer carrying it was wrecked off the coast of England.[7] But the accident, as things turned out, had no bearing on the final outcome in Rome. Grace had made his case persuasively enough, and his own prestige within the curia, which stood higher perhaps than he had realized, proved enough to win the day. "There can be no doubt," read the final Propaganda report, "that Mgr. Grace has earned the favor he asks; during the sixteen or seventeen years he has ruled the Diocese of St. Paul, he has consistently displayed wisdom, great zeal, and sincere attachment to the Holy See." The one legal obstacle which remained Propaganda cavalierly brushed aside: the canonical requirement for a terna could be waived in this case, the congregation decreed, because it was a matter simply of translating a vicar apostolic to another mission, a process done all the more easily since the subject had not only not taken possession but had not even been consecrated.[8] On May 9, 1875, Pope Pius IX appointed John Ireland coadjutor bishop of St. Paul, with right of succession.

So it was that John Ireland attained episcopal rank by a process of elimination, and a rather sloppy process at that. But once he put on the miter in 1875, he wore it for the remaining forty-three years of his life with immense pride and carried out the functions of the office it signified with extraordinary vigor. Born in Ireland in 1838, he came to Minnesota as an immigrant boy of fourteen. A year later the first bishop of St. Paul, Joseph Cretin, sent young John to France, where he spent four years in a *petit seminaire* and four more in a *grand*. In 1861, fluent in French and armed with a conventional but by no means inadequate seminary education,[9] he returned to St. Paul—no more at that date than a frontier village on the edge of the wilderness—to be ordained by Cretin's successor, Thomas Grace.

The civil war had begun even before Ireland returned from France, and within months of his ordination the young priest was named chaplain to the Fifth Regiment, Minnesota Volunteer Infantry. He participated in the campaign which culminated in the Battle of Corinth, Mississippi, October 3 and 4, 1862, and wrote at the time a lively, and largely accurate, account of that battle.[10] He reminisced often in later life about his military career, and indeed tended to romanticize it. Thus, in a memoir of 1892, he characterized "my years [sic] of chaplaincy [as] the happiest and most fruitful years of my ministry,"[11] when in fact his time of service had lasted less than ten months. Ireland at any rate clearly took great satisfaction in the sobriquet commonly applied to him in Minnesota—"the fighting chaplain of the fighting Fifth"[12]—and when, many years after the war, the story circulated nationally that at a crucial point in the Battle of Corinth Chaplain Ireland had saved the day by distributing cartridges to the soldiers in the line, the old archbishop could not be got to deny it.[13]

Veterans' memories are notoriously suspect; perhaps they glamorize the few moments of adventure they can recall in order to forget fear and tedium and carnage, the ordinary coin of their military experience. However that may be, John Ireland's army service, brief as it was, had a profound and lasting effect upon him. Scarcely more than a boy when he joined the regiment, fresh from the contemplative quiet of a French seminary, Ireland learned to be a man and to be a priest amidst the crash of artillery, the shrieks of maimed and dying men, the whine of the miniball, and the blood-curdling "rebel yell" of charging Confederate infantry. He learned also to be an American. In later years, at innumerable GAR encampments, John Ireland proudly claimed a place among the million men who, in their youth, had rallied to save the Union. Like them he had earned the right to wear the badge of an American patriot. "We were the soldiers of Abraham Lincoln," he once told a group of veterans. "This the praise we covet; this the memory we yearn to transmit to the coming years."[14]

In the spring of 1863 Father Ireland brought that aspiration back with him to St. Paul, where he served successively as curate and then rector of the cathedral parish there. His earliest notoriety stemmed from his abilities as a pulpit orator in an age which expected, and appreciated, long and fulsome sermons.[15] More than one eloquent young clergyman has found himself the object of the spiteful envy of his confreres by reason of that very eloquence. John Ireland avoided this fate, at least with regard to the only confrere who mattered. Bishop Grace, with whom Ireland resided in the rectory next door to the cathedral, possessed a serene appreciation of his own worth, which kept him preserved from the least pang of jealousy. The success of others did not trouble or threaten Thomas Langdon Grace.

This quality proved crucial in his relationship with Ireland, and had much to do with the latter's development. Grace was never a leader who initiated policies, but neither would he obstruct a subordinate who did. John Ireland's restless genius, with all its rough edges, thus found an ideal superior in Grace, a genuinely cultivated and conscientious man who gave his gifted younger colleague free rein and always bestowed credit where credit was due. So it was that early on Father Ireland—and even more so Coadjutor Bishop Ireland after 1875—plunged into a host of endeavors in which he enjoyed the confidence but also the detachment of his ordinary. An instance of this was Ireland's fierce advocacy of the cause of total abstinence from alcohol, a cause to which Bishop Grace, though he routinely condemned the evil of excessive drinking, never subscribed. Another of Ireland's projects, which his ordinary treated with benign neglect, was the colonization movement, whereby Ireland and other like-minded laymen and priests, invoking an almost Jeffersonian model, proposed to lure westward Catholic immigrants, huddled in the slums of eastern cities, and turn them into sturdy, prideful, land-owning yeomen. Though the colonizers' ideal did not succeed nationally, it was realized to some degree in southwestern Minnesota, where Ireland's ten colonies prospered and to this day stand, thriving communities, as a tribute to his energy and foresight.[16]

The colonists, however, made up only a tiny fraction of the people for whom Grace and Ireland were responsible. The diocese of St. Paul in those days included the entire state of Minnesota and two-thirds of what are now the states of North Dakota and South Dakota—166,000 square miles altogether. Catholics represented roughly twenty-five percent of a population that was growing with great rapidity, as settlers poured into the vast area seeking cheap land and a new chance. The immigrant character of the church was a reality which John Ireland encountered every day of his active ministry. The sometime chaplain of the Fifth Minnesota Volunteers judged it to be his duty to encourage his flock to adopt American ideals and standards as he, also an immigrant, had done so wholeheartedly and so successfully. Much of his activity was prosaic enough; brick and mortar were basic necessities if Catholics were to have a roof over their heads and possess the simple physical setting necessary to the practice of their religion. Allied to this concern was the attainment of that bourgeois respectability which, for Ireland, was a goal only slightly less important than eternal salvation. "Be ambitious," he pleaded with his fellow Irishmen; "seek to elevate yourselves, to better your lot; too often we are too easily satisfied. When a man is poor, let him live in a hovel. I esteem him; at any moment I tender him the right hand of fellowship; but if by labor, by energy, he can secure to his family comfort and respectability, and does not, then I despise him."[17]

But there were other, headier considerations, too. It was a volatile time and place, and perhaps it is not too much to say that in these malleable immigrants Ireland discerned a raw material which might be fashioned into a Catholic people freed from old world shibboleths and ready to assume leadership in the new, twentieth century which, he was convinced, would be dominated by the American ethos. A marriage made in heaven, and one which promised mutual benefit. "It is true," Ireland proclaimed in his great speech in Baltimore in 1884, "[that] the choicest field which providence offers in the world to-day to the occupancy of the Church is this republic, and she welcomes with delight the signs of the times that indicate a glorious future for her beneath the starry banner. But it is true, also, [that] the surest safeguards for her own life and prosperity the republic will find in the teachings of the Catholic Church, and the more America acknowledges those teachings, the more durable will her civil institutions be made."[18]

John Ireland, articulate indeed as he consistently proved himself to be, and highly intelligent, was nevertheless a man of action rather than a man of thought. This characteristic revealed itself strikingly in his ecclesiology, the best expression of which appeared in a sermon preached in 1873. "This Church," he said, "[is] the most stupendous organization on the face of the earth. She is the most complete, perfect organization, possessing, in a supereminent degree, all the elements of corporate life, a well-defined constitution, a powerful hierarchy, clearly-stated laws binding together into one solid body the governing and the governed. Her children number over two hundred millions; she has extended her power over every continent and every isle, [even] the most remote, and, while widespread, still remains everywhere the same, so wondrous is her unity, professing everywhere the same creed and acknowledging everywhere the same governing power."[19]

Governance was what fascinated John Ireland, the capacity to organize and direct. He never troubled himself unduly about the goals toward which the directing and organizing were ordered, goals that he largely took for granted. Nor was he interested in raising large constitutional questions. The Roman Church of the nineteenth century, with its strong centralizing tendencies, was for Ireland simply a fact, and therefore something not to be theorized about but to be accepted, to be used, and, on occasion, to be manipulated. The pattern he discerned in his own elevation to the episcopate served him as a kind of model in his dealings with the curia. That he should himself participate in the ruling function he never doubted for a moment. Indeed, he seldom entertained doubts of any kind. And amidst the struggles which dominated the middle portion of his career he remained steadfast in the conviction that his domestic enemies—Germans, Jesuits, and, above all, the hated archbishop of New York, Michael Augustine Corrigan—could best be dealt with in the corridors of power at the Vatican.

John Ireland first traveled to Rome late in 1869, when Bishop Grace dispatched him as his proctor to the first Vatican Council. Nothing substantive came of this assignment, because the legal status of the conciliar proctors ranged between the ambiguous and nugatory.[20] Ireland was in effect a tourist, savoring his first taste of *romanit,* understood here as that peculiar magic worked by Rome upon the visitor, especially if that visitor is from a northern land. Not that the council itself assumed minor proportions in Ireland's mind. The color and drama associated with it were precisely calculated to appeal to his powerful imagination. The coming together of more than seven hundred bishops representing every continent and every culture served to reassure the priest from the American frontier and to confirm his favorite boast that he and his people belonged to "the most stupendous organization on the face of the earth." If circumstances consigned him to an observer's role at the council, he did not seem to mind; it did not keep him at any rate from reveling in the celebration of what proved to be the last Christmas of old papal Rome.[21]

Not until 1886, after the passage of more than sixteen years, did Ireland return to Rome. He came again in 1892 and 1899. On these occasions the place looked much the same as it had before, still the baroque city of Bernini, all domes and fountains and obelisks, stucco façades of dark yellow fronting the streets and behind them sumptuous gardens and courtyards. The ruins of a half-dozen proud civilizations still lay casually about, the same stone angels stood guard on the Ponte Elio, and, atop the Janiculum, the inevitable umbrella pines were pasted against the sky.

But profound changes had occurred nonetheless. The papal Rome of a thousand years had given way to the capital of the new kingdom of Italy. The grand liturgical ceremonies Ireland remembered were held no more, for the pope, cabined up within the walls of the Vatican, removed himself from Roman public life as a way of protesting the aggression which had deprived him of his temporal power. The pope now was the sophisticated Leo XIII, in character and temperament a marked contrast to his flamboyant predecessor, but no less dedicated than Pius IX had been to a restoration of at least some measure of the papacy's civil princedom. To achieve that end he was prepared to employ the tools of diplomacy rather than those of denunciation.

And John Ireland in the interval had changed too. No longer the young traveler from afar, wide-eyed at the first sight of the splendors of *la citt,* he moved with the brisk, authoritative air of a man of affairs, a middle-aged bishop with important business to attend to. He was an ordinary in his own right now—Grace had retired in his favor in 1884 and within a few years he would become a metropolitan—and since the Third Plenary Council of Baltimore he had begun to forge for himself a national reputation. He had also formed those friendships which were crucial to the direction of his career: with James Gibbons, archbishop of Baltimore, and soon to be cardinal; with John J. Keane, rector of the fledgling Catholic University of America; with Denis J. O'Connell, mercurial rector of the North American College and man-about-the-curia—the three musketeers, as it were, with Ireland himself in the role of D'Artagnan, the nucleus of what came to be called the Americanist party.

It might be well to digress here for a moment in order to suggest in what sense the word "Americanist" can be usefully applied to John Ireland. One will look in vain through his words and deeds to find any theoretically coherent formulation of Americanism or indeed of any other ism. Ireland—it bears repeating—was a practical man, not given much to speculation. His rhetoric, to be sure, extolled to the skies the glories of the political and economic achievements of the United States, but in this he was hardly different from a host of self-conscious spokesmen of the gilded age. Michael Corrigan and the German archbishops of Milwaukee were wont to say much the same things. And Ireland tempered his public enthusiasm with many an indictment of the venality and degradation which were, he charged, all too common in American life.[22] Certainly experience had taught him the advantages for Catholicism in the religion clauses of the First Amendment, especially when compared to the virulently anti-clerical and even anti-Catholic policies rampant in so many Latin European countries, in which there remained a formal union between church and state. But his adherence to the principle of separation stemmed more from pragmatic than from speculative considerations; it was precisely because the American model of church-state relations had succeeded so well that he believed a universal application of it would have been a boon to Catholicism. But he did not express this view, even in private, as freely as did, say, Denis O'Connell.

What Ireland surely did want was the speedy amalgamation of Catholic immigrants into the mainstream of American life. He was surely an Americanizer.[23] This was why he was so ardent a civic booster in Minnesota, and why he was a colonizer, and why he ardently supported the Catholic University of America. His continuing preoccupation with the temperance issue flowed in large part from the same desire; how could the immigrant take his rightful place in American society if he constantly fell into alcoholic excess? Likewise, the imperative he felt to lift the immigrant masses to the level of American middle class respectability—as defined by the platforms of the Republican Party of which he was a faithful adherent—explains Ireland's eagerness that Catholics should accommodate themselves to the public school system; his consistent opposition to efforts—mounted by Corrigan and others and supported by Rome—to categorize harmless fraternal organizations, such as the Oddfellows and the Knights of Pythias, as the American equivalents of Masonic lodges headed by the likes of Mazzini or Clemenceau; and his violent dislike of the relatively prosperous and cohesive German Catholic community and its strong dedication to the language and customs of the old country. All these various strands of conviction tended after a while to coalesce in Ireland's mind and in the programs he sponsored, so that when his opponents branded him an "Americanist" they were in effect accusing him of disdaining parochial education, supporting secret societies, and tyrannizing over ethnic—that is, non-Irish—minorities, even to the point of a Waspishly puritanical interference with their drinking habits.

John Ireland was, finally, what might be called a home-ruler. A strong local hierarchy, dealing with local concerns, was for him a practical necessity for the health of the church. Whether this stance should be labeled a manifestation of Americanism, or whether it is better explained by the predictable and, by and large, the healthful tension which has always existed between pope and bishop—ever since Paul "withstood Peter to his face"—may be debatable. It implied in any case no theoretical objection to papal primacy; indeed, it implied no theory at all. "The difficulties," Ireland once observed to the prefect of Propaganda, "encountered by the Church in America due to diverse populations coming to our shores, are immense. The only remedy, I am convinced, is to strengthen the authority of the bishops. It is the only way to bind the different elements together and prevent chaos and schism."[24] This is not to say that Ireland was ever prepared to share such authority himself, or that he would have ever dreamed of promoting the kind of structures that have emerged in our own time, like priests' senates or diocesan councils. Participatory democracy was not his style. On the contrary, he was a natural autocrat; he ruled his diocese and, to some degree, his province later on with an iron hand. His notions about consultation can perhaps best be summed up by an entry in the *ad limina* report he filed with Propaganda in 1900: "There has been no provincial or diocesan synod, because there has been no opportunity or need for one. The Archbishop has conferred yearly with appropriate people in order to determine the means to achieve the spiritual well-being of the archdiocese, and this has seemed sufficient."[25] The same jealousy of his episcopal prerogatives helps explain Ireland's relentless vendetta against uniate Catholics and his suspicion of all religious orders of men. The Society of Jesus was his particular bugbear in this regard, so much so that it was said that a Jesuit dared not even change trains in St. Paul during Archbishop Ireland's lifetime.

Ireland's visits to Rome in 1886, 1892, and 1899 all dealt in one way or another with the bitter quarrels which divided the American Catholic community during the generation following the Third Plenary Council. All of them were in effect lobbying attempts on Ireland's part to persuade the pope and his curia to support the Americanists—the terms "liberals" and "progressives" seem hardly to apply—rather than to side with Corrigan and McQuaid, or the Jesuits, or the Germans, or an alleged cabal composed of representatives of all those groups. Some of the subjects under discussion at the Vatican and at the various curial congregations turned merely upon competition over turf or upon considerations of ego. Others, however, were matters of substance, issues serious enough to affect the vitals of the young American church. These included support for the Catholic University in Washington; resistance to proposals, associated first with Peter Abbelen and later with Peter Paul Cahensly, to impose an ethnic quota system upon the hierarchy in the United States; rescue of the Knights of Labor from a threatened condemnation which might well have triggered an anti-Catholic reaction among the entire American working class; approval of the celebrated Faribault school plan; and appointment of a nuncio or apostolic delgate to the United States. Ireland and his allies won more of these battles than they lost, but enough ambiguity remained, even after the smoke had cleared, to allow contenders on both sides to save face.

Ireland's greatest defeat, of course, was the issuance, early in 1899, of the papal letter *Testem Benevolentiae*.[26] He had hastened to Rome in an attempt to prevent the promulgation of this curious rebuke of "Americanism," a phenomenon, the letter appeared to say, which distorted principles acceptable enough in the United States by attempting to apply them to a European setting. "All that giant will could do," Ireland insisted "was done by me to prevent the publication. But the forces against us were enormous—Jesuits, Dominicans and Redemptorists fought for very life. . . . Archbishop Corrigan too. . . . Fanatics conjured up an 'Americanism'—and put such before the pope. . . . I cannot pray that God forgive them." What was condemned in *Testem*, he protested, was "a nightmare," a few bizarre ideas "set afloat in France." "Who ever 'preferred' natural to supernatural virtues? Who ever taught that the practice of natural virtues was not to be vitalized and supernaturalized by divine grace? Who ever taught that in hearkening to the H[oly] Ghost the Christian was not to be constantly guided by the magisterium of the Church?"[27]

These rhetorical questions were perfectly appropriate, since the strictures of *Testem Benevolentiae* seemed to have little to do with any program Ireland had ever advanced. The letter concerned itself with matters like spiritual direction, the cultivation of personal spirituality, and the charisms of the Holy Spirit, and had nothing to do with the kind of practical and political problems with which Ireland had been wrestling all through his public life. The archbishop of St. Paul was quick to offer a formal renunciation of the "errors" condemned by *Testem*, not, however, without drawing a sharp and, to him, obvious distinction. "I repudiate and condemn," he wrote in the *Osservatore Romano* on February 24, 1899, "all the opinions which the Apostolic Letter repudiates and condemns . . . [but I] cannot but be indignant that such a wrong should have been done us—our Bishops, our faithful people, and our whole nature—as to designate, as some have come to do, by the word 'Americanism' errors and extravagances of this sort."[28]

But the irony was that if "errors and extravagances" "set afloat in France" had led to Ireland's severest setback in his relations with the Vatican, his earlier victories there had likewise stemmed from a French connection. Take the events of 1892 as an example. Ireland had come to Rome to argue in behalf of his Faribault school plan. During the third week of February he had his first audience with the pope. It lasted an hour. "He was most affectionate," Ireland reported, "most eulogistic, most familiar. He talked of social questions . . . of his general democratic policy, of French affairs."[29]

The pope's eagerness to converse with the archbishop of St. Paul about "French affairs" and "democratic policy" suggested that the old diplomat—as Leo XIII liked to consider himself—had on his mind something besides the means of educating Catholic children in far-off Minnesota. His first political concern remained the reassertion of papal sovereignty over, or at least independence within, the city of Rome. To achieve that goal intervention by one or another of the European powers was, to him, an obvious necessity. Early in his pontificate he had reposed some hope for aid in Austria or Germany, but the anti-clerical Italians had checkmated him by entering into the Triple Alliance with the two German-speaking empires in 1882. When that agreement was renewed five years later, the pope began to contemplate a rapprochement with France, the natural rival of Italy and Germany.

But this was an initiative which bristled with difficulties. The French Third Republic had carved out a strong anti-clerical program of its own, though the more virulent features of it had subsided by the late 1880s. Significantly the struggle between church and state in France had centered upon the secularization of education, the very matter in dispute in the United States. The pope was wise enough and realistic enough to realize that French Catholics' devotion to monarchism was a lost cause, and that so long as it was entertained the church in France condemned itself to futility and isolation from public life. Therefore Leo proclaimed his policy of *ralliement,* the "rallying" of French Catholic allegiance to the republic.

Here was where the archbishop of St. Paul came in. Ireland, who had visited Paris on his way to Rome in 1892, had witnessed first-hand how stubbornly his French co-religionists clung to their monarchist illusions. "Intense confusion," he wrote, "prevails in France among Catholics—the Pope pressing upon them the Republic, they in large numbers resisting, respectfully but firmly."[30] But could not Ireland—a Francophile from his youth, fluent in the language, and, above all, the most visible exponent of the harmony between the church and republicanism—could not Ireland play a role in rallying French Catholics to an endorsement of the pope's policy? Little wonder that Leo welcomed Ireland warmly and listened with sympathy to a description of the Faribault plan—lilting French name! The Faribault school plan was duly approved in the spring of 1892, and Ireland, on his way home, returned to Paris. He held a private interview with the president of the republic, and, on the evening of June 18, he addressed an overflow crowd of twelve hundred distinguished persons, the light, he said later, of Parisian society. He spoke in French, and nostalgically recalled the time "when I spoke it by day, and dreamed in it by night." The speech was a paean of praise for America, a loving montage of history and of political and religious commentary which only toward the end made its real point, an explicit if muted recommendation of the pope's call for a *ralliement:* "Arriving in Rome a few months ago, I heard from the summit of the Vatican Hill: 'Of all the forms of civil government which the Church has recognized, and of which she has made trial, she cannot say from which she has received more harm or more good.' Just now she is resolved to make trial in France of the Republic; and I, as a citizen of a republic, say to the Church: 'In this experiment thou shalt succeed.' "[31]

But by 1899 the experiment had clearly failed. The policy of *ralliement* lay in tatters, the victim—as was so much else in French political life—of the Dreyfus affair.[32] A new generation of anti-clerical politicians had come to the fore in Paris, and they were intent upon destroying once for all that union of church and state which, it could be argued, went back to the time of Clovis, king of the Franks. And amidst the gloom that such developments produced upon Vatican Hill, there came the rumors, ever stronger, about certain French intellectuals— Alfred Loisy, Marcel Hebert, Albert Houtin were the names most frequently mentioned—who were raising radical questions about the nature of Catholic dogma and who, it was maintained by certain elements within the curia, were clearly encouraged in their extravagances by the French version of that ill-defined phenomenon called Americanism. Was it outlandish to wonder if those who displayed such enthusiasm for a country like the United States, filled with masons and heretics, might question even the divinity of Christ?

So it was that by the spring of 1899 John Ireland's world had turned upside down. Perhaps he pondered the transitoriness of all human affairs as he stalked across the Place Vendôme. More likely, given his nature, his pessimism subsided as he thought about the two cathedrals he was going to build—one in St. Paul, the other in Minneapolis. They would be the biggest, and therefore the best, he could possibly provide. He was, after all, a man of the American gilded age.

Abbreviations

APF-A: Archives of Propaganda, Acta

APF-NS: Archives of Propaganda, New Series

APF-SCOG: Archives of Propaganda, Documents cited by General Congregations

CHS: Ireland Papers, Archives of the Catholic Historical Society, St. Paul

MHS: Archives of the Minnesota Historical Society

NC: *Northwestern Chronicle,* St. Paul diocesan weekly

Notes

1. John Ireland, "Jeanne d'Arc, the Patron Saint of Patriotism," *The Church and Modern Society,* 2 vols. (St. Paul, 1904), 2: 58.

2. *La libre parole,* quoted in James H. Moynihan, *The Life of Archbishop Ireland* (New York, 1953), 147.

3. See "Prologue" to my *Patriarch of the West. A Biography of John Ireland* (St. Paul, forthcoming 1988). Humphrey Moynihan, the secretary, gave this account to Philip Hughes, who told it to me.

4. APF-A, 243 (1875): 284.

5. St. Paul *Dispatch,* February 16 and 27, 1875.

6. APF-A, 243 (1875): 283–285.

7. CHS, Ireland to Pius IX and to Grace, St. Paul, April 22, 1875. A diver recovered the mail pouch, and Ireland's packet was returned to him.

8. APF-A, 243 (1875): 285, which includes Grace to Barnab, Rome, April 30, 1875.

9. See CHS by date for correspondence and school notebooks.

10. St. Paul *Press,* November 1, 1862.

11. James P. Shannon (ed.), "Archbishop Ireland's Experiences as a Civil War Chaplain," *The Catholic Historical Review,* 39 (1953): 305.

12. Minneapolis *Tribune,* September 2, 1886.

13. For the cartridge incident and its publicity see Helen Angela Hurley, "John of St. Paul," unpublished typescript, MHS, 116–120.

14. In Buffalo, September 4, 1897. See Hurley, 120–121.

15. A large number of Ireland's manuscript sermons survive, CHS, most by date, some undated.

16. The definitive study is James P. Shannon, *Catholic Colonization on the Western Frontier* (New Haven, 1957).

17. CHS, "Virtues and Faults of the Irish, at Home and Abroad," March 17, 1865.

18. Ireland, *Church and Modern Society,* 1: 129–165 for the whole text.

19. CHS, "The Church," n. d. [January 1873].

20. See James Hennesey, *The First Council of the Vatican: the American Experience* (New York, 1963), 53–54.

21. For Ireland's colorful descriptions see *NC,* October 16 and November 27, 1869, and February 5 and 13, 1870.

22. See, e.g., CHS, "The Saloon," April 1888, and "Social Purity," June 1893.

23. For a helpful discussion of the terminological problem see Philip Gelason, "Coming to Terms with American Catholic History," *Societas,* 3 (1973): 292–295 and 301–305.

24. APF-SCOG, 1041 (1893): 208–209, Ireland to Simeoni, St. Paul, July 13, 1891.

25. APF-NS, 194: 846–862.

26. Full English text in Thomas T. McAvoy, *The Great Crisis in American Catholic History, 1895–1900* (Chicago, 1957), 379–391.

27. Ireland to Deshon, Rome, February 24 and March 16, 1899, q. in McAvoy, 284–285.

28. Text in *NC,* March 3, 1899.

29. CHS, Ireland to Caillet, Rome, February 14, 1892.

30. CHS, Ireland to Caillet, Paris, January 28, 1892.

31. Published as "America in France," *Church and Modern Society* 1: 365–395.

32. See Alexander Sedgwick, *The Ralliement in French Politics, 1890–1898* (Cambridge, Mass., 1965), 157–159, who argues "connection" rather than "cause."

Gerald P. Fogarty, S.J.

The Vatican and
the American Church
Since World War II

At the end of World War II, the Catholic Church in the United States was a sleeping giant. Its intellectual life had been virtually snuffed out at the turn of the century. First came the condemnation of Americanism, the American Catholic praise of religious liberty, in 1899. But scholarship in the American church was then only in its infancy and was still largely derivative from Europe. The condemnation of modernism in 1907 and the witch hunt that followed it took its toll on several European scholars who had taken up posts in American universities and seminaries. At the Catholic University of America, the Dutch-born Father Henry Poels was dismissed because he would not sign an oath that in conscience he believed that Moses was the author of the Pentateuch. At St. Joseph's Seminary, Dunwoodie, New York, the French-born Father Francis Gigot and several other Sulpicians withdrew from their society rather than face increasing censorship for his progressive writings on scripture. In 1908, the journal edited at the seminary, *The New York Review,* ceased publication after only three years. For the next four decades, Catholic theology in the United States was largely a repetition of Roman manuals—a repetition that led to the identification of theological interpretation with the authentic teaching of the church.

Yet the Holy See recognized the importance of the American church. In his first consistory in 1946, Pius XII elevated four Americans to the college of cardinals: Archbishops Francis J. Spellman of New York, Edward Mooney of Detroit, Samuel Stritch of Chicago, and John J. Glennon of St. Louis. With Cardinal Dennis Dougherty in Philadelphia, the American church had the largest number of cardinals in its history, although Glennon died before returning to the United States. But the bishops of the 1940s and 1950s were primarily builders and defenders of Catholic interests, not thinkers. Spellman was typical. To many Americans he represented the American hierarchy, although he never came to dominate the inner circle of the National Catholic Welfare Conference (NCWC), the organization of the American bishops, first formed in 1919 as the National Catholic Welfare Council and renamed "Conference" in 1922 after the Vatican had issued a condemnation of the original organization. In 1947 he had his coadjutor, James Francis McIntyre, appointed archbishop of Los Angeles. McIntyre, only the second ordinary of the western see, was a shrewd businessman and realtor. He presided over the development of Los Angeles into one of the major sees in the world. The United States was still expanding and continued to receive new immigrants. The needs of the church and the type of bishop best suited to meet those needs had changed little over the previous century.

But at the end of the war, the United States had emerged as the superpower of the west. Though many Vatican officials continued to harbor suspicion about American religious liberty, they had to take the United States seriously as the strongest bulwark against communism. Some Americans, too, raised questions about how American the Catholics could be, as the nation witnessed a new outbreak of anti-Catholicism. This was the framework as the Church in the United States settled into the post-war years that would lead to Vatican II.

I. The Holy See, the United States Government, and American Society

The relations between the Vatican and the United States government, though informal, had never been more cordial than in the opening years of the war. In an effort to win over Vatican opinion and to consolidate joint efforts for peace, President Franklin D. Roosevelt had named Myron C. Taylor as his "personal representative" to Pope Pius XII late in 1939. Basically a compromise for the formal diplomatic relations that Pius wanted and for which Francis Spellman had been working since 1935, first as auxiliary bishop of Boston and then as archbishop of New York, the designation of a personal representative had enabled the government to have a listening post in the Vatican during the war. When the United States and Italy went to war, Taylor's assistant, Harold H. Tittmann, a professional foreign service officer, was named chargé d'affaires, a formal diplomatic title that allowed him to take up residence in Vatican City. An early sign of tension after peace was restored, however, came with the State Department's query as to how he had been granted the title.[1] The tension between the Vatican and the government would increase in the coming years. One sign of the tension was renewed Vatican suspicion of American religious liberty on both the practical and the theoretical level.

In the fall of 1947, for example, the Vatican tried unsuccessfully to have the American hierarchy work to have a clause guaranteeing religious liberty removed from a forthcoming treaty of friendship, commerce and navigation between the United States and Italy. Another source of tension was the hostile reaction in the United States to the continuation of the Taylor mission after peace was restored. Possibly to assuage this hostility, President Harry S Truman instructed Taylor to see other religious leaders while he was in Europe to see the pope. Placing the pope on the same level as these other religious leaders brought forth a Vatican protest to Spellman in May 1949. When Spellman failed to respond, Monsignor Domenico Tardini, substitute secretary of state for the extraordinary affairs of the church, complained to Cicognani that in an audience with the pope, Taylor had suggested that Protestant attacks on the church would "cease if he were at the same time the representative to the various religious groups"—"a thing," added Tardini, "which is evidently impossible."[2] Cicognani passed on Tardini's letter to Spellman, who immediately attempted to make an appointment with Truman. Receiving no reply, he again wrote asking for a "ten minute appointment," only to receive word that the president had no time.[3]

Spellman's rebuff was the prelude to the manner in which the United States government ended the Taylor mission. In January 1950 Taylor submitted his resignation to Truman. With no formal notification to the pope that the mission was ended, Taylor's office in Rome was simply closed. Paradoxically, at this very period, Spellman begin maneuvers to establish formal diplomatic relations between the United States and the Holy See. Among those he attempted to enlist in his cause was James Byrnes, former senator from South Carolina, secretary of state, and supreme court justice. In January 1951 Byrnes, an ex-Catholic, was about to be inaugurated as governor of South Carolina. Spellman was on cordial terms with Byrnes and wrote him to congratulate him and to seek his assistance in establishing diplomatic relations. When he sought the assistance of Karl J. Alter, archbishop of Cincinnati and chairman of the administrative board of the National Catholic Welfare Conference, to gain the support of Senator Robert F. Taft of Ohio, he encountered less than enthusiastic support. Alter queried about the timing of these negotiations when the Holy See had recently prohibited Catholic membership in the International Rotary, a decision that had "caused so much bewilderment and unfavorable discussion among our fellow citizens."[4] He later confided that he and other leading members of the hierarchy were actually opposed to establishing diplomatic relations with the Holy See.[5]

Spellman's overtures—with little support of the rest of the hierarchy—led in October 1951 to Truman's nomination of General Mark Clark as ambassador to the Vatican. The announcement brought immediate negative reaction from the whole spectrum of American Protestants. In retrospect, it is difficult to determine whether Truman was serious in making the nomination. First of all, Clark had little chance of being approved by the Senate Foreign Relations Committee. Clark's use of the Thirty-Sixth Texas Division in the bloody battle of the Rapido River had aroused strong opposition in Texas, one of whose senators, Thomas Connolly, was chairman of the committee. Second, Truman made the nomination when congress was out of session, perhaps to make an apparent response to what he perceived to be a Catholic interest while at the same time assuring that the public debate would force the withdrawal of the nomination before any senate debate. In any event, Clark withdrew his name in January 1952. Although Truman made tentative overtures about making another nomination, he never did so.[6]

Most American Catholics were probably either ignorant to or indifferent about establishing diplomatic relations with the Holy See. The issue did, however, serve as a focal point for a renewed outbreak of anti-Catholicism. In 1948 Paul Blanshard had published his *American Freedom and Catholic Power* which argued that Catholicism was incompatible with American culture. He even went so far as to argue that the bishops should be obliged to register as foreign agents, since they received their appointments from the pope. His voice was one of many emanating from Protestant and Other Americans United for the Separation of Church and State (POAU) which held that Catholics could not be truly Americans. For him and his associates, the proposal of diplomatic relations with the Holy See was one more example of the Catholic Church's attempt to undermine the United States.

In 1953, while attending Pius XII's second consistory, Spellman told the pope about the failure to gain diplomatic relations. He then wrote to Monsignor Giovanni Battista Montini, substitute secretary of state for the ordinary affairs of the church, that a poll, taken at the time of Clark's nomination, indicated that only nine out of ninety-six senators would have supported the nomination even if it had reached the senate floor. For some time, however, Montini had been in correspondence with Spellman about the need to counter Blanshard's attacks. Montini now combined the issues of an answer to Blanshard together with the American opposition to diplomatic relations. On March 12, 1953, he informed Spellman that

> the Holy See cannot remain indifferent to the unreasonable and unreasoning attitude of non-Catholics in the United States. In connection with this matter of diplomatic representation and on other occasions in the recent past, there have been repeated, vulgar, bitter and entirely unjustified attacks against the Holy See, with unwarranted deductions and unmerited conclusions that are scarcely compatible with the "freedom" of

which the United States claims to be the champion and the custodian.

These attacks, he continued, had "greatly added to the burden of sorrow that weighs upon" Pius XII. He concluded by stating: "I cannot conceal from Your Eminence that it is felt here that such attacks on the part of non-Catholics did not arouse an adequate reaction on the part of the Catholic community in the United States, that neither orally nor in the press has there been a sufficient response or any particularly authoritative voice raised in defense of the Holy See."[7]

Spellman did not lightly accept such a reprimand. He expressed his "surprise and pain" at Montini's charge that the American Catholic community had not adequately defended the Holy See. Then he compiled a dossier of representative Catholic statements. While he had already himself sent clippings about these statements, he now forwarded them to Montini, "to save your Excellency from any inconvenience in locating them in the Vatican archives." Deftly he reminded Montini of the role of Italian-American Catholics in persuading their Italian relatives not to vote for the Communists in the election of 1948. "Your Excellency is well aware," he said, "of the Communist threats to the Church and her institutions even in countries where the great majority of the people are Catholic." Although American Catholics were in the minority and were frequently "hated in the same way by many fanatical people in this country," they had been able "to retain control of our schools and charitable institutions and own our own church properties without taxation or interference." In response to Montini's reference to "the burden of sorrow" weighing upon the heart of the pope, Spellman could only note his own indescrible "poignancy of grief," because he knew "that the Hierarchy, the priests, the religious and faithful of the United States are second to the people of no country in the world, I repeat, of no country in the world, in their devotion to the Vicar of Christ." As evidence for this, he thought that far "more precious" than the more than $200,000,000 distributed during the previous decade through the Catholic Relief Services were "the numbers of religious men and women from the United States who are leaving their homeland to bring the Gospel of Christ to the pagan world, and even to countries assumed to be almost Catholic."[8]

Spellman's response to Montini ran five pages, single-spaced; at the bottom of one copy, he noted that he never received a reply. His references to communism were well taken. He had mobilized Italian-Americans in 1948 to write their Italian relatives to vote against communism. The Vatican asked him to do the same in 1953. He noted the irony for a friend in Rome—"only two weeks ago I wrote to Monsignor Montini defending the Bishops of the United States, and here now the Holy See asks the Bishops of America to defend the Holy See in Italy!!!!!!!!!!!!"[9] The campaign against communism would ultimately bring the United States and the Vatican closer together and contribute to the assimilation of Catholics into American society. But there were other American issues that drew Vatican attention.

In 1786 John Carroll had formally distinguished between membership in and full communion with the Catholic Church. Unfortunately, this distinction was lost on Father Leonard Feeney, S.J. A poet and popular speaker, Feeney was assigned by his Jesuit superiors to St. Benedict's Center in Cambridge, Massachusetts, to serve the spiritual needs of Catholic students at Harvard University and Radcliffe College. By the late 1940s, however, Feeney, together with several lay professors at Boston College, began to assert that there was no salvation outside the Catholic Church. A charismatic man, he influenced several students to withdraw from Harvard and Radcliffe to attend courses at St. Benedict's Center, which he had had chartered by the Commonwealth of Massachusetts. Next, he began attacking several Catholic colleges for being lax in their teaching about salvation outside the Catholic Church and he induced several students publicly to resign from those schools. He refused to accept another assignment from his provincial superior and was ultimately suspended from the priesthood for hearing confessions in Boston after his faculties for the archdiocese had expired. The issue came to a head in Holy Week, 1949. On Good Friday Feeney's followers picketed several Catholic churches in Boston distributing literature describing their position that there was no salvation outside formal communion with the Catholic Church, accusing Feeney's Jesuit superiors and colleagues of heresy, and denying Archbishop Richard J. Cushing's authority over them. Cushing then placed St. Benedict's Center under interdict and wrote to the Holy Office that, for the time being, Feeney's suspension was sufficient. But Feeney continued to escalate his attacks. Finally, on July 27, the Holy Office issued a decree, with papal approval, stating that actual incorporation into the Catholic Church was not necessary for salvation. Now that Rome had spoken, the decree continued, Feeney and his followers could no longer claim to be in good faith. Quite to the contrary, "their bond of duty of obedience toward the Church is much graver than that of those who as yet are related to the Church 'only by an unconscious desire' . . . to them apply without any restriction that principle: submission to the Catholic Church and to the Sovereign Pontiff is required as necessary for salvation."[10]

Despite several more overtures, Feeney refused to submit and was excommunicated—he and some of his followers were restored to communion with the church in 1972. While his teaching about the meaning of "no salvation outside the church" was an aberration from what had been the American Catholic interpretation of the dictum, the Holy See's public condemnation of him did serve to assuage American Protestant fears that the church did indeed teach that one had to be a Catholic in order to be saved. The condemnation, moreover, had universal implications and was specifically cited in Vatican II's dogmatic constitution on the church.[11]

While the Feeney case was a painful episode in American Catholicism, the issue of communism was to have a long-range impact on both Vatican relations with the United States government and American Catholics' position in American society. A relatively minor event signaled closer rapport between the Vatican and the government. In 1943 Roosevelt had written Pius XII about the impending Allied invasion of Italy proper. He guaranteed that the American forces had been instructed to respect "the neutral status of Vatican City as well as of the Papal domains throughout Italy." In 1944 there were four American bombing raids that did substantial damage to the papal villa at Castel Gandolfo. Relations between the Holy See and the United States had already been severely strained by the two bombings of Rome the previous summer. Now Spellman and other Catholic leaders publicly protested the new raids. At the end of the war, the War Department rejected a Vatican suit for $1,000,000 on the grounds, later upheld by the State Department, that Roosevelt had no right to bind the government and that "the Papal domains damaged were not territory of a neutral state, but had the status of a neutral diplomatic mission located in the territory of a belligerent."[12] Special appropriations would have to be made by congress that would arouse the charge that the government was giving money to the church.

In 1955 Spellman proposed that the NCWC pay the damages, but the administrative board allocated only $150,000 in addition to the $500,000 annually sent to the pope for relief purposes. Spellman considered using funds of his own archdiocese, but, as he told his friend and confidant of Pius XII, Enrico Galeazzi, "I thought . . . that it would be most pleasing to our Holy Father if the Administrative Board of Bishops all cooperated in this assistance, knowing the bitter anti-Catholic debate that would have taken place in Congress if the matter of an appropriation came up."[13]

The settlement of the issue had all the earmarks of a complicated plot for a spy novel. First, in April 1955 Joseph Kennedy proposed an undisclosed plan to Galeazzi that would not involve congressional appropriations. Galeazzi recommended that he follow Spellman's advice. In September Allen W. Dulles, director of the Central Intelligence Agency, paid a visit to Rome. Galeazzi prepared a memorandum for him outlining the Vatican's position. Recounting their conversation to Kennedy, Galeazzi said Dulles "was somehow worried about the stern attitude of the State Department about the necessity of the representation to the Congress of this matter." The secretary of state at the time was, of course, Dulles' brother, John Foster Dulles. Then Galeazzi revealed what may have been the prime motivation in bringing the government to settle the claims with the Vatican. He and Dulles had expressed the hope "for the establishment of ever more close relations between the Holy See and the U.S. Government at this stage, as there is such a great need of communion in the efforts to keep Communism back, especially in the social, cultural, and spiritual fields." Dulles promised to confer with Kennedy whom Galeazzi urged to "go on insisting that the main scope of the U.S. Government should be that of ending this pending question in the best and quickest way possible."[14]

While Galeazzi was encouraging Dulles and Kennedy to work on a non-legislative settlement, in October 1955 he received another visitor, Senator John F. Kennedy, Joseph Kennedy's son. They discussed a legislative approach. Late in February 1956 Representative John W. McCormack (D-Mass.), the house majority leader, and Representative Joseph Martin (R-Mass.), the minority leader, introduced a bill for the appropriation of $1,523,810.98 for damages. Clare Booth Luce, the United States ambassador to Italy, recommended that Spellman speak to "friendly members" of the appropriations committee. The State Department then modified its earlier position. While it still argued that Castel Gandolfo was not neutral territory, it recommended that, as a "matter of grace" and not to set a precedent, the sum of $964,199.35 be paid to the Vatican. The reason for the lower sum, it said, was that the higher figure was derived from the loss of works of art that were irreplaceable. Early in June congress approved this appropriation.[15] In retrospect, it was a minor affair, but it was one which symbolized the desire of both the Vatican and the United States to have closer relations as they waged their common battle against communism.

The campaign against communism would have a more direct effect upon the assimilation of Catholics into American society. Senator Joseph R. McCarthy's witch hunt for communists had at least one advantage for Catholics in the United States. A Catholic, he presented the public image that a Catholic could not be a communist. Anti-communism began to cancel out anti-Catholicism, despite Paul Blanshard's efforts to keep the issue alive. Socially, the way was being paved for the election of the first Catholic president.

In 1958 Senator Kennedy announced his candidacy for the presidency. Immediately Blanshard and the POAU demanded that all candidates declare their positions on two issues: diplomatic relations with the Vatican and federal aid to parochial schools. In an interview Kennedy declared his opposition to diplomatic relations because the divisiveness that would result would undermine the effectiveness of any ambassador. He likewise declared that he was bound to uphold the supreme court's decisions in regard to aid to parochial schools. In his 1960 campaign he addressed these same questions in his address to the Greater Houston Ministerial Association—to them he also added the questions of birth control, divorce, censorship, and gambling. He made it clear that in dealing with such issues as president, he would make his decision "in accordance with what my conscience tells me to be in the national interest and without regard to outside religious pressure. And no power or threat of punishment could cause me to decide otherwise." If any remote situation should occur, he continued, "when my office would require me to violate my conscience, or violate the national interest, then I would resign the office, and I hope any other conscientious public servant would do likewise." One questioner interpreted Kennedy's statement to mean that he would resign the presidency "if it were in real conflict with your Church." Kennedy immediately corrected him by saying: "No, I said with my conscience."[16]

Kennedy's speech before the Greater Houston Ministerial Association was a critical factor in his election to the White House. His statement may well have reflected the civic faith of many American Catholics. Upon closer analysis, however, his sense of the relationship between the presidency and his conscience, but not his Church, could be construed as making religion essentially private. At the time he could get away with the answer because the questions were different. In regard to diplomatic relations with the Vatican and aid to parochial schools, Catholics were legitimately divided. In regard to divorce and birth control, there was increasing dissent within the American church which had, in any case, accommodated itself, at least in regard to divorce, to recognizing a pluralism of moral views within American society. On other issues, there was still a general moral consensus within that society. Twenty years later, the answer would be seen as inadequate as that consensus broke down and different questions, e.g. about abortion, would be asked of prospective candidates. Even as Kennedy was waging the campaign that would bring the first Catholic to the White House, however, theologians were seeking to address the question of religious liberty and the precise Catholic doctrine on the relationship between church and state.

II. Theological Tensions Between the Holy See and the United States

From the condemnation of Americanism in 1899 to 1943, Catholic reflection on the question of religious liberty as guaranteed by the first amendment to the constitution had been mute. American theologians took for granted that the American situation was at best an accommodation, an "hypothesis," to be tolerated because Catholics would never be numerous enough to have their church officially united to the state.[17] Simultaneously, other theological issues that had been long dormant came to the fore in the post-war years, notably in the field of biblical scholarship. But, for the moment, religious liberty was the principal concern of American theologians.

In 1943 Father John Courtney Murray, S.J., professor of theology at Woodstock College in Maryland, began a series of articles in *Theological Studies* on the official church teaching about the relationship between church and state. His concern was the growing secularism of American society. To combat this, he saw the need for "intercredal cooperation," that is, cooperation between Catholics, Protestants, and Jews—he would later add secularists as well—for the sake of the common good. To achieve this goal, he sought to determine what was the official teaching in regard to church-state relations. In his early writings he pointed out that in the encyclicals of Leo XIII, there was a development of doctrine on the issue. Initially this brought him into conflict with some members of the hierarchy who gradually came to his point of view. But it also brought him into conflict with Monsignor Joseph C. Fenton, professor of dogmatic theology at the Catholic University of America, who was not to be won over. In Fenton's mind, if Murray said the American separation of church and state was more than a merely tolerable "hypothesis," he was in violation of *Longinqua Oceani,* an apostolic letter Leo XIII addressed to the American church in 1895. If Murray argued that papal statements had to be adapted to particular cultural situations, he was guilty of watering down doctrine that Leo had condemned in his apostolic letter *Testem Benevolentiae* against Americanism. Fenton made both these apostolic letters infallible pronouncements and accused Murray of being an Americanist.[18]

There was a certain irony in Murray being accused of being an Americanist, for in the nineteenth century his Jesuit predecessors had been opposed to the movement. The crisis developed from a new interpretation of the papal magisterium after Vatican I. In the immediate aftermath of Pius IX's Syllabus of Errors in 1864, some bishops continued to state that the pope was condemning only the absolute position, demanded by European radicals, that the church had always to be separated from the state. Archbishop Martin John Spalding of Baltimore, for instance, issued a pastoral letter publicly stating that the pope had not condemned the American proposition. While Spalding failed to get an official Roman statement in support of his position, he also received no reprimand.

Thirty years after the Syllabus, however, theologians gave the condemned proposition a different interpretation. First, they argued that, in condemning the separation of church and state, Pius IX was teaching that there should be a union of church and state. Leo XIII came close to but fell short of this in *Longinqua Oceani,* when he had warned American Catholic leaders that they should not think their form of the separation of Church and state was suitable for the church everywhere. In his mind, the American church had indeed prospered, "but she would bring forth more abundant fruits if, in addition to liberty, she enjoyed the favor of the laws and the patronage of the public authority."[19] Second, theologians increasingly emphasized the papal magisterium without distinction between various levels of authority. When Leo condemned Americanism in 1899, for example, Archbishops Michael A. Corrigan of New York and Frederick J. Katzer of Milwaukee thanked the pontiff for the exercise of his infallible office. This was the theological tradition to which Joseph Fenton was heir and against which Murray had to react.

Fenton represented a well established theological school of thought. In Rome, Alfredo Ottaviani, elevated to the college of cardinals in 1953 and named secretary of the Holy Office, publicly stated that, where Catholics were in the majority, the church should be united to the state. Where Catholics were in the minority, the church should be guaranteed freedom. His argument was a simple one—there should be two standards for truth and error, for error has no rights. Though Ottaviani specifically alluded to the controversy then waging in the United States—he actually gave the page references to one of Fenton's articles—he did not mention Murray by name. Although the full text of Ottaviani's address was never published, his position was embodied in the concordat that the Holy See was then negotiating with Spain, and the Spanish bishops openly proclaimed that union of church and state was Catholic doctrine, despite what Murray was saying. But there were mixed signals coming from Rome. Late in 1953 Pius XII gave an address in which he definitely seemed to repudiate Ottaviani's position. At least, that is the way Murray understood it and publicly stated it in a speech at the Catholic University of America in March 1954. This brought him Ottaviani's increasing opposition. In the summer of 1955 Murray learned from his superiors in Rome that the censors could not approve two of his articles because of Holy Office hostility. On his own initiative Murray abandoned his writing on the separation of church and state and on religious liberty—at least for the time.[20]

Murray, however, was not the only theologian to fall under ecclesiastical suspicion during the 1950s. In 1937 the Catholic Biblical Association had been formed, originally to make a revision of the Douay-Challoner-Rheims translation from the Vulgate. An exclusively clerical group at its inception, it was the first organization to be comprised of priests from various dioceses and religious orders since the specific condemnation of such associations in *Pascendi Dominici Gregis* in 1907. American Catholic biblical scholarship had fallen victim to the anti-modernist witch hunt at the beginning of the century. As had happened with church-state relations, theological opinion had become confused with authentic teaching. In 1943, however, Pius XII issued *Divino Afflante Spiritu* which opened the doors to Catholic biblical scholars who were instructed to use the same historico-critical method that had been condemned at the beginning of the century. By the 1950s American Catholic biblical scholarship was coming into its maturity. Under the editorship of Edward Siegman, C.Pp.S., associate professor of scripture at the Catholic University, the *Catholic Biblical Quarterly* had become a scholarly journal. But then biblical scholarship met opposition from a now familiar source, Monsignor Joseph C. Fenton.

Fenton began his attack on biblical scholars almost as soon as Murray ceased writing. As editor of the *American Ecclesiastical Review,* a journal widely circulated among priests, Fenton published accusations that the new scholars were guilty of modernism. In 1958 he received an important ally in the new apostolic delegate, Archbishop Egidio Vagnozzi. In the summer of 1961 Vagnozzi gave the commencement address at Marquette University and challenged the orthodoxy of, among others, biblical scholars. Fenton published the text of the address. Later that summer the CBA met at Cincinnati. In a dramatic session the members passed a resolution against the *American Ecclesiastical Review* for its attacks on biblical scholarship. Among the articles the resolution specifically cited was Vagnozzi's address. Under pressure from Vagnozzi, however, Archbishop Patrick A. O'Boyle of Washington, who gave the imprimatur to the *Catholic Biblical Quarterly,* the published resolution referred to the attacks without any specific reference to the *American Ecclesiastical Review.*[21]

As the church prepared for Vatican II, Vagnozzi did all in his power to prevent the Americans from being ready. And he could be vindictive. Late in the summer of 1961 Siegman suffered a heart attack. While he was recovering, his provincial received a terse telegram from the rector of the university, Monsignor William A. McDonald, that Siegman had been replaced. It was obvious to observers that Vagnozzi and Fenton were responsible. The graduate school faculty unanimously passed a resolution censoring the rector; with two votes in the negative, the theological faculty passed a similar resolution. Rather than appeal to Rome, as some of his friends advised, Siegman quietly accepted the decision.[22]

Biblical scholars did find a champion, however, in the unlikely person of Cardinal Spellman. He indicated his attitude in 1960. The Paulist Press had just published the first volumes in the Bible Pamphlet Series. The purpose was to place on a popular level what modern scripture scholarship was doing. Vagnozzi asked Spellman to withdraw his imprimatur. Spellman, instead, first consulted the editor of the Paulist Press and his own canonical and theological advisors. Then he wrote to Vagnozzi declaring that the series represented legitimate scholarship, according to the norms of Rome, that he had consulted several men from the Pontifical Biblical Commission with doctorates in scripture, and that he had no intention of withdrawing his imprimatur. Conservative though Spellman may have been, he knew that as a delegate Vagnozzi had no right to interfere with the rights of an ordinary.

On the eve of Vatican II, American Catholic scholarship was in disarray. Murray continued his silence in regard to church-state relations. Biblical scholars were on the defensive. And the hierarchy had a papal representative who was intruding into its affairs on issues ranging from scripture scholarship and religious liberty to discussion of the use of the vernacular in the liturgy. The very experience of a council was foreign to the bishops. Cardinal James Gibbons of Baltimore was the last surviving participant in Vatican I and in the Third Plenary Council of Baltimore, held in 1884. He had died in 1921. A prevailing ecclesiology implied that councils were indeed superfluous with an infallible pope. Gustave Weigel, S.J., Murray's colleague at Woodstock, for example, used the analogy of the pope as the "primary receptor" for the radio stimulus of the Holy Spirit; all other "receptors" or local bishops were tuned into the primary receptor.[23] The analogy came close to saying that bishops were merely the delegates of the pope and not active participants in expressing the magisterium. Vatican II would challenge all these theological presuppositions.

III. Vatican II: Resolution or Source of New Conflicts

To a great extent, the first session of Vatican II was a learning experience for the American bishops. As the council opened Murray was not present; he had been "disinvited," to use his term, at the request of Ottaviani and Vagnozzi. Present was Fenton as a *peritus* for Ottaviani.[24] Ottaviani's theological commission had produced several schemata that it expected the bishops simply to accept. Its schema on the church contained a chapter stating that a union of church and state was normative wherever Catholics were in the majority. Its schema on revelation spoke of the "sources" of revelation. But John XXIII had also established the Secretariat for Promoting Christian Unity under the presidency of Cardinal Augustin Bea, S.J., a scripture scholar. Under instructions from the pope to carve out its own territory, the secretariat had drafted a document on ecumenism, one chapter of which was on religious liberty. The reaction of the bishops to the proposed schemata gave the Americans their first practical experience of a theological concept familiar to their nineteenth century predecessors—episcopal collegiality. They discovered the bishops of other nations acting in consort on the schemata. For many American bishops, for example, the idea of scripture and tradition as separate sources of revelation was the church's official doctrine, derived from the Council of Trent.[25] When the bishops at the council failed to gain an absolute majority to reject the proposed schema, John XXIII personally intervened to withdraw it. At the end of the session, the bishops had approved only the constitution on the liturgy. But, as Joseph Ratzinger noted at the time, this constitution had important ramifications for the concept of collegiality, for it placed aspects of liturgical change within the hands of episcopal conferences, which were then under consideration in another schema. Ratzinger pointed out that episcopal conferences, where they existed, were formerly "of a merely deliberative character," but "now that they possess as a right a definite legislative function, they appear as a new element in the ecclesiastical body-politic, and form a link of a quasi-synodal kind between the individual bishops and the pope."[26] Of more immediate importance to Americans was Spellman's intervention to gain the appointment of John Courtney Murray as a *peritus.*

During the summer of 1963 John XXIII died, and the conclave elected as his successor Cardinal G. B. Montini, with whom Spellman had had such a sharp exchange of letters only a decade earlier. Paul VI's personality would be an enigma for many as the second session of the council opened in the fall. The American bishops for their part showed that they had not completely learned the signficance of collegiality. On the one hand, Spellman, who made more interventions at the council than any other American bishop, learned that religious liberty was being dropped from the council's agenda. He then led the American hierarchy in approving a position paper drawn up by Murray, drafting a joint letter to the officials of the council, and petitioning that religious liberty be discussed at the council. Had it not been for this united stance of the American bishops, Murray thought at the time, the council might not have considered the issue.[27] On the other hand, at the very time of this petition, Spellman spoke in the council against certain aspects of collegiality. Since "the authority of the Supreme Pontiff is supreme and full in itself," he said, "it is not necessary that he share it with others, even if they are bishops whose collaboration in governing the universal Church can be asked for by the Supreme Pontiff himself, but is neither necessary nor essential."[28] Spellman had not yet learned to see the connection between the action he had just taken and the theology of collegiality.

The complete story of Vatican II and of American participation in it has yet to be written. Here it will have to suffice to touch upon some important highlights. During the third session in 1964, the schema on religious liberty had been separated from the one on ecumenism. Just as the bishops were prepared to vote on the document on November 19, however, it was withdrawn from discussion. The bishops hastily gathered signatures for a petition for Pope Paul VI to override the decision, but he remained adamant. He did, however, promise that the topic would be the first on the agenda in the next session. Murray later admitted that the schema then under consideration was one of the weakest versions drafted by the Secretariat for Promoting Christian Unity. It had been largely the work of himself and Pietro Pavan, a professor at the Lateran University whom Pope John Paul II named a cardinal in 1985. It had stressed the limitations of the state over religious matters. The opponents to the schema fell into two groups. First, some believed that religious liberty was contrary to the doctrine of the church. This was the position of Archbishop Marcel Lefebvre, who would lead a schism in the church twenty years after the council. Second, others thought that the position taken by the English-speaking bishops and some Italians was based on juridical and political arguments. What was needed was an adequate theology of the person.

Such a theology was even then being developed in a schema that at first blush had little to do with religious liberty—the dogmatic constitution on divine revelation. The new schema reflected the work of modern biblical scholarship—and, for that matter, of an older American Catholic theological tradition. It spoke of scripture and tradition constituting a single source of revelation. As Joseph Ratzinger later commented, the pen was that of Yves Congar, O.P., but the theology was that of the Tübingen school of the nineteenth century. American bishops who thought this was indeed a change in the teaching of Trent may have been surprised to learn that Francis P. Kenrick, bishop of Philadelphia and later archbishop of Baltimore, had specifically referred to Tübingen and to the work of Johann Adam Möhler in his *Theologia Dogmatica* in 1838.[29] In 1833 their predecessors, gathered for the Second Provincial Council of Baltimore, used similar language in their pastoral letter. They had argued for witnesses who not only testified to what was the word of God but also "proclaimed in the name of the Catholic Church, and with its approbation, the interpretation of the Holy Bible, whether they were assembled in their councils or dispersed over the surface of the Christian world."[30]

The constitution on revelation gave a new emphasis to the relationship between faith and revelation. Revelation as the object of faith was the word of God culminating in the Word made flesh. Faith was then the acceptance of the Word, the person of Jesus Christ. Pierre Benoit, O.P. was the primary draftsman of this section. During the fourth session of the council he was appointed to help draft the final version of the declaration on religious liberty. The final document, accepted by the bishops, stated that "the act of faith is of its very nature a free act," because "man, redeemed by Christ the Savior and called through Jesus Christ to be an adopted son of God, cannot give his adherence to God when he reveals himself unless, drawn by the Father, he submits to God with a faith that is reasonable and free."[31] The two documents on revelation and religious liberty, when taken together, present a theology that emphasizes God's freedom in communicating himself and the human being's personal freedom in responding through faith. It is not the theology of subjectivism that the Holy See feared in Americanism and modernism at the beginning of the century, but of personalism that had its roots deep within not only the European but also the American Catholic tradition.

The approval of the declaration on religious liberty represented a victory for Murray and other Americans who had argued that the situation of the church in the United States was not merely a tolerable "hypothesis." But the document, as approved by the church in council, had moved considerably beyond the original discussion on church-state relations. One source of tension and misunderstanding between the Vatican and the American church had been overcome. But new tensions were now to arise.

For most American bishops, the concept of episcopal collegiality, so familiar to their predecessors in the nineteenth century, was something new. Though they had had their NCWC since 1919, it had initially been held suspect and was merely consultative. Vatican II now made such national conferences mandatory. In the United States, two new entities took the place of the old NCWC: the National Conference of

Catholic Bishops (NCCB) and the United States Catholic Conference (USCC), which maintained permanent departments in Washington to represent Catholic interests. As the NCCB became more active, it addressed many issues that would have been off-limits to the NCWC. By the 1970s the bishops were critical of national policy in war and in Latin America. They were exercising their rights as American citizens and religious leaders; their predecessors had to prove that Catholics were loyal Americans and that frequently meant patriotic service in the nation's wars. In 1983 they challenged the nation's policy on nuclear arms. In 1986 they addressed the question of the nation's economic policies. For many American Catholics this new episcopal activism was a deviation from the legitimate spiritual sphere of the Church. For others it represented the bishops recognizing their role in not becoming identified with the national culture. For some Roman officials the activism of the NCCB and other national conferences has raised the question of the canonical status and teaching authority of episcopal conferences. Do they play a legitimate role in expressing the magisterium or do their statements, including pastoral letters, merely express the non-binding opinions of the bishops who signed them?

In the years since the council, there have continued to be tensions with both the Vatican and American society. But there is added to this a new tension with the laity. To some extent this new tension is a product of the increased educational status of the laity coupled with theological confusion. While the laity are well educated in various professions, they are not versed in theology. Some confuse the theological opinions they learned in the pre-conciliar church with irreformable doctrine. Others misunderstand the meaning of some conciliar statements. To cite but a few examples: "collegiality," used by the council primarily to express the relationship of bishops with the pope, and secondarily to indicate the relationship of priests with their bishops, is construed to mean full lay participation in decision making; the declaration on religious liberty has come to mean freedom of thought within the church; and the biblical term "people of God," used in the dogmatic constitution on the church, has become synonymous with the democratic expression "We the People." Still other Catholics believe that the election of John Kennedy signaled the full acceptance of Catholics as Americans, but few have taken the time to analyze Kennedy's statement at Houston, given above; many have made their religion strictly a private matter. Into the vocabulary of American Catholicism, moreover, has been introduced the term "dissent." The bishops first used it in their pastoral letter of 1968 in speaking of adherence to Paul VI's encyclical on birth control. A question arises whether the term "dissent" in this context is derived from the proceedings of civil law, in which a "dissenting opinion" recognizes the legal binding force of the majority of a court's decision, while expressing arguments against that decision. In the legal context, dissent means disagreement with but not rejection of the majority decision. Dissent within American society at large, however, has come to mean not only disagreement but also rejection. The concept of a "loyal opposition" is part and parcel of the British and American legal tradition, but it remains foreign to the continental experience and the church's practice. As happened at the end of the last century with Americanism, American cultural experience and practice cannot help but create confusion in Vatican circles.

Pope John Paul II and other Roman officials are portrayed as seeing American Catholicism as a smorgasbord religion in which the people pick and choose what doctrines they will accept. Frequently, however, this impression arises more from American Catholic misinformation than practice. Many Catholics think that dissent from the ordinary teaching on birth control is rejection of the defined doctrine of papal infallibility. Far from being guilty of heresy or rejection of defined doctrine, their actions and words flow from ignorance of the church's authentic teaching. Their education in Catholic doctrine is not commensurate with their education in secular fields.

Many of the issues that formerly seemed to militate against acceptance of Catholics as Americans have ceased to exist. Relations between the Vatican and the United States government have become increasingly cordial. In 1970 President Richard M. Nixon reestablished the office of personal representative to the pope by appointing Henry Cabot Lodge to the post. President Gerald R. Ford, Jimmy Carter, and Ronald Reagan continued the practice until 1984 when the Holy See and the United States announced the establishment of full diplomatic relations. Although there were official protests and court cases against the action, the issue to which Kennedy had to address himself in 1959 and 1960 led to no domestic strife. One could well read the 1984 action as an attempt on the part of the government to insert itself into the affairs of an activist hierarchy. Diplomatic relations may relieve the tensions between the United States and the Holy See, but may increase friction between the government and the American hierarchy.

Notes

1. National Archives of the United States, RG 59, DS 121.866A/4-1345, Memorandum on the Personal Representative of the President of

the United States to His Holiness Pope Pius XII, Apr. 11, 1945. On the background to the Taylor mission and Tittmann's appointment, see Gerald P. Fogarty, S.J., *The Vatican and the American Hierarchy from 1870 to 1965* (Wilmington, Del.: Michael Glazier, Inc., 1985), pp. 259–266, 279–280.

2. Archives of the Archdiocese of New York, Tardini to Cicognani, Vatican, July 4, 1949, translation attached to Cicognani to Spellman, Washington, July 9, 1949.

3. *Ibid.,* Spellman to Truman, New York, July 31, 1949 (copy); Matthew Connelly to Spellman, Washington, Aug. 3, 1949.

4. AANY, Alter to Spellman, Cincinnati, Jan. 22, 1951.

5. See Fogarty, pp. 321–326.

6. See Fogarty, pp. 328–329.

7. AANY, Montini to Spellman, Vatican, Mar. 12, 1953.

8. AANY, Spellman to Montini, New York, Apr. 17, 1953 (copy).

9. AANY, Spellman to Enrico Galeazzi, New York, May 25, 1953 (copy).

10. Archives of the Archdiocese of Boston, Marchetti-Selvagiani to Cushing, Aug. 8, 1949. For reasons unclear, the full text was not published for three more years and then, not in the *Acta Apostolicae Sedis,* but in the *American Ecclesiastical Review,* 127 (Oct. 1952), 307–315. See DS, 3866–3873.

11. *Lumen Gentium,* Dogmatic Constitution on the Church, in Austin Flannery, O.P. (ed.), *Vatican Council II: The Conciliar and Post Conciliar Documents* (Collegeville, Minn.: The Liturgical Press, 1975), no. 16, n. 19, p. 367.

12. AANY, State Department memorandum on Vatican claims, June 11, 1953 (copy).

13. AANY, Spellman to Galeazzi, New York, Apr. 5, 1955 (copy).

14. AANY, Galeazzi to Kennedy, Vatican, Sept. 7, 1955 (copy) enclosed in Galeazzi to Spellman, Vatican, Sept. 8, 1955.

15. *Congressional Record,* 102 Pt. 7 (1956), 9570–9571.

16. *New York Times,* Sept. 13, 1960, p. 22.

17. Even John A. Ryan, the progressive director of the Social Action Department of the NCWC, held this view. See Francis L. Broderick, *Right Reverend New Dealer: John A. Ryan* (New York: The Macmillan Company, 1963), pp. 119–120.

18. Donald E. Pelotte, S.S.S., *John Courtney Murray: Theologian in Conflict* (New York: Paulist Press, 1975), pp. 154–173.

19. Given in John Tracy Ellis (ed.), *Documents of American Catholic History* (3 vols.; Wilmington, Del.: Michael Glazier, 1987), II, 502.

20. Fogarty, pp. 370–380.

21. See Archives of the Catholic Biblical Association, Catholic University of America, "Paraphrased Record of the Business Meeting . . . of the Catholic Biblical Association of America, Thursday, August 31, 1961"; *CBQ,* 23 (1961), 470.

22. The documents on this episode are in the archives of the Catholic Biblical Association and the archives of the Congregation of the Most Precious Blood, Carthagena, Ohio.

23. Patrick Wincester Collins, "Gustave Weigel: Ecclesiologist and Ecumenist," Unpublished Ph.D. dissertation, Theology Department, Fordham University, 1972, p. 327.

24. Pelotte, p. 77.

25. For the truncated quotation of Trent in Vatican I and its influence on the subsequent theology of tradition, see Yves M.-J. Congar, O.P., *Traditions and Tradition: An Historical and a Theological Essay* (New York: The Macmillan Company, 1967), pp. 48–49.

26. Joseph Ratzinger, "The First Session," *Worship,* 37 (1963), 534.

27. Pelotte, p. 82.

28. Vincent A. Yzermans (ed.), *American Participation in the Second Vatican Council* (New York: Sheed and Ward, 1967), 382.

29. Francis Patrick Kenrick, *Theologia Dogmatica* (4 vols.; 2nd ed.; Baltimore: John Murphy & Co., 1858), I, 288. On this point, Kenrick did not change his treatment from the first edition of 1838.

30. Hugh J. Nolan (ed.), *The Pastoral Letters of the American Hierarchy, 1792–1970* (Huntington, Ind.: Our Sunday Visitor, 1970), p. 52.

31. *Dignitatis Humanae Personae,* in *Documents of Vatican II,* no. 10, pp. 806–807. Compare this section, which cites Eph 1:5, with *Dei Verbum,* in *ibid.,* pp. 750–751, which refers to Eph 1:9.

Agnes Cunningham, S.S.C.M.

The Power of the Keys:
The Patristic Tradition

In an interesting article entitled, "One Woman's Confession of Faith,"[1] Lee Oo Chung, a Korean woman theologian, calls our attention to the fact that, in the gospel of Mark, the disciples of Jesus frequently seem to have missed the point of their master's teaching. She cites Peter's lack of comprehension when Jesus began to speak of his suffering and death (Mk 8:31–33), the disciples' failure to understand the prediction of the passion and resurrection of the Son of Man (Mk 9:32), the wonderment of the twelve as the Lord tried "to tell them what was going to happen to him" in Jerusalem (Mk 10:32–33).

This author's argument is not unlike one presented by Donald Senior in an article on discipleship which appeared in the *New Catholic World* in 1982.[2] Those who were "called to be with Jesus . . . the ones to whom he will entrust his mission" are clearly flawed by human weakness. Along with what Senior calls "positive affirmations" of the disciples' participation in the ministry of Jesus and their recognition of him as the Christ, there are also "stunning glimpses," especially in Mark, "into the disciples' obtuseness and failure."

Think, for example, of the faith of the woman cured of a twelve year hemorrhage and the disciples' reaction in that scene (Mk 5:25–31). Listen to the proclamations of the leper who was cleansed by Jesus and note the silence of his disciples (Mk 1:45). Again, the family's "astonishment" is recorded by Mark when the daughter of Jairus is called back from death, while Peter, James and John stand by with nothing to say, it would seem (Mk 5:42).

To anyone familiar with the age of Christian antiquity, these articles and the theses suggested by their authors carry a familiar resonance when the "power of the keys" and the "patristic tradition" are proposed as a topic of study and reflection. One of the most striking phenomena of the patristic era is what seems to be the absence of the bishop of Rome from the great doctrinal controversies of the first four centuries. Theological acumen and leadership emerge from other ecclesial centers: Antioch, Lugdunum, Carthage, Alexandria, Milan, Hippo. Between the First Epistle to the Corinthians of Clement of Rome and the Tome of Leo the Great, we look in vain for significant contributions from Rome to a developing articulation of trinitarian and christological doctrine.

What, then, was the role of the bishop of Rome in the early church? The question has been asked repeatedly by authors who have recently

143

undertaken studies of the Petrine office. For example, Jean Tillard in *The Bishop of Rome*[3] invites us to follow him in a new reading of the "function of the bishop of Rome," in light of both Vatican I and Vatican II. When did the pope become "more than a pope"? Tillard asks. What was it like in the beginning? What was the successor of Peter meant to be and to do in the church? How is he to exercise the "power of the keys"?

I propose to address these questions by assembling evidences from the age of the fathers of the church (c. A.D. 97–A.D. 608). First, I shall review the interpretation of Matthew 16:17–19, as that passage was understood by several early fathers. Then I shall attempt to examine a few selected events which reveal underlying attitudes toward the bishop of Rome, as these were expressed in the life and praxis of the church. Finally, I shall present the teaching of the fathers regarding the successor of Peter, as theological articulation contributed to the development of the apostolic traditio. I hope to demonstrate that, in the centuries between Clement of Rome and Gregory the Great, the perception and exercise of the Petrine office were diverse and, at times, ambiguous. The development of the authority of the bishop of Rome moved along a continuum that provided for both emulation and abuse by later popes.

Matthew 16:17–19: Patristic Exegesis

Before we consider the understanding which prevailed among the fathers of the church regarding Matthew 16:17–19, a word about patristic exegesis is in order. The first Christians read their scriptures—that is, the Old Testament—christologically. The inspired texts spoke to them of Christ and his mission as Lord and risen savior. Documents that, in time, would be assembled and known as the "New Testament" confirmed the ancient prophecies. The sacred writings were used in the proclamation of the good news, as exhortations to gospel living or in explanation of the savior's message, transmitted through the preaching of the apostles and their successors.

The allegorical interpretation of scripture developed in Alexandria was used to discover the hidden, "secret" meaning of the text. According to Origen, the first Christian biblical scholar, the "soul" and the "spirit" of the scriptures were more important than the "body," the words. In contrast and opposition to this method, the school of Antioch presented a more literal, "scientific" reading of the sacred writings. By the time of Augustine and Chrysostom, characteristics of both schools can be found reflected in the sermons, homilies and commentaries of the great fathers. A failure to take the complex nature of patristic exegesis into account can lead to a misunderstanding or a distortion of the teaching of the fathers. Their choice of texts as well as the purpose of the choice and their explication of a text are, at times, as amazing or confusing—to us—as they are inspiring.

What, then, of Matthew 16:17–19? The earliest important reference to this passage seems to have been made by Tertullian (+ post A.D. 220).[4] As he moved from orthodox Christianity to Montanism, Tertullian subscribed to a more rigorous position on the forgiveness of sin than that practiced by the church. He denies to the church the power of the keys. That authority was given to Peter for himself alone; it was not meant for the rest of the bishops.[5] For Tertullian, Montanist, the authority to bind and to loose was entrusted to "spiritual men." Thus, in his departure from the Catholic Christian understanding of the scriptures, he witnesses to the fact that Matthew 16:18–19 was taken to apply to the role of the church in the forgiveness of sins.

A different understanding of Matthew 16:18–19 is found in another North African theologian, Cyprian of Carthage (+ A.D. 258). Cyprian reads Matthew's text as an argument in support of the unity and unicity of the church built upon Peter.[6] This teaching is clear. What appears less evident is Cyprian's application of the text to the question of the primacy of Rome.

Chapter four of the *De unitate* has been preserved in two versions, one of which stresses the primacy of Peter. This longer text has been rejected by scholars in the past as a later corruption with interpolations. More recent studies have reversed this opinion. The longer text is now perceived as (1) a version revised by Cyprian himself or even (2) the original text (c. 251), rewritten later in shorter form, to reflect Cyprian's claim that every bishop answered to God alone.[7]

In light of Cyprian's controversy with the bishop of Rome (c. 256) on the question of "rebaptism" of heretics, his reticence to ascribe to the bishop of Rome an authority above that of any other bishop is understandable. The bishop of Rome, according to Cyprian, is the center of the unity of the church, enjoying a primacy of honor as *primus inter pares*. Cyprian never taught that the bishop of Rome possessed a primacy of jurisdiction; neither did he ever openly deny it. As Bévenot points out, Cyprian provides us with "a good example of what a dogma can look like while still in an early stage of development."[8]

Other fathers of the church invoked Matthew's pericope in their teaching. Origen (+ A.D. 253/254) read the text to emphasize Christ's promise to preserve his church from "the gates of hell."[9] Firmilian of Caesarea (+ c. A.D. 268), in a letter to Cyprian of Carthage, stated that "the power of forgiving sins was given to the apostles," to the churches they established and "to the bishops who succeeded them by being ordained in their place" (75, 16). Pope Damasus I proclaimed that the Roman church received the primacy "not by the conciliar decisions of other Churches, but . . . by the evangelic voice of our Lord and Savior. . . ."[10]

Cyril of Jerusalem (+ A.D. 386) identified Peter as the one who "carries about the keys of heaven." Pacian of Barcelona affirms that "absolutely nothing . . . whether it be great or whether it be small" was to be excluded from the power to loose and to bind. From Ambrose of Milan comes the acclamation: "Where Peter is, there is the Church. And where the Church, no death is there, but life eternal."[11] Jerome argues with Jovinian that, although "the strength of the Church depends equally" on all the apostles, "one among the twelve [was] chosen to be their head in order to remove any occasion for division."[12]

Augustine addresses the text from Matthew in several instances. At one time, before giving us a list of the bishops down to and including Anastasius (+ 401),[13] he refers to the "order of episcopal succession" that is to be numbered "from Peter himself." In another, he relates the words of Christ in Matthew to the church's power to forgive sin.[14] In still another, he invokes the charge entrusted to Peter to affirm the "unity of the Church, which received the keys."[15] "The gates of hell shall not conquer her."[16]

This review of the reading of Matthew 16:18–19 by some of the great fathers of the early church reflects the diversity of meanings attributed to Peter's role as "rock" and receiver of the keys. From this and other biblical texts, the fathers derived an understanding of a certain primacy of the church of Rome and the conviction that the bishop of Rome was to assure the unity of the church. It would be difficult to formulate a clear doctrine of the power and authority of the Petrine office from nothing other than patristic exegesis. For this reason, it is important to examine other evidences that help us understand the development of teaching regarding the papacy in the patristic age.

The Voice of Tradition

Scholars seem to agree that, from the second century of the Christian era on, the bishop of Rome was regularly asked to make decisions in matters of controversy. From the fourth century on, we find other bishops appealing to Rome for the protection of their rights. Rome—that is, the bishop of Rome—became the "court of appeal" in matters of law. Further, once a decision was made by the bishop of Rome, any attempt to challenge that decision was presumed to be inadmissible. It seems clear that by the fourth century there was no doubt that the successors of Peter were to be found in Rome.[17]

These positions cannot be verified in any formal treatise on the primacy or, indeed, on the papacy. They are found (a) in the gestures and documents which record the perception of the churches regarding the church of Rome, (b) in statements which reflect the bishop of Rome's understanding of his role and function in regard to the whole church, and (c) in the theological literature which has been preserved from the centuries when christological and trinitarian doctrines were being formulated. I will consider each of these areas of evidence individually.

The Churches Look to Rome

Ignatius of Antioch is the first witness. His salutation to the church of Rome has long been signaled and disputed by scholars. What seems certain is the meaning of two phrases in his letter to that church: (1) this is the Church which presides in love (*praesidens caritatis*); (2) this is the church which has "never grudged" anyone, but, rather, has "taught others." His desire, on the way to Rome and to martyrdom, was to live the lessons by which this church initiates candidates to the life of true discipleship (III, 1).

Like other Christians—Catholic or heterodox—who chose to visit Rome in what strike us as great numbers[18] for the time, Ignatius recognized certain treasures in the church of Rome. This was the church founded by two apostles, a church enriched by a twofold apostolic tradition. It was the capital of the empire. The Roman *regula fidei,* the rule of faith, had already been adopted by other churches and used as the basis of several baptismal creeds, in both the east and the west. The Roman *lex orandi,* the law of prayer, was also held in esteem and regarded by many as the norm.[19] In the eyes of Ignatius, the church of Rome had been faithful to the mission entrusted to her by both Peter and Paul (IV, 3).

A second witness is Irenaeus. From this second century father we have the earliest list of the uninterrupted succession of bishops in the church of Rome, beginning with Peter. Irenaeus understands this phenomenon to attest to a pre-eminence that is both doctrinal and disciplinary, a pre-eminence that is more than a primacy of honor. Scholars disagree less and less about the interpretation of the problematic passage in *Adversus haereses* (III, III, 2: III, XIX, 2). In light of his ecclesiology, it is not an exaggeration to accept the opinion of those who understand Irenaeus to insist "that all Churches must agree" with the church of Rome and that, by communion with her, "the faithful of all countries [preserve] the Apostolic tradition."[20]

An accumulated witness emerges from the words and actions of church fathers from Cyprian of Carthage through Augustine and Jerome in the west, and from the Cappadocians and John Chrysostom in the east. We have noted earlier the ambiguity of Cyprian's relationship with the bishop of Rome. Despite this, the African bishop acknowledges his duty to report matters of major significance to Rome in at least two instances, when he had acted first without consulting the bishop of the Roman see.[21] Cyprian recognized in the Roman church a *principalis* based on its authority, its antiquity ("anteriority") and the permanent principle of unity to which it gave witness.[22]

The writers of the golden age of patristic literature are not less eloquent and direct. For Augustine, the teaching office of the Roman church was invested with an "infallible" authority. This was attested to by the universal councils which Rome convoked, by the teaching of the bishop of Rome in matters of doctrine, and by the power of jurisdiction which that bishop exercised.[23] Augustine equated the chair of Peter with the apostolic see. In his controversy with the Pelagians, Augustine submitted at least one of his writings to the bishop of Rome for approval. Augustine held that the authority of Rome in matters of doctrine was definitive. The decisions of that church were equivalent to those of the entire church.[24]

Other fourth century writers acknowledged the pre-eminence of Rome. For example, Hilary of Poitiers seldom refers to the "supremacy" of Peter. In his eyes, supremacy was based on the office confided to Peter as the rock on which the church is founded. He saw the "power of the keys" exercised in the anti-Montanist and anti-Novatian decisions of the bishop of Rome.[25] Optatus taught that communion with the church of Rome was the guarantor of the legitimacy and the divine authority of all other churches.

Among the Cappadocians, it is especially Gregory Nazianzen—the theologian—whose teaching addressed the function of the church of Rome and the relationship of this church to the other churches. Rome is the president of the churches. She has always gone straight to her goal. Her influence in the west has been particularly salutary.[26]

More than any other Christian writer in the fourth century, Epiphanius upheld the concept of tradition, which he equated with the "ordinary" teaching of the Church. Because the Church is built on Peter, the immovable foundation of faith, the privileges of Peter are entrusted to the bishop of Rome.[27] A somewhat different point of view is expressed by Maximus the Confessor several centuries later. In a homily for the feast of St. Peter and St. Paul, Maximus attributes to Peter the "key of power" (*clavis potentiae*) and to Paul the "key of knowledge" (*clavis scientiae*).[28]

Over and above all the other fathers of the fourth century, John Chrysostom emerges as one of the most outstanding witnesses to Roman primacy. Rome's defense of Chrysostom during his life and even after his death is paralleled only by Chrysostom's loyal defense of the authority and jurisdiction to which he appealed in times of persecution and exile.

Other instances can be cited. From Syria, Ephrem defends and praises Peter from whom all priests receive the power of sanctifying. It is Peter who has the right to watch over all the apostles and bishops who uphold the church by their teaching. Following the deposing of Liberius (A.D. 367), the bishop of Caesarea admitted that the pope (Damasus) had the right to reestablish bishops who had been deposed as well as to confirm the election of new bishops. Finally, the Council of Constantinople (A.D. 381) declared the universal primacy of Rome and accorded to Constantinople, New Rome, a primacy of honor.

The Voice of Peter

Defense of Roman primacy, authority and jurisdiction comes from three bishops of Rome in the patristic era. They are: Clement of Rome, Leo the Great and Gregory the Great.

The First Letter of Clement to the Corinthians has been called "one of the most important documents of the period of transition from the 'Apostolic Church' to the 'Catholic Church.' " It has also been identified as a document that "confronts scholars with one of the 'thorniest problems of the Church.' " What is that problem? It is precisely the question that occupies our attention in this conference: "the question of office and ministry; its origin, its authority and power; and the question of a supreme authority in the Church."[29]

Patrologists have always found a certain, if indirect, claim to primacy in 1 Clement. The authoritative language and tone of the letter support this opinion, as do what are perceived as signs of prophetic awareness, of what seems to be a charism of universality and of personal conviction that what the author does is right, in admonishing the rebellious Corinthians and calling for obedience "to the things which we have written through the Holy Spirit" (63, 2).

Recent studies by both Protestant and Catholic scholars have led to a new reading of 1 Clement and new opinions regarding the position and function of the person we call Clement of Rome. Despite the absence of any mention of Clement's name from the letter, the existence of such a person does not seem to have called for much debate. Following von Harnack, leading Protestant scholars arrive at a negative view of 1 Clement. They agree that the "situation of the time" required a development from the Pauline organization of the church to one in which order, hierarchy and leadership dominate. Clement seems to have been realistic and futuristic in his vision, reading the circumstances and events of the times as a sign of the Spirit and directing the Church to meet the challenge before it.

These scholars, however, challenge Clement's justification of the new order as one that is valid for all eras because it is willed by God and instituted by the apostles. They admit the "remarkable reception" of the letter, its strong sense of the universality of the church and the fact that it was meant for a wider audience than the church to which it was directed. They regard the question of a claim to primacy as "historically misconceived and anachronistic."

Catholic scholars, for their part, have reread 1 Clement in light of the understanding and evaluation of office and ministry following developments in New Testament exegesis in the last fifty years. Catholic authors no longer cite 1 Clement as an *apologia* with the same energy as in the past. Catholic scholars hold that Clement's theory of office has an historical basis, but their analysis of the document has been strongly influenced by ecumenical considerations as well as by the pastoral and theological rethinking of office in the Church since Vatican II. It seems clear that "[a]s the historical evidence that Rome was ruled by one bishop or a clearly defined president becomes more uncertain, scholars are more hesitant to take up the question of a primacy." Despite these judgments, 1 Clement reflects a privileged view of the self-image of the church of Rome through the words of one who spoke in the name of that church.

Leo the Great, of course, is recognized as the bishop of Rome who "both in theory and practice . . . contributed to the development of the primacy of the Apostolic See of Rome."[30] Building on ideas of some of his predecessors, Leo is credited with having perfected the doctrine of the primacy of the apostolic see. "Peter," he affirmed, "who was united to Christ, the true founder and pastor of the church, in a singular way, continues even now to exercise his primacy over all the churches; the bishop of Rome, the heir and successor of Peter, renders this primacy visible in the community of all the Christians. Just as Christ transmitted his mission to the Apostles *per Petrum,* so are the faith and the ecclesiastical order guaranteed by the See of Peter."[31]

Leo founded his teaching on juridical, political and christological principles. The political-juridical aspects appear in his use of categories such as: *dignitas, sollicitudo, potestas, auctoritas* and the more philosophical concept of *forma.* His christological basis is found in his teaching on the *integritas* of the church, where the *communio sanctorum* and the *communio sacramentorum* are assured by the presence of Christ. Leo's awareness of his role was based on his understanding of the special relationship that existed between Peter and Christ. Leo was too good a theologian to think solely in political or juridical terms. Peter, following Christ, is meant to be a model and guide for all pastors. Leo saw that his *praesidium* was to be exercised especially through making present the action of Christ, chief pastor and true shepherd. Leo's first sermon as pope echoed the words of Christ: *Holy Father, keep in thy name those whom thou hast given me.* However, Leo identified his ministry more directly with that of Peter than with the ministry of Christ. He understood that Christ was to be an inspiration not only for him, but for all bishops and, even, for the emperor. Leo tells us that the pre-eminence of Rome is due to the unity of faith in the Church and to the accord of the clergy with Rome, as much as to the primacy of Peter and his successors, the bishops of Rome.[32] Leo seems also to have been the one person most responsible for transposing the idea of "*Roma aeterna, caput orbis terrarum*" into the Christian concept of the "*Urbs sancta.*"[33]

About one hundred and fifty years after Leo shepherded the church, Gregory the Great was unanimously chosen by the Roman clergy, senate and people to be bishop of Rome. The bishops of Rome who preceded Gregory had never claimed any specific title for themselves. Terms such as *papa, apostolicus, vicarius Christi, summus pontifex* and *summus sacerdos* referred to other bishops as much as to them. Congar points out[34] that terms like *vicarius Christi, caput, regere,* and *potestas* came to underlie ecclesiastical power in the medieval period. Gregory, with his concern for the honor of his brother bishops, did not depart from the earlier practice. The title Gregory did choose for himself was: *servus servorum Dei.* His affirmation of the primacy of his office was revealed primarily in his efforts to restore and preserve the apostolic tradition and the heritage of the Christian past.

Gregory sought to govern in peace and to promote peace in an age when the church was faced by challenges from New Rome, a declining Byzantine world and an ascending barbarian population. At the same time, Gregory knew he had to distinguish the *principatus* which was the legacy held by the bishop of Rome from Peter and the rights which he held as metropolitan over certain other churches. As Battifol has pointed out, Gregory, as pope, exercised a primacy of solicitude in his responsibility for the universal church.[35] Because his honor was the honor of all the bishops, Gregory knew how to move energetically when attempts were made to usurp his functions.

We find him acting with a decisiveness that derived from awareness of the rights of his see. He reached out in response to appeals from Spain, Gaul, and Great Britain. He sought to heal schismatic ruptures in the church. He promoted the evangelization of pagan lands. He knew how to be both "a bishop for bishops" and the "servant of the servants of God." Gregory appears, at the dawn of the middle ages, as a witness to unity, tradition and continuity. He had built well on the work of Leo the Great. He left the apostolic see of Rome and the papacy enhanced by an "active, beneficent spiritual primacy."[36]

Gregory left to the church a model to be remembered and emulated. If later popes were—to reverse Tillard's expression—*less* than popes, because they were less than pastors and, even at times, less than Christians, it was, perhaps, because they selected and remained paralyzed in one mode of governance which had been a stage in the long, gradual development of a unique ministry in the church.

In addition to their contribution to an understanding of papal primacy, authority, power and jurisdiction, Leo and Gregory bequeathed to the church a rich heritage of pastoral, spiritual and doctrinal theology. Their writings speak to us today. Their message still carries vitality and inspiration. As representatives of the church of Rome, however, they are unique as theologians. The Roman church is strikingly absent from the works which contributed to the development of theological discourse and doctrinal teaching in the patristic era.

Theologians of the Patristic Age

The professor who would offer a good basic course in patristic theology will not have to look far or long for representatives from the age of Christian antiquity. Although documentation is somewhat limited in the period prior to Nicaea, there is still sufficient material available. There are the Letters of Ignatius of Antioch with their rich theological insights, unique imagery, and mystical intuitions. Justin, philosopher and martyr, belongs to that group of apologists—intelligent, well-educated laymen—who, some scholars would say, were the first Christian theologians.

The name "father of Catholic theology" is reserved for Irenaeus, the second century bishop of the church of Gaul. In his two works—*The Proof of the Apostolic Preaching* and the *Adversus haereses*—he has given us both a witness to the apostolic traditio and a model of theology as the "enculturation of belief."[37] The theory of recapitulation in Christ proposed by Irenaeus influenced subsequent doctrinal developments by reason of its contribution to nearly every aspect of theology. In fact, Irenaeus, himself, can be looked upon as a "bridge" or even a "watershed" in theological development. His teaching can be found reflected in the works of Tertullian and Cyprian in North Africa, and in those of Clement and Origen in Alexandria. The quality and quantity of patristic works continued to multiply after Irenaeus. We sense a growing ferment in Christian thought as we read the documents which have been preserved from the ante-Nicene era.

With Athanasius, the golden age of patristic literature is inaugurated. Here, we encounter the great controversies that were to challenge the church in both doctrine and discipline. As one heterodox movement after another appeared, theologians in both the west and the east took up the challenge to defend the faith of Nicaea. The history of theological reflection, articulation and discourse at this time is rich and complex. We are overwhelmed at the number of extant works attributed to Ambrose, Augustine and Jerome, to the Cappadocians, Cyril of Jerusalem, and John Chrysostom. It is not surprising that patrology courses in the past were taught either from an *Enchiridion* of selected, brief texts on specific topics or from selected writings of Augustine (representing western theology) and Chrysostom (representing eastern Christian thought). There is too much to cover in one single course.

In addition to the major theologians, there were many secondary writers whose theological endeavors are not to be rejected. The development of theology in the age of the fathers of the church contributed to the development of doctrine and to the eventual formulation of dogma. Our knowledge and understanding of God, Christ, church, scripture, tradition, prayer, liturgy and the Christian lifestyle have been influenced and frequently molded by the theology of the fathers. Even though theological developments continued beyond the patristic era, many of their initial insights and reflections have merit today. The *consensus patrum* remains a reality in the life of the church.

The purpose of this seemingly disparate "thumbnail sketch" is surely evident. Nowhere among the great patristic theologians prior to Leo the Great do we find the name of a bishop of Rome. What, then, was the teaching role of the pope in Christian antiquity? How was it perceived in the patristic era? Perhaps it is time to attempt some analysis of the evidences assembled in this paper.

Reflection and Considerations

Nearly seven centuries elapsed between the time of Clement of Rome and the age of Gregory the Great. During those years many factors contributed to the clarification and development of the role of the bishop of Rome as successor to Peter, as a bishop among other bishops, as symbol and guardian of unity and as teacher of orthodox doctrine.

Five critical "moments" provide the context within which this clarification and development took place.

The first is the writing of 1 Clement. The significance of this document is not to be disputed. Irenaeus and Eusebius recognize Clement as author. The church of Corinth "received" the intervention of the church of Rome favorably. The entire church considered it part of the scriptures for a surprisingly long period of time and attributed a universal character to its message. 1 Clement marked one point of development in the primacy accorded to the church of Rome and to its bishop.

A second critical "moment" was the occasion of the Quartodeciman controversy. Polycarp and Irenaeus, respectively, restrained Anicetus and Victor when Rome sought to impose a uniform observance of the paschal feast on the entire church. The argument of alternate apostolic traditions, which allowed for diversity of praxis where unity of faith was assured, carried the day. When the Roman practice was decreed for the whole church, it was the decision of a council (Nicaea, A.D. 325). The relationship of the bishop of Rome to other bishops—individually or in conciliar assembly—is to be noted in this critical "moment."

The baptismal controversy which raged in north Africa in the third century is a third critical "moment." Here, regional bishops in synod arrived at a decision contrary to that upheld by Rome. Cyprian and the bishops of north Africa insisted on "rebaptizing" persons initiated into the Christian community by "heretics" in time of persecution. Cyprian taught that bishops in communion with one another—even when not in communion with the bishop of Rome—were able to teach true doctrine and were in union with the true church. Cyprian and his colleagues proved to be wrong. The validity of baptism by anyone intending to do what the church intends was affirmed. Another stage of development was realized for the question of papal primacy.

A fourth critical "moment" occurred by reason of two events: the emergence of the "Constantinian" church and the establishment of New Rome. In the first instance, the church adopted a number of structures and offices because of the interest and support of the emperor. In the second, civil and political responsibilities fell to the bishop of Rome because of the absence of the emperor and the transfer of his interest and presence to New Rome. By this time, the understanding of Roman primacy and the authority of the bishop of Rome had developed far beyond 1 Clement.

A final critical "moment" was one that reached across the entire patristic era. It consisted in the theological stimulus which major theologians—usually, but not always, bishops of other churches—provided to the bishop of Rome. He was the one who was challenged to exercise the charism of his office by *discerning* what was faithful to the authentic teaching transmitted by Jesus to the apostles and "traditioned" by them to their successors. In other words, the church, through its theologians, called the bishop of Rome to orthodoxy. He in turn, through his teaching office, called the church to fidelity and to unity.

A number of questions seem to emerge from the above considerations.

What constitutes papal primacy for the fathers of the church? The answer to this question takes us back to the patristic understanding of the mandate entrusted to Peter by the Lord Jesus. This mandate was certainly transmitted in the renaming of Simon as "rock" and in the "power of the keys" (Mt 16:16–19). In the mind of the early fathers, however, this mandate was frequently understood in relation to Peter's responsibility to strengthen his brothers (Lk 22:31–32) and in light of that apostle's triple affirmation of love (Jn 21:15–17). Aside from direct interpretation of these and other scriptural texts, an "image" of "Peter," in himself and in his successors, can be formed from the way his name is used in the documents of the first Christian centuries. One classic definition of the primacy in the patristic era identifies three essential points: (1) doctrinal unity; (2) the unique and sovereign importance of the Roman church as witness, guardian and origin of the apostolic tradition; (3) the superior pre-eminence of the church of Rome and its bishop in the whole of Christendom.[38]

What is the relationship of the bishop of Rome to the other bishops in the church? The answer to this question is already inscribed in the reading of the scriptural texts which pertain to Peter. He never stands alone, but, in every significant moment, is always with some of or all of the other apostles. Peter speaks in their name. His denials and affirmations are known by them. He is "chief" in relation to them. So, too, the fathers understood that the bishop of Rome was, in a very real sense, "Peter" with them and for them. From the beginning of the patristic age, it was important—even necessary—to appeal to him, to seek his counsel, to know his position. As we read the patristic texts, we discern an easy tension, a delicate balance, between the acknowledgement of the bishop of Rome as *praesidens* or pre-eminent and the awareness that he was so only because there were bishops in other churches, standing in other apostolic legacies. Peter and the apostles provided the paradigm for the bishop of Rome and the bishops of the Catholic Christian world.

How is the bishop of Rome to exercise the "power of the keys"? The fathers of the church understood this "power," first of all, in terms of "binding" and "loosing." Their understanding meant, certainly, the forgiveness of sins and the designation of the sins that were to be forgiven. It came to include the identification of criteria for membership in the Catholic Christian community and the "overseeing" of the churches where these questions were at issue. While the "leadership" in theological acumen emerged from other bishops and lay members of the church, the bishop of Rome was never far removed from central developments. We think, for example, of Polycarp and Anicetus, of Irenaeus and Victor, of Cyprian and Cornelius, of Chrysostom and Innocent, of Liberius and Damasus. Clement, Leo and Gregory appear as jewels of fire-water brilliance in a sky of lesser stars. They are not solitary exceptions proving a rule, but peak-achievers in a trajectory and a continuum.

How are we to assess the patristic tradition in light of contemporary studies? At every point in our consideration of the Petrine office, we have seen signs of a growing awareness and a developing teaching of what came to be formulated subsequently in the church as official teaching and, eventually, as dogmatic truth. Contemporary studies, such as those examined by Fuellenbach in his work,[39] are especially noteworthy. If there is a difference between Clement of Rome and Leo the Great, there is also a difference between the church of the second century, the church of the fifth century and that of the twentieth. As Newman saw over one hundred years ago, the development of doctrine is at the heart of Christianity. The fathers would offer two *caveats* to results of recent studies of the Petrine office and to our understanding of the manner in which the "power of the keys" is to be exercised.

The first caution is that we not forget to take into account the authentic apostolic *traditio*. This may be more easily said than done. The last twenty years have taught us how difficult it is to distinguish *tradition* from *traditions,* for example, in the reform of the liturgy. Patristic texts are always at least one remove—and, frequently, more than one—from us: linguistically, culturally, philosophically, existentially. It is not immediately evident that exegetical principles suited to biblical interpretation are in themselves appropriate for the analysis of texts which derive from the world of classical Greek literature.

The second word of advice speaks to us as citizens of a democratic society. At least, that is what we claim to be. Actually, our mode of democracy is unique in a world of possible—or real—democratic modes. The founders of our nation called us a "republic," and we might do well to reflect on the implications of that designation for our own political experience. At any rate, the ecclesiology of Vatican II has sounded in our ears very much like democracy. "Collegiality" and the "people of

God" are only two terms which seem to have endorsed the American experience of being Catholic. We still face the challenge of defining more clearly than we have until now the "truths" we hold to be "self-evident" in relation to the values of the gospel as it has been "traditioned" to us. We have yet to learn how Catholics can be truly American and Americans can be authentically Catholic. As Newman said, we have to learn to be "primitive Christians" in our own space and time.

What can we learn from the patristic tradition for an understanding of the function of the Petrine office? The recent visit of Pope John Paul II to our country makes this question particularly germane to the issues that we have been reflecting on these past several days. Our learnings from the patristic age for this question—as for any issue of importance in the church today—are few and simple. By all the reasonings of human logic, Christianity ought not to have survived the second century. The odds against it were overwhelming and we can recognize that fact, even today. There are those who say today that Christianity will not survive this century and perhaps is already "dead." We would like to know how to face and survive, as the early Christians did, the life-and-faith-threatening dangers of our "empire" and our "colosseum." We know, however, that the scenario has changed. We cannot do it *their* way, but we can look to them for guidelines.

We can strive to be, as they were, women and men immersed in our age and culture. We can seek to listen to the world that is ours, to take its questions seriously, to recognize the gifts it has to bring to a more effective proclamation of the good news. We can also be, as they were, totally committed to the implications of baptism into the dying and rising of the Lord. We can strive to understand what it means to bear witness to our faith in the risen Christ. We can bring the wisdom of God to convict error of its waywardness and sin of its evil.

Finally, we must learn, as did the Christians of the first centuries, that the second coming is not "around the corner." This awareness introduces a note of realism into our strivings and aspirations for a church that resides not as a stranger in Corinth or Ephesus or Smyrna but in some idealized utopia. The pope's spontaneous admission, at one point in his visit to the United States, that "it's a long, long way to Tipperary" is a humorous, if cautionary affirmation of a process that has been proven true throughout the history of the church.

In the meantime, we ought to read and reread the documents of the patristic era in order to be able to identify for our own time what I have referred to in another context as the "discontinuity that necessarily exists between [the person of Jesus] and every Christian leader who comes after him . . ." and, at the same time, "the continuity that binds the leadership exercised in subsequent stages of the community's life to the Lordship of Christ."[40]

Notes

1. Lee Oo Chung, in *New Eyes for Reading,* John S. Pobee and Bärtel von Wartenberg-Potter, eds.; World Council of Churches, 1986, pp. 18–20.

2. "To Be a Disciple: Synoptic Images of the Christian Life," vol. 225, no. 1345, pp. 4–9.

3. J.M.R. Tillard, O.P., *The Bishop of Rome;* John de Satgé, trans. Wilmington, Delaware: Michael Glazier, Inc., 1983.

4. Cf. "On Modesty" 21; Rev. S. Thelwall, trans. Ante-Nicene Fathers IV. A. Roberts and J. Donaldson, eds. New York: Charles Scribner's Sons, 1925, pp. 74–101. *De pudicitia;* CSEL 20, pp. 219–273.

5. Cf. Johannes Quasten, *Patrology II.* Westminster, Maryland: The Newman Press, 1964, pp. 334f.

6. Cf. "The Unity of the Catholic Church," 4; Maurice Bévenot, S.J., trans. Ancient Christian Writers 25. Westminster, Maryland: The Newman Press, 1957, pp. 43–68. *De ecclesiae catholicae unitate;* CSEL 3, 1, pp. 207–264.

7. Quasten, *op. cit.,* pp. 349–352, 375–378.

8. *Op. cit.,* pp. 7–8.

9. Cf. *Commentaries on John* 5, 3; William A. Jurgens, trans. *The Faith of the Early Fathers,* Volume One. Collegeville, Minnesota: The Liturgical Press, 1970, p. 202. GCS, 10, pp. 1–574.

10. *The Decree of Damasus* 3 (A.D. 382). Cf. *"Decretum Gelasianum,"* e.g., PL 13, 373–376.

11. *Commentary on Psalm 40,* 30. *Enarrationes in Psalmis,* PL 14.

12. *Adversus Iovinianum;* PL 23, 211–338.

13. *Letter to Generosus* 53, 1, 2. Sister Wilfrid Parsons, S.N.D., trans. The Fathers of the Church 12. Washington, D.C.: The Catholic University of America Press, 1951. PL 33.

14. *Exposition of Psalm 101.* A Cleveland Coxe, trans. LNPF 8, ser. 1; PL 36.

15. *Sermones de Sanctis* 295, 1. PL 38.

16. *Sermones de tempore: In redditione Symboli* 6, 14. PL 38.

17. Cf., e.g., Cayré, *Manual of Patrology* I and II, *passim;* Quasten, Patrology (4 vols.), *passim;* DTC 13, *"Primauté du Pope,"* G. Glez, ccls. 247–344 (esp. 247–300).

18. Notice the number of voyages to Rome recorded by Eusebius in his Ecclesiastical History, *passim.*

19. Consider the role played by Polycarp and Irenaeus in the Quartodeciman controversy. The decision of Victor (189–198) to call for councils throughout the church on this question was respected. The intervention of Irenaeus averted serious division, but Roman tradition in the observance of the Easter feast was generally accepted.

20. Cf. Bardenhewer, *Patrologie* I, p. 234. Paris: 1905. *Les Pères de l'Eglise, leur vie et leurs oeuvres,* 3 vol.

21. I refer to Cyprian's consecration of Fortunatus (cf. Letter 59, 9) and his defense of having left Carthage during a time of persecution (cf. Quasten, *Patrology* II, pp. 376–377).

22. Cf. Dom John Chapman, *Studies in the Early Papacy.* Port Washington, N.Y./London: Kennikat Press, 1971.

23. Cf., e.g., *De doctrina christiana* XVII, XVIII. PL 34; *De natura et gratia.* PL 44; *Liber de perfectione justitiae hominis.* PL 34; *De baptisimo* II, 1, 2. PL 43; *Epist.* XL II, VII, 7. PL 33.

24. Cf. *Commentary on Matthew; De sermone Domini in monte.* PL 38, 1238.

25. Cf. *Commentary on St. Matthew* IX, 917. PL 9, 917–1078.

26. Cf. *Oration* 26, 9. PG 35.

27. Cf. Haer. LIX, 7, 8. PG 41.

28. Cf. PL LXVII, 403.

29. Quotations are taken from the dust-jacket advertisement of *Ecclesiastical Office and the Primacy of Rome,* John Fuellenbach, S.V.D. Washington, D.C.: The Catholic University of America Press, 1980.

30. Quasten, *Patrology* IV, p. 607.

31. *Ibid.,* citing *Epistle* 10, 1 and 9.

32. Cf. Sermon 3, 2; 4, 1; *Epistles* 80, 1–2; 10, 12, 14, 28, 69. Sermons 2–5; 82–83. LNPF 12, ser. 2. PL 54–56.

33. I have relied heavily on Quasten, *Patrology* IV, pp. 600–611, for this section.

34. Yves Congar, O.P., "The Historical Development of Authority in the Church: Points for Christian Reflection," in *Problems of Authority,* John M. Todd, ed. Baltimore: Helicon Press, 1962, pp. 148–150.

35. P. Battifol, *Saint Grégoire le Grand.* Paris: 1928, pp. 188–189.

36. DTC, *art. cit.,* cols. 291–294.

37. I owe this phrase to Reverend Charles R. Meyer, professor of Systematic Theology at Mundelein Seminary.

38. L. Duchesne, *Les Eglises séparées,* p. 119. Paris, 1905.

39. Cf. *op. cit.*

40. *The Ministry of Governance,* James K. Mallett, ed. Washington, D.C.: Canon Law Society of America, 1986, p. 83.

Selected Bibliography

The Office of Peter and the Structure of the Church, Hans Urs Von Balthasar; trans. Andrée Emery. San Francisco: Ignatius Press, 1986.

Peter in the New Testament, ed. Raymond E. Brown, Karl P. Donfield, John Reumann. Minneapolis: Augsburg Publishing House; New York: Paulist Press, 1973.

Ecclesiastical Authority and Spiritual Power in the Church of the First Three Centuries, Hans von Campenhausen; trans. J.A. Baker. London: Adam & Charles Black, 1969.

Studies in the Early Papacy, Dom John Chapman. Port Washington, N.Y./London: Kennikat Press, 1971.

L'Episcopat Catholique: Collégialité et Primauté, Jean Colson. Paris: Les Editions du Cerf, 1963.

Ecclesiastical Office and the Primacy of Rome, John Fuellenbach, S.V.D. Washington, D.C.: The Catholic University of America Press, 1980.

The Ministry of Governance, ed. James K. Mallett. Washington, D.C.: Canon Law Society of America, 1986.

The Emergence of the Catholic Tradition (100–600) (THE CHRISTIAN TRADITION, 1), Jaroslav Pelikan. Chicago and London: The University of Chicago Press, 1971.

The Bishop of Rome, J.M.R. Tillard, O.P., trans. John De Satgé. Wilmington, Delaware: Michael Glazier, Inc., 1983.

Problems of Authority, ed. John M. Todd. Baltimore: Helicon Press, 1962.

Frederick R. McManus

Local, Regional, and Universal Church Law

Although this topic falls under the subheading of "Theology of Papal Power" in this volume, with it we turn rather sharply from history and doctrine to the canonical, juridical, and legal. The purpose is simple enough: to survey the church's law in the strictest sense of "canon law"—certainly not the most important facet of church life and mission, but not the least important.

We may take heart, as well as a starting point, from the conciliar constitution on the church *Lumen Gentium* (LG). In its first chapter that document moves from the church as mystery and communion and from the diverse biblical metaphors for the *ecclesia* to the social and the external (LG 8). It moves to the dimension of the church community which demands the articulation of order and responsibility, of the rights and behavior of the Christian people as that people makes progress toward the fulfillment of the gospel and the mission embodied in the gospel.

There is less dichotomy than unity in these potentially polarized aspects of the church called together by God, if indeed the mystery or sacrament of the church stands in some contrast to its external structure, order, and law.

The opening words of the conciliar fathers in the first decree of Vatican II are an eloquent description of the church in which the internal and the external are not only acknowledged but proclaimed:

> It is of the essence of the Church to be both human and divine, visible yet endowed with invisible resources, eager to act yet intent on contemplation, present in this world yet not at home in it; and the Church is all these things in such wise that in it the human is directed and subordinated to the divine, the visible likewise to the invisible, action to contemplation, and this present world to that city yet to come which we seek (*Sacrosanctum Concilium* [SC] 2).

Because the church is human, visible, active, and present in this world, because the church is a people, a community of communities, a communion of churches, it has need of order and rule and law. That this dimension is less important as a value, that it is means and not end, that it seems far down the scale from the word of God or the total ecclesial mission, far less than sacrament and faith—none of this is reason to apologize for or to denigrate church law or canon law. If the smallest community and the nuclear family need order and rule, surely the assembled local church—which less felicitously the canons call the particular church—and the communion of local churches need law.

The sticking point comes with the extent of such law. How much law and how much specificity of law are needed to govern the Christian people as a whole and to determine rights and responsibilities, especially the rights of all and the responsibilities of those who hold office in the community. Should it be minimal? Should it be expansive?

An inevitable paradox will be apparent in the pages that follow. It is easy to advocate a minimal intrusion of law and decree into the Christian life of God's people and at the same time to acknowledge—and also advocate—the necessary or useful exercise of lawmaking ecclesial power. When it comes, moreover, to such canonical institutes as the Roman synod of bishops and the national conferences of bishops, their real or potential power is a healthy, human, and Christian instance of the creative tension between the bishop of Rome and the other bishops who represent their local churches or among the members of the order of bishops as they assemble in their several nations or regions.

Yet, to stay with these examples, the weaknesses of the national conferences and the universal synod are evident too. One may not place his or her Christian hope in the human side of parliaments or congresses. Fortunately such bodies of the sacramentally ordained heads of the local churches resemble ecclesiastical legislatures, parliaments, or congresses only in a small fraction of their activity. But this activity too is moved by the Spirit of God which fills the church community and is a strength and potential in the total mission of the church.

The topic proposed for this paper was originally stated as "Local and/or Universal Church Law." I have enlarged it to "Local, Regional, and Universal Law," for reasons that I suspect are evident—if only because our general theme is not simply the Petrine office or papacy and the individual diocesan churches of the United States, but rather the Petrine office and the total church in the United States, the *ecclesia americana,* if one dares use the term.

Let me begin with a curious source. The logical beginning is not in the "universal" canon law but rather in the particular canon law: diocesan, provincial, national, regional, and "ritual." But in the yearbook of the Roman See, the *Annuario Pontificio,* there is an impressive page that enumerates the titles of Pope John Paul—not unlike the enumeration of royal or monarchical titles, I am afraid. Hardly updated in style since the Second Vatican Council, it does illustrate the theme "local, regional, universal." The text reads:

> John Paul II
> Bishop of Rome
> Vicar of Jesus Christ
> Successor of the Chief of the Apostles
> Patriarch of the West
> Primate of Italy
> Archbishop and Metropolitan of the Province of Rome
> Sovereign of the State of Vatican City
> Servant of the Servants of God

We may quickly pass over several of these titles as less significant for our juridical purpose, but they deserve a word.

"Vicar of Jesus Christ," given typographical emphasis in the *Annuario Pontificio,* is a title shared by the pope and the other bishops. The attempt of the Second Vatican Council to make this point in an *obiter dictum* (LG 27) has fallen on deaf ears, at least those of the editors of the *Annuario* and indeed of the redactors of the 1983 Code of Canon Law, who introduced "vicar of Christ" into canon 331 on the bishop of Rome, but not in reference to the other bishops.

Strangely enough, the more ancient and more meaningful papal title is "vicar of Saint Peter." This is reflected in the term "Successor of the Chief of the Apostles," and in conciliar usage, "Head of the College of Bishops," carefully added to canon 331 if not to the Vatican yearbook.

"Sovereign of the State of Vatican City" is a secular title of course, since the pope is one cleric who exercises a civil office, possibly dispensing himself from canon 285 3. It is, by the way, not as sovereign of Vatican City that the pope sends nuncios and receives ambassadors, as is so often thought.

And "Servant of the Servants of God," dating from the sixth century, is a title echoing the gospel itself. The pope is servant of his own church of Rome and of the other bishops, the servants who preside over the other churches.

More concretely, the listing of papal titles may be reduced by those which illustrate the several levels of church structural life which are verified throughout the church and thus illustrate the levels of local, regional, and universal church law. Pared down for this purpose, the list is briefer:

Bishop of Rome
Successor of the Chief of the Apostles (the Vicar of Saint Peter and
    thus the *Collegii Episcoporum caput*)
Patriarch of the West
Primate of Italy
Archbishop and Metropolitan of the Province of Rome

The pope's total ministry within the church—and thus also his role
of governance and even his role as lawmaker—begins with his ordination as bishop of the local church of Rome. Pope Paul VI, faithful to the
conciliar teaching about the sacramentality of the episcopate from which
the other functions and powers are derived, determined explicitly: One
who is already an ordained bishop becomes bishop of Rome and pope,
chief bishop and head of the other bishops, simply by election and
acceptance of election, no more. In the unlikely event that a presbyter,
deacon, or layperson is so elected, he must first be ordained or consecrated bishop of Rome before entering upon the papal office.

The bishop of the church of Rome and successor of Peter is given
other titles in the listing above. He is called the archbishop and metropolitan of the immediate region, the ecclesiastical province of Rome. He
is the primate of Italy, the chief bishop of the particular national church
of Italy. He is the patriarch of the west, the chief of the bishops of the
Latin church or Roman patriarchate.

This introductory discursus is not intended by any means to be a
reflection on the Petrine office as such, but the list of titles at the several
levels can be a paradigm for those who exercise the pastoral office of
bishop and for the churches which they shepherd. It can also be a paradigm for the canon law of the church and thus for this essay.

The canon law is not only local, not only universal, but also "regional" or perhaps "intermediary"—and that at several levels: province,
nation, region larger or smaller than a nation, and, from antiquity,
patriarchate. The particular councils of bishops of the first centuries,
antedating the councils that were received as ecumenical, are evidence
enough of the collegial action of groups of local churches—dioceses we
now say—represented by their respective bishops. Nor need we look,
rather fancifully, to the biblical role of Titus and Timothy as the Second
Plenary Council of Baltimore insinuated (*Acta* 78) to vindicate the office
of metropolitan—a personal presidency or primacy of the chief bishop of
a church province—or other "superior bishops" such as primates and
patriarchs. The ancient tradition is still seen in that list of papal titles.

Whether in the construct of proclaiming the gospel or in exercising
the *episkope,* whether in exhortation or in lawmaking, whether in the

modern political categories of executive, judicial, and legislative powers, the human law of the Christian community—which we call canon law—may be determined not only locally and universally but also at the several levels summed up here by the term regional, intermediary between local and universal.

One of these levels that deserves prior, special mention is the level of the autonomous particular church, that is, the group of local churches which in the providence of God has a special distinctiveness. It may be called a patriarchal church (or matriarchal); it may be called autocephalous in the eastern style or ritual church *sui iuris* in the Roman style of the 1983 code (canons 111–112). The Second Vatican Council explained the development of conferences of bishops in the nineteenth and twentieth centuries—closely analogous to the most ancient traditions of both east and west—in these terms:

> By Divine Providence it has come about that various churches established in diverse places by the apostles and their successors have in the course of time coalesced into several groups, organically united. These groups of churches, preserving the unity of faith and the unique divine constitution of the universal Church, enjoy their own discipline, their own liturgical use, and their own theological and spiritual heritage. Some of these churches, notably the ancient patriarchal churches, as parent-stocks of the faith, have begotten others as daughter churches. With these they are connected down to our own time by a close bond of charity in their sacramental life and in their mutual respect for rights and duties. This variety of local churches with one common aspiration is particularly splendid evidence of the catholicity of the undivided Church. *In like manner today* the conferences of bishops are able to render a manifold and fruitful assistance, so that the collegial sense (*collegialis affectus*) may be put into concrete application (LG 23; emphasis added).

This is not the place to disentangle the complexity of the papal roles. The bishop of Rome, as the vicar and successor of Saint Peter, acts as both head of the episcopal college, a truly universal role, and as patriarch of the west, a ministry confined to the Latin church and comparable to that of the several eastern patriarchs. From the outset, however, we note the Latin church's usage of often referring to its general or common law as universal. But we can postpone for the moment any speculation about the modern conferences of bishops and their (limited) resemblance to the ancient patriarchal structure in order to deal first with the local church and its law.

Local Church Law

Often the student recalls with clearest memory what first impressed him or her in earliest studies. This canonist was struck early on by a professor, Edward Roelker, who repeatedly made the point that the celebrated Code of Canon Law—in those days it was of course the first Code of Canon Law in the church's history, initiated by Pius X and published by Benedict XV in 1917—was by no means the totality of the canon law. Revolutionary in that, perhaps unwisely, it attempted to replace nineteen centuries of church discipline, the 1917 Code of Canon Law was a stunning achievement and a practical convenience for student and pastor alike. (Its ecclesiological foundations and pastoral orientation aside, the 1917 code was superior as a technical and professional piece of work to its 1983 successor.)

The Code of Canon Law for the Latin church, whether of 1917 or of 1983, is only a small part of the canon law of the church of Christ. For all its importance the Latin church code cannot embrace the canon law of the Eastern churches—whether in communion with the Roman see or not—or of the non-Roman western churches and ecclesial communities, which have their own law, sometimes highly developed. It cannot embrace the liturgical law, the concordat or treaty law, the unwritten law of custom—all of equal standing, for the Latin or western church, with its Code of Canon Law. In particular it does not embrace the canon law of the individual local churches or dioceses.

And the law of the local church is just as appropriate a starting point as the universal law. The law of each diocesan church is the law of the total church of Christ as realized and actualized, as concretized and fully present in the local gathering of God's people assembled with its head, the bishop, empowered by the Holy Spirit, and its ministers, its presbyters and deacons.

Beginning with the particular church, and thus with its law, is no denigration of the catholicity or universality of the church of Christ, which is a communion of local churches. But to begin with the local church can be a still necessary corrective to the common misconception of the universal church as some kind of pyramidal structure—which it is not entirely facetious to compare with a multi-national corporation.

Without going back on the fiercely papal orientation of the First Vatican Council or the necessity of communion, indeed the full communion, of the local churches, the Second Vatican Council on occasion made the point with some eloquence, indicated here by the emphasis added to each quotation:

> The individual bishops are the visible principle and foundation of unity in their particular churches, formed in the image of the universal Church (and) *in and from which* (particular or local) *churches there comes into being the one and only catholic Church.* For this reason each individual bishop represents his own church, but all of them together in union with the pope represent the entire Church joined in the bond of peace, love, and unity . . . (LG 23).

> This Church of Christ is *truly present in all legitimate local congregations of the faithful which, adhering to their pastors, are themselves called churches in the New Testament* (LG 26).

> A diocese is a portion of the people of God, which is entrusted to a bishop to be shepherded by him with the cooperation of the presbyterium. Thus, adhering to its pastor and gathered together by him in the Holy Spirit through the Gospel and the Eucharist, this portion constitutes a particular church *in which the one, holy, catholic, and apostolic Church of Christ is truly present and operative Christus Dominus* ([CD] 11).

Theologians and bishops themselves have expressed this doctrine, perhaps more clearly understood in the east than in the west, still more forcefully. For example, Cardinal Godfried Danneels of Malines-Brussels quotes Leonard Boff:

> What is the particular church? The particular church is the universal church (the salvific will in Christ through the Spirit) in its phenomenal or sacramental presentation.

> The particular church is the universal church concretized; and in being concretized, taking flesh; and in taking flesh, assuming the limits of place, time, culture and human beings.

> The particular church is *the whole mystery of salvation in Christ—the universal church—in history, but not the totality of the history of the mystery* of salvation in Christ. For each particular church is itself limited and, precisely, particular. Accordingly each particular church must be open to others, which

likewise, each in its own manner, concretize and manifest the same universal salvific mystery—that is, the church universal.

The particular church is the church wholly, but not the whole church. It is the church wholly because in each particular church is contained the whole mystery of salvation. But it is not the whole church because no particular church exhausts by itself the whole wealth of the mystery of salvation. That mystery can and must be expressed in other particular churches and in other particular forms. (*Origins,* September 17, 1987; emphasis added.)

What does this have to do with the canon law of the local or particular church? Perhaps the answer can best be given in a series of propositions or observations.

1. *The (strictly limited) need for local church law.* Since the church, present and operative in the local congregation of the faithful, is primarily mystery and sacrament, its structures and its laws are secondary—but nonetheless necessary and useful for the church's order and indeed mission. To its canon law may be applied the conventional axiom: the best law is the least law. But that law, if moderate and clear and certain, may be a powerful instrument of unity and a useful means to the achievement of the church's mission.

2. *Local law in relation to universal law.* There is need to explore the relationship of local norm, rule, and law to the general canon law (as well as to the regional ecclesiastical law that will be considered later). I draw attention especially to a basic principle and presumption, if not the practice, that is sacrosanct in the general law and has been faithfully repeated in the 1983 Code of Canon Law of the Latin church: ". . . a universal law in no way derogates from a particular or special law unless the [universal] law itself expressly provides otherwise" (canon 20).

The same principle applies equally to the unwritten law or customary law, which enjoys a privileged place, again in principle if not in practice, in the canon law. Custom, says the draft of the code for the eastern Catholic churches, "corresponds to the activity of the Holy Spirit in the ecclesial community." The 1983 Code of Canon Law retains the axiom, "Custom is the best interpreter of laws," and says of particular customs: ". . . unless it makes express mention of centenary or immemorial customs, a [written] law does not revoke them, nor does a universal law revoke particular customs" (canon 28).

The older canonists—I am tempted to say the old-fashioned canonists—had a twofold explanation for the principle that the more general law does not revoke particular law. More profoundly, because of the breadth of territory and the diversity of peoples the church judges prudently that not everything should be reduced to a uniformity which may hurt rather than help. More formally, it used to be suggested, with Pope Boniface VIII as authority, that the general legislator could not be knowledgeable about all the circumstances and conditions which support local legislation.

Unfortunately each time there is a new general or universal code—there have been only two—the principle has been gravely weakened by canonical dispositions directly revoking contrary particular law (canon 61, n. 2). And papal legislation often goes to great lengths to revoke contrary particular or local dispositions. But the principle found in the canonical tradition is sound, and far greater respect needs to be shown to the diversities of local canon law and practice.

3. *The diocesan bishop in relation to the general canon law.* The 1917 Code of Canon Law did not adopt explicitly the faulty ecclesiology that would have the bishop of the local church a vicar or auxiliary of the bishop of Rome. Whatever its mindset, that code did not at any point derive the canonical authority of the diocesan bishop from the Roman bishop. Nevertheless the mindset was almost a convention, and the explicit affirmations of the Second Vatican Council were surely needed: the bishop of Rome is not the bishop of Worcester, nor is the latter his vicar, representative, or branch manager.

At the same time the Second Vatican Council overturned an existing presumption of church law: that the diocesan bishop might dispense from the general canon law only by virtue of a faculty, grant, or concession from the pope. The text is significant and is well understood by canonists:

> Each diocesan bishop has the faculty, in particular cases, of dispensing from the general law of the Church the faithful over whom he exercises authority in accord with the norm of law, as often as he judges it useful for their spiritual good, unless a special reservation has been made by the supreme authority of the Church (CD 8b; see canon 87).

When it was introduced in 1965, this conciliar norm was deliberately revolutionary. Since then, however, aside from the expected list of special reservations, it has been attenuated so as to exclude from episcopal dispensing power any non-disciplinary law, constitutive law, procedural law, penal law, and even—according to the gratuitous but faulty assertion of some—liturgical law. More seriously, the bishops of the local churches have seemed reluctant to employ this dispensing power of theirs. Attention to this provision of the conciliar decree on the pastoral office of bishops in the church seems, moreover, to have drawn attention away from the still more basic and positive principle stated in the same context:

> As successors of the apostles, bishops per se enjoy, in the dioceses entrusted to them, all the ordinary, proper, and immediate power required for the exercise of their pastoral office. But always and in all matters the power which the Bishop of Rome has, by virtue of his office, of reserving cases to himself or to some other authority remains intact (CD 8a; see canon 381, 1).

Again the responsibility acknowledged in the local church or now restored to it—in the person of its pastor—may in some sense be considered revolutionary. It has not begun to be tested in actual church use and life; some feel that it has been inhibited in the retrogressive years since the great council.

4. *The episcopal office of governance and lawmaking.* The pastoral office of the diocesan bishop embraces far more than the ruling function. In fact, he is teacher and priest, herald of the gospel and president of the sacred mysteries, pastor and head, before he is governor and moderator. The jurisdictional office (or, according to the current canonical euphemism, the power of governance or regimen) deserves third place—and even then the lawmaking power is not the usual or preferred means of guiding the Christian community of the local church. This is another way of saying: the less canon law in the Christian community of love, the better.

Nonetheless there is a lawmaking role of the bishop in the local church, and it deserves our attention. It is said to be exercised in synod or outside of synod.

5. *Synodal laws and decrees.* The sacred canons of our code follow the western tradition in saying that the bishop is the single ecclesiastical lawmaker in the local church (canon 466). It is a statement that is susceptible of a wrongful interpretation—as if the bishop might act unilaterally in his lawmaking or as if his laws and statutes were subject to no reception by the church community unless the latter, in which the Spirit also resides, interprets or even revokes the written law by its life and action.

The canons do not, of course, support this wrongful view when the diocesan synod is described as the first of the institutes in the "internal ordering of particular churches," however rarely such synods are convoked by the bishop in consultation with the priests' council (canon 461, 1). For one thing, the very canon which calls the bishop "the sole legislator at a diocesan synod" speaks of the consultative vote of the other members of the synod. The principle at stake, according to the canonical tradition, is that those who are consulted have an authentic role and responsibility: it is not merely the bishop's law but the synodal law.

Elsewhere the canons, in a rather different context, explain what consultation means: "although in no way obliged to accede to their recommendation, even if it be unanimous, nevertheless the superior should not act contrary to it, especially when there is a consensus, unless there be a reason which, in the superior's judgment, is overriding" (canon 130, 2, n. 2).

There are happy signs that diocesan synods, certainly in the United States, will not concentrate on lawmaking alone or be mere exercises in solemnity and formality. There are equally happy signs that the preparatory process of synods will be a process of searching and renewal itself. Just as important, the (consultative) membership of the diocesan synod has been redefined, newly adding not only the members of the presbyteral council but also:

lay members of the Christian faithful and members of institutes of consecrated life [religious and members of secular institutes], to be selected by the [diocesan] pastoral council in a manner and number to be determined by the bishop or, where such a council does not exist, in a manner determined by the diocesan bishop . . . (canon 463, 1).

Almost as important, the 1983 code opens the door to a still wider participation of Catholic members of a synod and of observers from other churches and ecclesial communities:

Others can be called as members to the diocesan synod by the diocesan bishop; these can be clerics, members of institutes of consecrated life, or lay members of Christian faithful.

If he should judge it opportune, the diocesan bishop can invite as observers to the diocesan synod some ministers or members of churches or ecclesial communities which are not in full communion with the Catholic Church (canon 463, 2–3).

An assembly, a diocesan congress or parliament, of this makeup should be so truly representative of the local church that its acts, including its laws published by the singular authority of the diocesan bishop, would have a new moral as well as canonical weight vis-à-vis the regional law and the universal law.

6. *Extra-synodal laws and decrees.* But such an idealistic image of local church law, the fruit of deliberation and consensus, dims beside the more usual extra-synodal model of diocesan regulation, norm, statute, decree, and law. Yet the episcopal authority of the diocese is not monarchical; it is exercised "with the church," in collaboration with the presbyters and ministers and at the service of all.

In abstract theory, the head of the local church may make ecclesiastical law without consultation—as in abstract theory the bishop of Rome, as head of the college of bishops, may make universal ecclesiastical law without consultation. Fortunately this does not happen, although the Christian community may well be dissatisfied with the extent of the collaboration and consultation that precedes "unilateral" lawmaking.

The new general law provides two diocesan bodies or councils which surely belong in the legislative process, apart from the occasional celebration of the diocesan synod. One is the mandatory priests' council or presbyteral council, "like a senate of the bishop, representing the presbyterate," to be set up "to aid the bishop in the governance of the diocese according to the norm of the law, in order that the pastoral welfare of the portion of the people of God entrusted to [the bishop] may be promoted as effectively as possible" (canon 495, 1). Again, with every acknowledgement that governance and, specifically, the making of laws and decrees are far, far from the principal concerns of either the bishop or the presbyteral council, it should go without saying that in the area of legislation the presbyteral council has a primary role of collaborating with the bishop.

Despite some regression from the image of the presbyteral council found in the conciliar decree *Presbyterorum Ordinis* (n. 7; CD 27) and developed by Paul VI, the essentials of the council or senate have been preserved in the new Code of Canon Law. Unfortunately the Second Vatican Council neglected to specify that this body, acting on behalf of the diocesan presbyterate, should be truly representative and should replace the canonical function of such bodies as the diocesan board of consultors and cathedral chapters of canons. But the unexpected anomalies of the council's ceasing upon the vacancy of the see and of long periods permitted without such a council (canon 501, 2–3) do not invalidate either its moral significance or its canonical status. It needs only to be strengthened.

The second body which should be consulted before the promulgation of diocesan law is the pastoral council. Here again, perhaps too trustingly, the Second Vatican Council was not very specific (CD 27). The 1983 code is somewhat more emphatic, but only slightly so. It has a saving clause about the very establishment of such a council ("to the extent that pastoral circumstances recommend it") that might be interpreted to circumvent the conciliar intent. It too ceases during the vacancy of the see. And its definition of purpose leaves something to be desired: "to investigate under the authority of the bishop all those things which pertain to pastoral works and to ponder them and to propose practical conclusions about them" (canon 511; 513, 2).

This is in some degree a regression from the norms by which Pope Paul VI implemented the conciliar decree's commendation of pastoral councils. As expressed in his 1966 apostolic letter *Ecclesiae sanctae* (n. 16), the purpose of such councils is to "promote the conformity of the life and activity of the people of God with the gospel." It was expected that "prior study would precede the common work" of the council with the help of "institutes and offices," presumably those of the pastoral council itself. The (consultative) participation of the diocesan pastoral council in any necessary or useful episcopal lawmaking should be self-evident, if indeed the bishop is to act "with the church."

The local or particular diocesan church remains free, in its laws as well as in its institutions and pastoral style, to move forward from the general or universal law, without contravening the latter. The initiative remains in the local church, whether the principle of subsidiarity is adduced to explain it or not. The starting point is in the local church, where the whole church of Christ is realized, actualized, present.

Regional Church law

My passing reference to the principle of subsidiarty, which is now unaccountably disdained in revisionist circles, provides a point of transition to what I have called regional church law. Subsidiarity and decentralization may well be political terms, but after some generations of overdoing the analogy of the church as a "perfect society" with the other perfect society, the state, we may be excused for using such language. Subsidiarity here is a kind of shorthand for the relationship between the local church and the total or universal church—and also for the relationship of both universal church and local church to intermediary ecclesial structures (whether personal, like patriarchs and metropolitans, or conciliar, like councils and conferences).

It was Pius XII who in 1946 applied subsidiarity as an ecclesiological principle to the church, and it was among the principles adopted by Paul VI and approved by the universal synod of bishops in 1967 for the revision of the Code of Canon Law. The reference here serves to introduce the matter of regional church law. One significant and in a sense very traditional body, which may on occasion be a legislative assembly, the conference of bishops, is now under challenge.

As should be obvious, it is an oversimplification to speak of regional law, which can mean many things, and to offer observations principally on the conferences of bishops. A word is in order first about the multiple levels of supra-diocesan church structures as these include the lawmaking function.

The first of these is the traditional ecclesiastical province, confirmed in its structure by the Second Vatican Council. The council asked the conferences of bishops to review the boundaries of provinces and required that particular churches should indeed be incorporated in such provinces, with the suppression of the practice by which dioceses would be exempt from metropolitan jurisdiction and directly subject to the apostolic see (CD 41; see canon 431, 2).

At this level of church governance, the role of the lawmaking provincial council remains on the books, but it may be an unlikely force in church life in the future. The primacy of the presiding bishop of the ecclesiastical province—the metropolitan who is the archbishop of the principal local church of the province—lacks any substance in non-judicial matters, despite Vatican II. His position as an intermediary authority, providing both an immediate administrative tribunal and what is called hierarchical recourse in disputed matters needs to be appraised and possibly restored.

This issue of recourse and appeal would take us too far afield from law and lawmaking. But a major disappointment in the 1983 Code of Canon Law was the unexplained disappearance of the planned administrative tribunals to resolve complaints and grievances at the regional and national levels. Nor was there any rethinking of "hierarchical recourse," which in principle should go from the diocesan bishop to the metropolitan and from him to the president of the conference of bishops (the "primate" in the older canonical tradition)—and only then to the Roman see. Instead the intermediate church authorities have no acknowledged role in canonical recourse.

The Second Vatican Council also recognized the potential of ecclesiastical regions consisting of several provinces, that is, within a given nation. This provision has been carried into the 1983 Code of Canon Law in a refined and perhaps attenuated form. The possibility of regional church law at such a level is acknowledged in the new canons, but only with reluctance (CD 40, 3; canons 433–434). And this is the place to mention, if only in passing, the other possibilities of regional church law enacted by councils or conferences of bishops within a nation that has linguistic or even ethnic divisions and also the supra-national levels at which councils and conferences of bishops may have a role to play.

It is, however, at the level of the nation or country that the particular church—in the sense of a group of local or particular churches—may have the greatest interest and impact for our overall topic of the papacy and the church in the United States. The following observations and propositions may be pursued.

1. *The broader role of national conferences of bishops.* As with the diocesan synod or the bishop as lawmaker, as with the councils of ecclesiastical provinces and the like, the total particular church of a given nation engages in the church's mission in innumerable ways. Together its bishops lead in the exercise of the church's teaching and sanctifying and pastoral offices in ways that may be vastly more significant and more frequent than the making of laws. The repetition of this thesis may be tiring, but it is essential not to overstress the legislative or even the governing role.

We have only to look at the living and successful experience of the American conference of bishops: the smallest fraction of its ecclesial enterprise is done in terms of laws, decrees, statutes, or canons. On the one hand, this makes our topic of regional law at the national level a narrow one; on the other hand, the legislative function appears to be a testing point and a symbol of either strength or weakness, of acceptance or rejection, of the very institute of conferences of bishops.

Before the 1985 extraordinary session of the Roman synod of bishops the conferences of bishops were challenged in several ways. And although there was very broad support afforded by the presidents of the conferences, elected by the vote of the bishops of their respective bodies, a theoretical question found its way into the final statement:

> Since the episcopal conferences are so useful, indeed necessary, in the present-day pastoral work of the Church, it is hoped that the study of their theological "status," and above all the problem of their doctrinal authority, might be made explicit in a deeper and more extensive way, keeping in mind what was written in the conciliar decree *Christus Dominus* n. 38 and the Code of Canon Law, canons 447 and 753.

It is a little late to question the ecclesiological status of the conferences in view of *Lumen gentium* 23, which compared them to the ancient patriarchates or, for that matter, in view of the ecumenical council of Nicaea. In the fourth century that council was satisfied that it was legiti-

mate to continue the older tradition of particular councils. It enjoined
that provincial synods of bishops be held semi-annually. And it would
have seemed strange indeed to the bishops assembled at Elvira (300/306)
that they could not appropriately teach the doctrine of matrimonial
indissolubility, at Arles (314) about baptism, at Sardica (343–344) about
the primacy of the bishop of Rome, at Carthage (397) about the canon
of the scriptures or (418) original sin, or at Orange (529) about original
sin, grace, and predestination.

The drafters of the final report of the 1985 synod knew what they
were about and referred positively to a canon which had escaped the
efforts, which I shall mention shortly, to lessen the role of the conferences of bishops in the 1983 code:

> Although they do not enjoy infallible teaching authority, the
> bishops in communion with the head and members of the college
> [of bishops], whether as individuals or *gathered in conferences of
> bishops or in particular councils,* are authentic [authoritative]
> teachers and instructors of the faith for the faithful entrusted to
> their care; the faithful must adhere to the authentic [authorita-
> tive] teaching of their own bishops with a religious assent of soul
> [*religioso animi obsequio*] (canon 753; emphasis added).

A similar point is made about the teaching office of groups of
bishops, associated in conferences or councils, in connection with the
ministry of the divine word. This ministry, carried on by both ordained
and lay, principally by preaching and catechetical instruction, is exercised in the local church by the individual bishops

> Since within [the particular church] they are the moderators of
> the entire ministry of the word; sometimes, *several bishops
> simultaneously fulfill this office jointly for various churches at
> once* in accord with the norm of law (canon 756, 2; emphasis
> added).

The opposition to the conferences of bishops today is not substan-
tively different from that of the minority of the college of bishops at the
Second Vatican Council in 1962–1965. The irony is to see the minority
position, which was then roundly defeated, resurrected today in a different guise. Nor, from an American viewpoint, is the current opposition
much different from the position—again a minority position—taken in
the early 1920s by those who opposed any power in the American conference of bishops at its general meeting or in its instrumentality, the

incorporated National Catholic Welfare Conference (now the United States Catholic Conference).

2. *Regional councils: plenary or national.* Since we are confining ourselves largely to the lawmaking responsibility and the possibility of church law at the national level, traditional priority belongs to the potential national council. It is called "plenary" council in the canons, so as to embrace any kind of supra-provincial council.

The argument has been made, reasonably enough, that the particular church of a nation should enact its canon law only when assembled in the traditional and formal council. Given the infrequency of such councils in the modern period—the last in this country was held in 1984—that position is hardly tenable. And I am not so sure that the added formalities and solemnities of councils are truly needed to enhance the legislative function. Perhaps it is better to say that the conference of bishops, like every ecclesiastical legislator or legislature, should exercise its lawmaking power sparingly.

In the formulation of the 1983 Code of Canon Law, the proposal that even particular councils should lose their legislative power was simply ruled out. In fact, following the favorable if unrealistic words of encouragement offered such councils by Vatican II (CD 36), the code took a fresh look at the makeup of particular councils. Should a national council be held, its non-voting participants may now be greatly enlarged, according to canon 443:

> 4. Presbyters and other members of the Christian faithful can also be called to particular councils with only a consultative vote; their number is not to exceed half of the number of those mentioned in 2–3 [i.e., those specifically designated by the law].

> 6. Others can be invited to particular councils as guests [i.e., in addition to the members with either deliberative or consultative vote] if it seems advantageous in the judgement of the conference of bishops in regard to a plenary council. . . .

3. *Conferences of bishops as legislatures.* From the canonical viewpoint of ecclesial structures, the differences between a particular council at the national level and a national conference of bishops are largely secondary and incidental. The latter is a continuing or permanent body, with regular meetings of the member bishops. Other differences have their significance in the extent of the conferences' lawmaking powers.

During the Second Vatican Council the modern conference of bishops was carefully redefined. When at the beginning of the nineteenth century the few bishops of the United States assembled, they represented the particular churches of the new province of Baltimore and took for granted the right to enact ecclesiastical law for the country. A hundred and fifty years later the spirit of ecclesial conciliarity had risen and then fallen among the American bishops, as Gerald Fogarty has brilliantly recounted in *The Vatican and the American Hierarchy from 1870 to 1965.* In 1965, however, along with the rest of the episcopal college, the American bishops acknowledged, among other things, a legislative power in the conferences clearly analogous to that of particular councils.

From the modern practice of particular councils the decree *Christus Dominus* borrowed the formality of a required Roman review of the binding decrees of the conferences of bishops. This institute, called *recognitio,* dates from the sixteenth century and deserves special attention later. But the concerns of the conciliar fathers about the possible intrusion of the conferences into the affairs of the local or particular church—strangely, few seemed exercised over the more likely intrusion of the Roman see or of preeminent prelates on its behalf—resulted in severe strictures on the otherwise open-ended authority of the conferences.

The first safeguard, now written into the Code of Canon Law, requires consensus of two-thirds of the members for binding decisions, rather than the usual simple majority required at particular councils. A second safeguard was the novel limitation of areas of competence: instead of matters of faith and discipline not already determined by the general canon law—this is the competence of particular councils—the conferences of bishops are limited to matters enumerated in the general law or conceded to them by the apostolic see at its own initiative or upon request (CD 38, 4; canon 455, 1–2).

Again, the general law of the Latin code preserves—it could hardly do otherwise—this pattern. Over and above the innate right of appeal from the decisions of conferences to the bishop of Rome, the role of conferences remains limited, at least in making binding canonical decrees. Evidence of the resurgent bias against the conferences and indeed against the conciliar spirit is the rather gratuitous norm newly added by canon 455:

> 4. In [other] cases [where it is not a question of general decrees] the competence of individual bishops remains intact; and neither the conference nor its president may act in the name of

all the bishops unless each and every bishop has given his consent.

We may thus be grateful that, at least in the United States, the moral weight of the corporate decisions of the conference, even when lacking canonical force, is so very great and that, especially in the case of the recent pastoral letters, the dissenting minority has been so very small.

4. *Conferences of bishops in the 1983 code.* This is not the place to tell the story of the faithful implementation of the letter and spirit of the Second Vatican Council by Pope Paul VI. A prime instance was in his regular enlargement of the enumerated cases of competence of conferences of bishops. In document after document, whether for practical or pastoral reasons or out of simple adherence to a major direction of the council, the late pope pointed the way to the corporate responsibility of the conferences for their respective nations or territories.

The evidence that this mode of action was agreeable to the Catholic episcopate is in the careful way in which their representatives circumscribed the criticisms of the minority at the 1985 synod, as already mentioned. In the meantime, however, the process of revising the Code of Canon Law had taken its toll. It has been estimated that about fifty instances in which the conferences of bishops were declared competent in early drafts of the code were suppressed at later stages and in the text promulgated in 1983.

The paradox is this. Whenever the members of the commission of revision raised this question in 1981, seeking to respect the intent of the council and the progress made under Paul VI, the commission's secretariat replied again and again that the consultation with the universal episcopate had revealed objections to the centralization of church power in the conferences—but apparently not elsewhere. The paradox is that those who raised the difficulty must have been from a minority— certainly a very small minority in the United States conference of bishops—namely, those bishops who had been opposed to the various decisions made by their respective conferences in the period from 1965 to the late 1970s.

And let it be noted that the regression in this matter is not limited to areas of competence dreamed up by the redactors of the early schemata of the new code. At times the code turns its back on the decrees of the Second Vatican Council. The canon on the power of the conferences of bishops in liturgical matters is a pale shadow of the conciliar constitution on the liturgy (SC 22, 2; 39–40; see canon 838, 3). The same is true of the responsibility of the conferences of bishops in relation to the missionary activity of the church (*Ad gentes divinitus* 38; canon 792). Fortunately in such instances the conciliar decree prevails unless certainly abrogated. No one has been more insistent than Pope John Paul that the Code of Canon Law must be read and interpreted in accord with the doctrine and discipline of the Second Vatican Council and not vice versa.

Another curious thing happened on the way to the 1983 Code of Canon Law. The Second Vatican Council had spoken rather generally of the canonical and disciplinary function of the conferences of bishops— always over and above their pastoral role in collaborative enterprises of all kinds. Its language, referring to "juridically binding force" of decisions, had been applied rather broadly in the time of Pope Paul VI to include all manner of executive and even judicial matters on occasion. Once again a canon, much too carefully crafted, appears to limit the "juridically binding force" of decisions exclusively to the form of general decrees and, as already noted, demands unanimity in all other matters. This canon may be viewed as inconsistent with many of the functions still attributed to the conferences in the Code of Canon Law or in their statutes (approved by the Roman see), but attention needs to be drawn to the tone and spirit of the general law.

5. *Future lawmaking responsibility of the conferences.* The more important proposition is whether, for the future, the broad role of the conferences of bishops in pastoral matters should continue to be inhibited when it comes to the making of canonically binding decrees. The traditional and canonical answer would be, once for all, to move forward to the point at which conferences would be as competent as plenary councils. This is not to advocate a multiplication of laws by conferences of bishops any more than by any other church authorities. It is rather a recognition of a legitimate and traditional level of subsidiary action in the church and, by and large, the success of the conferences under the movement of the Holy Spirit of God.

Surely the safeguards are sufficient to avoid majoritarian abuse: the required two-thirds vote, the review by the Roman see, the dispensing power of the diocesan bishop when appropriate, and the possibility, inherent in our understanding of the Petrine office, of recourse to the bishop of Rome.

A word had to be added about a canonical desideratum, namely, a redefinition of that modern institute by which Roman review (*recognitio*) is demanded for the decisions of conferences and particular councils. This review may be understood in different ways.

In the ordinary understanding it is a second look at particular legislation, an inspection to determine whether a decree, for example, contravenes the general law of the universal church, exceeds the authority of a council or conference of bishops, or contains anything contrary to Catholic faith or the common good of the other particular churches. In this ideal sense review may result in a strengthening of a law, an additional support to it.

At the other extreme, Roman review may be employed as an intrusion upon the legitimate responsibility of the conference of bishops, a denigration of the pastoral sense of the particular churches, a denial of the splendid diversity which has been so movingly proclaimed, and the replacement of diversity by uniformity and centralization.

To sum up, the principal instrument or structure at the intermediary level between local church and universal church has come to be the conference of bishops. It is an institute that is needlessly feared, but apparently not feared by the overwhelming numbers of bishops of the local churches. It is an institute that seems to attract the animus of the traditionalists who in many instances know so little of our Christian and Catholic traditions.

In spite of the revisionism and regression, the conferences of bishops seem alive and well. They are a wholesome point of leverage and strength between the local and the universal, as witnessed by the admirable statements of the four representative bishops during the 1987 pastoral visit of the Pope John Paul to the United States. And while no one would seek to turn the conferences into parliaments or legislatures, the current limitations upon their lawmaking role in matters necessary or useful for the particular churches might well be lifted.

Universal Church Law

It is necessary to begin with the reminder that, for convenience, "universal" church law has to be taken—in view of the size and predominance of the Latin church—in what is really a limited and actually misleading sense. The Latin church is not the universal church, but its general canon law is often considered universal.

1. *Conciliar Laws*. In a broader sense, the first point to make is that the legislature of the universal church does not meet very often: only three times in the modern period, 1545–1563 (Trent), 1869–1870 (Vatican I), 1962–1965 (Vatican II). The Code of Canon Law takes note of this. Following the Second Vatican Council, it states that the college of bishops exercises its supreme and full power over the universal church not only in an ecumenical council but also "through the united action of the bishops dispersed in the world, which action as such has been inaugu-

rated or has been freely accepted by the Roman Pontiff so that a truly collegial act results" (LG 22; canon 337, 2).

Since *Lumen gentium* was completed in 1964, insufficient thought has been given to the ways and means for this common action of the college of bishops, whether in teaching or in governing the communion of the churches which constitute the universal church. The code offers little: "It is for the Roman Pontiff, in keeping with the needs of the Church, to select and promote the ways by which the college of bishops is to exercise collegially its function regarding the universal church" (canon 337, 3).

What is unfortunate is that so little effort has been made to move beyond the Second Vatican Council, to seek means and methods of collegial action appropriate to this twentieth century by which the college, head and other members, may act together with all the visible signs of collegial solicitude for the churches—even without the forms and panoply of the ecumenical council. To say this, in relation to the making of universal church law, is in no way to deny or minimize the continuing responsibility and right of the head of the college, the bishop of Rome, to make church law.

2. *The synod of bishops.* Next is the still ambivalent role of the universal synod of bishops. At the behest of the conciliar fathers, Paul VI in 1965 established this central and permanent ecclesiastical institute, both Roman and universal. In turn the council adopted the pope's own language to describe the synod as representing or "taking the part of the entire Catholic episcopate" and as signifying "that all the bishops in hierarchical communion are sharers in solicitude for the universal Church" (CD 5). It is worth noting, with great concern, that this language was carefully eschewed in the 1983 Code of Canon Law.

The fear that the synod of bishops might somehow be or become or be received by the church as an ecumenical council, by deputation or representation of the episcopate, suggests that a groundless fear of medieval conciliarism is still alive. But whatever may be said about means to engage the entire college of bishops in united action outside a council, certainly the synod of bishops is or should be a first step.

A good deal too much has been made of the synod's purely or merely consultative role. Without even possessing legislative power—which, by the way, Paul VI and the Code of Canon Law envisioned as being conferred on the synod on occasion (canon 343)—it can have a moral weight and force far beyond that seen up to the present time. Critics have already demonstrated a kind of deterioration of the role of the synod in the short span of twenty years. This has gone from statements and resolutions and votes on matters of substance to more amorphous conclusions and subsequent apostolic exhortations that may or may not reflect the concerns of the members of the synod or of the universal episcopate they represent. The final report of the 1985 extraordinary session, for all its counterbalancing of hopes and fears, did appear in a more positive light; the 1987 synod has been characterized as a non-event.

A crucial weakness of the synod is the constitutive and influential role of the day-to-day advisors and ministers of the Roman See, specifically the heads of the curial offices. The counsel of the total episcopate, given by bishops of the other particular churches on behalf of their national groupings of churches, is needed by the bishop of Rome—as distinct from the counsel which is regularly given him by his own immediate assistants. The distinction is well made in canon 334; it is not verified in the makeup of the synod of bishops.

On the other hand, little attention has been paid to the positive distinctiveness of the so-called extraordinary sessions of the synod. At these the majority consists of the presidents of the national conferences. The presidents—although elected rather than attached to a particular major diocese and serving for only a term—are in some fashion the inheritors of the old position of national primates. Canon 438, however, fails to make the connection and treats the (national) primatial office as merely honorific.

Our subject, however, is law rather than exhortation or consultation, the latter of course being the formal purpose of the new synod of bishops. A major opportunity was lost when, after repeated reports made concerning the revision process to the several sessions of the synod beginning in 1967, the Code of Canon Law of the Latin church was not submitted for the deliberative vote of the synod that would have made it the law of the pope acting "in synod." The Code of Canon Law is no less the law of the Latin church for this omission, but there is a difference between the act of the unique legislator and the act of a legislative assembly, the head and the other members. This would have corresponded dramatically to the conciliar concept of the church's hierarchical structure.

The 1985 synod expressed the hope that the code for the eastern Catholic churches—those with which we are in full communion—would soon be completed and promulgated. Whatever one may think of a single code for such diverse autonomous churches and whatever the problems inherent in a Latinized canon law for them, the opportunity for a special, legislative session of the synod of bishops, to be limited to the eastern hierarchs, should be considered.

3. *The limits on lawmaking.* Perhaps enough has been said about

the need for restraint in the exercise of the lawmaking power in the church. Nowhere is this more important than at the level of the universal church. The canonist would recall the dictum of Gratian, following Isidore, about the "reasonable" law: "honest, just, possible, in accord with nature, in accord with the custom of the nation, suitable for the time and the place, necessary, useful, clear, to no private advantage, written for the common welfare." Perhaps few laws meet all these expectations. Certainly the proliferation of universal laws and their ancillary instructions and the like is problematical in the light of the diversity of the local churches.

One example is the projected juridical document on Catholic higher education (as if canons 807–814 were not enough and more than enough legislation in this area). Examples of expanding universal law— complicated by the supplementary regulatory categories of instructions, notifications, declarations, pastoral norms, circular letters, and the like—might be multiplied. At this moment one problematic area is the sacrament of penance: first, the sequence of initiation into eucharistic communion and first sacramental reconciliation (with little attention to a more substantive issue: the inversion of confirmation and eucharist in much of the Latin church); second, the troubled matter of general sacramental absolution without prior auricular confession. In both cases an ambiguously written general law is coupled with a failure to thrash out questions of a theological, cultural, pastoral, and even psychological character.

Conclusion

These considerations stress the tension between local church and universal canon law—not to mention the regional or intermediary levels, which themselves might serve to resolve some of the tensions and even have a mediating effect. This in turn raises, for church law as for other aspects of church life, the principle of subsidiarity. The latter is only a way of asserting the authenticity of the local or particular church, only a way of acknowledging also that from the very first centuries the local churches have assembled in the Spirit in groups of churches, without hurt or detriment to the universal communion of churches.

As we reflect upon the relationships and the tensions, however, the brightest side of the picture is the actual ecclesial reality and vitality of the people of God gathered in the Spirit. There remains, moreover, the living memory of the Second Vatican Council—if only that council were seen as an intermediate peak from which the pilgrim people move forward and upward to new peaks.

In the clear canonical tradition of the western church, there is no recourse from the bishop of Rome to a future general or ecumenical council. But there is, first, a diversity of levels of church laws and church authorities in a complex but providential pattern and, second, the continuing possibility of recourse from canon law, including the Code of Canon Law of the Latin church, to the letter and spirit of the Second Vatican Council.

In this we can acknowledge with gratitude the path laid down emphatically by Pope John Paul. He described the codification as "a great effort to translate the conciliar doctrine and ecclesiology into *canonical* language." He explained that the Code of Canon Law "must always be referred to this [conciliar] image [of the church] as the primary pattern which the code ought to express . . ." (*Sacrae disciplinae leges*). Most directly he has urged an "exegetical and critical comparison" of the new code of general law with the conciliar texts.

It might have been possible to consider the merits and demerits of canon law, especially the general or universal law, now in force within the church community. Instead these observations have presented some focal points of lawmaking power and proposed some rethinking, however unlikely at this time, along with a strong sense of restraint in the multiplication of laws.

James H. Provost

The Papacy:
Power, Authority, Leadership

T he role of the papacy is a central theme in any discussion of the bicentennial of the Roman Catholic hierarchy in the United States. The historical, theological and canonical dimensions of this theme are dealt with by other studies in this volume; I have been asked to assess the power, authority and leadership of the papacy as a distinct concern.

The attitudes of bishops in the United States toward papal power, authority and leadership have shifted over the past two hundred years.[1] During this same time, there have also been major shifts in general church thinking on this topic.

It is within these two centuries, for example, that the shift has taken place from thinking of power in the church as divided into the power of orders and the power of jurisdiction, to thinking in terms of the three-fold *munera* or powers of teaching, sanctifying and governing. The problems related to this paradigm shift are still being addressed in theory and practice.

If knowledge is power, then there is considerable significance for questions of power, authority and leadership in the church from the nineteenth and twentieth century developments in the understanding of "ordinary magisterium."[2]

Moreover, from the perspective of the lived experience of the popes themselves, these two hundred years have seen a dramatic shift from the captivity of the pope in Fontainbleau to a pope who acts as the bishop of the whole church, something which is lived out in the pastoral trips of the reigning pontiff. In addition, this two century period has seen the definition of the primacy of power and the exercise of the church's infallibility by the pope, adding doctrinal clarifications regarding papal power.[3]

It is important that canon lawyers, among others, pay attention to these historical developments. Otherwise we may fail to give the proper interpretation to such terms as "vicar of Christ" and *"servus servorum Dei,"* terms which are often associated with the source of papal power. Yet it is also important for canon lawyers, as a service to the church itself, to analyze papal power, authority and leadership as we find them today. I do not propose to rehearse here the debates of Vatican II, or the issues related to the agents of supreme power in the church.[4] Rather, I will set a preliminary context from considerations about the church itself, attempt to clarify some terms, then analyze the exercise of papal power, authority and leadership today with the help of some case studies, and finally conclude with a few personal observations.

I. Preliminary Considerations

To set the context for this study, some preliminary observations are called for on the use of analogy in this topic, the centrality of Christ to any consideration of power in the Church, and the all-pervasive character of power itself.

A. THE IMPORTANCE OF MYSTERY AND ANALOGY

"Power," "authority" and "leadership" are analogous concepts when used in the church. Only God has true power, authority and leadership. The key affirmation of the early Christians was that "Jesus is Lord" (Rom 10:9), a revolutionary claim over against the all-pervasive power of the Roman state. It was a claim that Jesus, not the emperor, is truly Lord. It was also a claim that Jesus is indeed Lord, the all-powerful God.

Jesus cautions his disciples to call no human being "father," "teacher" or "master," for "you have one," who is God (Mt 23:8–11). Ultimate "leadership" in the church is really the work of the Spirit, guiding and caring for God's people.

God is a mystery, as indeed is the church and any other object of faith. In this life we come to understand mysteries not by direct knowledge, but through analogy. That is, working from what we do know, we come to some knowledge of what we do not know because of a certain analogy or similarity between them; but when attempting to come to understand a mystery of faith, what we do not know remains more than what we do know. The *via negativa* remains uppermost in our understanding of the mysteries of faith.[5]

The analogy of faith controls our understanding of power, authority and leadership in the church. While secular realities may give us some glimmer of the mysterious reality within the church, they hide more than they reveal. Thus, for example, the church is not a democracy—nor a monarchy, oligarchy, or any other type of human political system, even though each of these systems may enable us to have some understanding of what true power, authority and leadership may be in the church.[6] The church is neither a governmental system nor a business enterprise, even though it shows striking similarities to both. Despite other similarities, it is neither a private, voluntary organization nor a public, necessary one. Analogy, not direct parallels, gives us the proper approach to understanding the realities of the church.

Genuine ecclesial power, authority and leadership operate at the level of faith. Those who exercise these functions must be persons of faith, and faith itself imposes limits on what they do with these in the church. Similarly, the claim which church authorities have on those in ecclesial communion is based on faith: those who are subject to that power, who follow the leadership and acknowledge the authority, do so ultimately because they are believers.

B. CHRIST AT THE CENTER

Power, authority and leadership in the church are fundamentally those of Christ. The analogy of the "mystical body of Christ" emphasizes the reality of Christ's continued, active presence, whether as the powerful source of unity within the body or as providing authoritative leadership as its head (LG 7). The messianic work of Jesus as priest, prophet and king leads to the continued teaching, sanctifying and governing work of the church as a whole (LG 9–13) and of the hierarchy within the church (LG 25–27).

In dealing with papal-episcopal relations, Vatican II emphasized that whatever power, authority and leadership there are in the church must be seen in relationship to Christ (LG 21). This applies not only to how the pope and the bishops relate to one another, but also to any such relationship, whether of pope to individual Christians, bishops to priests, or religious education directors to parents and children. All must somehow be related to Christ (cf LG 10).

There are various ways of being in relationship with Christ. Vatican II addressed at least three: charismatic, or through the operation of grace as freely given in the Spirit (LG 12, AA 3); sacramental, or though the operation of grace as it comes to us through the sacraments of the church (LG 11); institutional, as the institution is the external expression of that inner reality which is the grace of Christ's continued presence among us (LG 8). Each of these ways is vital to the continued life of the church. All three exist at every moment in the church's history.

C. POWER IS ALL PERVASIVE

Power is central to all of creation. This is clear at the inanimate level in the power of atomic and even sub-atomic particles, in the power of gravity, in the power of various physical realities. Power is also all-pervasive in the animate world: the power of life, the "vital force" which animates living beings, the power of biological realities. Power is also central to interpersonal relations, whether it is charismatic or institutional power, personal or social power.

Indeed, power is so all pervasive that it fills the background of our perceptions, and we can only get a partial grasp of its reality. Some have even abandoned any effort to define "power." Clearly, it is a foundational concept in relation to which other concepts such as authority and leadership are derived concepts.

Power is most apparent, or easiest to see, in situations of tension. In a sense, power does not exist "at rest," only the potential for it; power itself exists in interaction or tension.[7] For example, electric power is always a power in tension, and without that tension our electric lights would go out. Power in a social body, which is the topic of this study, is also a power in tension, the tension of interpersonal relationships.

D. CAUTIONS

In light of the above, clearly there are limitations to what is to follow. Our discussion must be framed in the context of analogy, so that what we discuss (i.e. the part of the analogy based on what we know already) is modest and certainly less that what we accept in faith. We are going to deal with the human component of the analogy, and thus only with power, authority and leadership in the visible, institutional structures of the church.

Since we are dealing with faith realities, and not merely human ones, there will be an attempt to relate these to Christ who is ever active in the church. But since they are also truly human realities, we must deal with insights from human sciences insofar as they illuminate this human dimension. Given how we usually come to understand power in human experience, looking at areas of tension may prove helpful in coming to a better understanding of power, authority and leadership as these exist in the church.

II. Clarifying Some Terms

Topics of power, authority and leadership are much discussed today. They are of concern to philosophers, business and industry, political science, the helping professions, military science, etc.[8] Yet there is no clear consensus on how to define or interrelate these terms. Any "clarification" which may be proposed here, therefore, is only tentative.

A. GENERAL CONSIDERATIONS

There are various forms of power in interpersonal relationships. "Force" acts directly on external reality and determines the world of others from the "outside." "Authority," on the other hand, is considered to work through the free consent of others in a common domain of reality, from the "inside."

Authority may be subjective, in the sense that because of personal qualities or expertise the "authority" exercises power over others, over their intellect and/or will. It may be objective, in the sense that because of a role, function or office, the authority's exercise of power is legitimate within the social group.

In practice there seem to be at least three factors which motivate people to accept the power of another as legitimate, and in this sense enable the other to lead. First, there is some legitimation by an external authority: the person is assigned by proper authority to a particular office, or is legitimately elected and accepts that office. Second, the person has what it takes personally to do the office, a sort of inner legitimacy in assuming the position. Finally, there is that legitimation which arises from acceptance by others. This legitimation is based on an interpersonal bonding which develops when mutual respect and trust reach the degree that the person in authority is truly credible, and those subject to him or her freely accept the authority's power rather than bend to it as if to force.

B. APPLICATION

For our purposes and as a working definition, "power" is considered the ability to produce effects, and "authority" is the legitimate exercise of power. The 1983 code gives some credence to this distinction. In various headings it refers to "authority," while in the canons within those headings it uses the term "power"—in other words, the legitimate use of power is structured within the framework of the church's law, so the code terms it "authority."[9]

"Leadership" is considered the actual leading of others in some direction, based on credibility (i.e. others consider the one who is leading to be credible, and so follow the leader). Leadership may be by someone with legitimate power (an "authority"), or it may be exercised by persons who lack "legitimation" in the full sense but nevertheless have effective influence within a group.

The key questions are not the *nature* of power, authority and leadership, but their source, exercise, and purpose. Significant in life is not the "what" so much as the "where's it coming from," "how's it being used," and "where's it taking us."[10] Thus in what follows, some clarity in the practice of papal power, authority and leadership will be sought by examining some areas of tension around the key questions of source, exercise and purpose.

III. Analysis of Papal Power, Authority and Leadership[11]

A. SOURCE: CHRIST

While all accept that Christ is the source of the papal role, there are varying views about how this power, authority and leadership are related to Christ. Since the middle ages this has been expressed in the formula "vicar of Christ." Today a more ecclesial framework is discussed.

1. Vicar of Christ

The claim has been that as the "vicar of Christ" the pope has a special and unique relationship to Christ, a source of power which no one else has in the church. But a brief look at the history of this title raises some questions about the claim.[12]

During the first millennium the term was used generally for all bishops who preside over local churches as vicars or legates of Christ. The pope, as bishop of the local church of Rome, was considered vicar of Christ—as was, for example, the bishop of Milan, Paris, or Pergamum. The specific role of the pope within the whole church was considered rooted in the Petrine function, as successor of Peter and bishop of the city where Peter and Paul gave the ultimate witness in their martyrdom.

Innocent III (+ 1216) seems to have begun the use of the term "vicar of Christ" as an expression of a special papal prerogative, describing the fullness of the pope's power. This usage gradually eclipsed the application of the term to other bishops.

In the fifteenth to nineteenth centuries, theories about church power developed in the context of tensions with the newly powerful nation states. The church was presented as having two types of power, one which was proper to it as with any sovereign state, the other which was the church's as a distinctly religious society.[13] The first type, parallel with any secular state, was proper to the church just as the state's was naturally proper to it; within the church such power related to the normal governing of the faithful and derived in a descending fashion from the pope. Analogous to the divine right of secular monarchs, the pope received this power directly from God upon accepting election. The second type, peculiar to the church and which the state did not have, related to the sacraments, dispensations from vows, dispensations of ratified but not consummated marriages, etc. Rather than being native to the church as such, it was a vicarious power rooted in a special command of Christ; as "vicar of Christ" the pope held this power in a special way.

Vatican II returned to an earlier perspective. All power in the church comes from Christ, so all power (whether the power to govern normal operations, or the power over the sacraments and other sacred realities) comes from Christ. In this sense, *all* power in the church is "vicarious." But on the other hand, all power (again, whether the power to govern normal operations or the power over the sacraments and other sacred realities) is "proper" to the church as a community of faith, as the body of Christ and the people of God.

The conciliar documents refer to the pope as "vicar of Christ" (LG 22) but use the same term in reference to bishops in their own dioceses (LG 27). Conciliar teaching also specifically rooted the power of bishops ultimately in the sacrament of order; that is, there is a *sacramental* basis for episcopal power (LG 21). The term "vicar of Christ," applied to both pope and bishops, is used with a clearly spiritual meaning and does not seem to provide a special relationship to Christ (and hence a special source of "power") distinct from sacramental episcopal consecration.

This being the case, can the phrase "vicar of Christ" continue to claim to be a special source of power for the pope, based on a special papal relationship to Christ different from that relationship which is established by sacramental episcopal consecration for any bishop?

2. Ecclesial Relationship

The pope may be considered as relating to Christ through the same means as others in the church, but as having a special role within the church. As mentioned earlier, the relationship to Christ can be through grace or charism, through sacraments, and through the church as an institution revealing God's continued presence among us.

a. From the perspective of grace, the pope is a man of faith, grace, charism and charity.[14] He may also have distinct personal gifts or charisms which led the cardinals to select him at the time of his election as pope.

He does not, however, have those charisms which were unique to the apostles, and which ceased with the death of the last apostle. Thus the pope cannot make a new "revelation," since public revelation ended with the death of the last apostle (cf DV 7–9). The pope is not, as pope, assured of the gifts to handle poisonous serpents, cast out devils, or any of the other special charisms usually associated with the apostolic foundations of the church.[15]

b. From the perspective of sacraments, as with other bishops the pope must be a fully initiated Christian (baptized, confirmed and admitted to the eucharist), and ordained. Fundamentally, he is the bishop of Rome (c. 331). Moreover, for him as for any Catholic the eucharist is the *culmen et fons*, the summit and source of ecclesial life (LG 11).

But the election and installation of a pope are not an eighth sacrament, or a new level of the sacrament of order beyond that of deacon, presbyter and bishop. The pope does not have a distinct sacramental basis for his power beyond that sacramental ordination as a bishop which he shares with the other bishop members of the episcopal college.

c. There are several ways to approach the pope's relationship to Christ through the church as an institution. Since the church itself is an object of faith, a mystery, it can be understood only analogically.

For example, the church is the body of Christ; Christ is its head. The pope stands in relation to the rest of the church as Peter did, not as Christ; that is, the relationship is between Peter and the rest of the apostles, and the pope and the rest of the bishops.[16]

The church can be viewed as the people of God. The people are God's because they have Christ for their head, the dignity and freedom of God's children for their heritage, the new commandment to love as Christ loved us for their law, and the kingdom of God for their goal (LG 9). The pope, and the rest of the hierarchy, are *within* the people of God. They have a special role of service within that people, and the pope has a distinct role in service to the unity of that people (LG 23).

The church can also be conceived as a communion on mission. Both "communion" and "mission" are theological realities.[17] That is, they are rooted in God—a communion of three persons who are known to us through their divine "missions." Christ, the communion of human and divine natures in one person, comes to us on mission as messiah—priest, prophet and king. The church, empowered by the Spirit to continue Christ's mission by exercising these *munera*, is itself a communion of disciples in whom the Spirit dwells and thus establishes a divine communion—a communion expressed sacramentally in the eucharist, in which these disciples are nourished by communion with God through communicating the body and blood of the Lord, and whose communion with one another is expressed and strengthened by the sharing in the one bread and the one cup (LG 7).

This communion, expressed in every local celebration of the eucharist under the authority of the bishop (LG 27), is not something in isolation but exists in an organized communion linked together by bishops, who themselves are related in hierarchical communion with one another (a communion of hierarchs) and under the pope (a hierarchy within their communion). Thus the Catholic Church is a communion of communions, expressed and assured through the hierarchical communion of the episcopal college, which succeeds to the apostolic college in the *munus* of pastoring (LG 22).

It is within this college that the pope has a special role as Peter's successor; it is within this communion of churches that the pope has the special responsibility of being a source and center of unity (LG 23).

The role of the pope—his power, authority and leadership—have their source in this function within the church. It is not something isolated and prescinding from the church, but within and understandable only in the context of the church.

Thus it is appropriate that attention to the power, authority and leadership of the pope form a significant theme in any discussion of the history of the church in the United States. The church in a particular country participates in the communion of churches which is the Catholic Church, and the Catholic Church is truly present in each particular church. The pope has a significant role in the particular churches and their expression on a national level, for his function is indeed ecclesial, that is, related to the reality of the church itself.

B. EXERCISE OF POWER

There are any number of issues which could be examined to analyze the contemporary exercise of papal power, authority and leadership. Given the constraints of time and space only four will be examined here: liturgical, sexual, truth, and justice issues. Regrettably, other issues which are perhaps even more obvious will have to be left for other studies.[18]

In what follows attention is given to the "apostolic see." Papal power, authority and leadership are exercised not only by the pope individually but also through those various offices and agencies which assist him in the exercise of the Petrine function within the church (c. 361). Moreover, since this study is being made in the context of the relationship between the apostolic see and the church in the United States, these exercises of papal power will be viewed especially from the context of their effect within the church in the United States.

1. Liturgical Issues

While Vatican II set the principles for liturgical renewal, it left much of the specifics up to the revision of the liturgical books. Indeed, the council left most of the practical decisions in regard to liturgical renewal for the apostolic see (SC 22, §1). This was not merely because the council did not have time to engage in all the details; it was also a recognition of the specific competence of the apostolic see in liturgical issues, a competence given renewed affirmation in the 1983 code (c. 838). The revision of the liturgical books is a clear example of papal power, authority and leadership.

What has been the experience of the exercise of this power?[19] At first, the revision of the books followed an uncertain path. Some portions of the mass, for example, could be celebrated in the vernacular but others still had to be in Latin.[20] Then it was decided to permit full vernacular celebrations.[21] The resulting printing of successive missals left many publishers disillusioned, to say nothing of the conflicting signals at the parish level. Moreover, the catechesis to prepare the people for these liturgical changes was often inadequate, ill-prepared, and sometimes not even possible to prepare, given the varying signals from the Vatican.

Centuries-old church practices were involved, so the task was of unusual difficulty, and some confusion could be expected. But the confusion that did occur was all the more regrettable given the deeper significance of what was involved. The symbols, gestures and words with which people relate to God reach deeply into the human psyche; they are examples of the basic "mythic" level of religious experience. Even if there had been a clear and systematic plan agreed to ahead of time, some resistance could be anticipated. As it was, the resistance assumed major proportions.

First, there was division within the offices of the Roman curia itself. As the agency responsible for carrying out the papal power, authority and leadership in this matter, such division did not bode well. The congregation responsible for liturgical matters included persons who were opposed to the reforms mandated by the council. This resistance was of special concern, given the responsibilities of the congregation involved. The issue was addressed on the basis of internal politics, rather than liturgical considerations. A Consilium for implementing the conciliar constitution was formed of experts who had assisted the conciliar commissions.[22] But the results of the Consilium's work were subject to approval by the curial Congregation of Rites. Eventually, once the initial revision of the liturgical books was completed, the Consilium was amalgamated into the revised Congregation for Divine Worship.[23] A further revision of the congregation's structure[24] led to the dispersal of the Consilium's membership; its leader, Archbishop Bugnini, was sent as apostolic delegate to Iran.

Subsequently there have been mixed signals as to how Roman authorities desire the revised liturgical books to be interpreted. The most evident tension has been over matters such as communion under both species and general sacramental absolution, where it would seem those now in charge of the congregation differ from the intent of those who drafted the revised rituals concerned with these issues.[25]

A second and more public resistance has been mounted by various organized groups, especially those connected with Archbishop Lefebvre. Lefebvre's case is of special interest, since it includes an explicit challenge to papal power, authority and leadership. But it also spills over into local bases of organized resistance to the liturgical changes mandated by Vatican II, challenging the role of local bishops which the Roman pontiff is supposed to "affirm, strengthen and vindicate" (LG 27).

What has been the response of the apostolic see to this direct challenge to its authority? It has been, quite frankly, a remarkable toleration of dissent.[26] When the validity of the eucharist celebrated by the Roman pontiff and those who followed the ritual promulgated by him was challenged, Rome did not declare the position to be heretical or schismatic; it tolerated such attacks, apparently in hopes of an eventual reconciliation. Dissent on the validity of the eucharist is not dissent on a peripheral issue; it goes to the very heart of the church, of its dogma and pastoral life. But such dissent by a bishop of the church and his followers has been publicly tolerated by the supreme authorities of the church for at least two decades. This in itself is a remarkable fact, given the official rejection of public dissent in other matters, which will be discussed below.

Lefebvre was suspended for disobeying a direct papal order and ordaining priests;[27] those priests he ordained are likewise suspended by the Catholic Church (c. 1383). The archbishop's ordination of bishops entailed a more serious split with the church—an automatic excommunication, to which the apostolic see added that those who remain in communion with Lefebvre are placing themselves in the same status, given the now declared schismatic nature of the movement.[28]

But prior to this ultimate act of dissent by Lefebvre, the Vatican was sending confusing signals to the local churches which were struggling with organized dissent within their territories. Although Lefebvre was operating a seminary without proper authorization, and without authorization continued to tonsure and ordain to minor orders which were no longer in effect in the Catholic Church, bishops were directed to accept the tonsure and minor orders of any former seminarians from Lefebvre's seminaries who may wish to study for the priesthood under proper Catholic auspices.[29] The liturgical dissent in these matters was not only tolerated, but was accepted as satisfying the present Catholic requirements prior to ordination.

More disturbing were the private letters on official stationary from individual cardinals in the Roman curia, affirming to inquiring individuals from the United States that they did indeed satisfy their Sunday obligation by participating in a mass celebrated by a Lefebvre priest. This was said despite the fact that such a celebration did not take place under the authority of the proper local bishop. While it could be argued that the wording of the new code may justify satisfying the Sunday obligation at a mass celebrated in any rite which may at one time have been authorized by the church,[30] there is nothing in the code which would seem to justify satisfying an obligation at a mass celebrated contrary to communion with the local bishop (cf LG 26).

Finally, the proposed arrangement which Lefebvre first agreed to, and then rejected, in May 1988 carried with it a mixed message concerning toleration of resistance to the earlier exercise of papal power, authority and leadership in the liturgical reform.[31]

To reflect on these events for a moment, it is clear that the reform of the liturgical rituals was an accepted area of papal responsibility. Yet the manner in which that responsibility has been exercised, both within the Roman curia and in dealing with organized resistance over the past twenty years, has led to confusion. It is difficult to see how this manner of exercising power, authority and leadership has not led to an erosion of the credibility of the apostolic see.

2. Sexual Issues

Historically this has been another area of papal exercise of power, authority and leadership in the church. Celibacy was imposed on the clergy in the western church through papal intervention,[32] not only in the fourth century but also through the general councils of the middle ages whose decrees appear to be more specifically papal than conciliar. Issues of sexual morality have been at the forefront of papal concerns in dealing with theologians for several centuries. Indeed, that there is "no parvity of matter in sexual issues" became a papally imposed principle which set clearly defined limits for theologians addressing such issues.[33] Finally, popes have paid special attention to sexual issues in marriage, even to the extent of judging authenticity of membership in the church on the basis of conformity to papal teaching on these matters.[34]

Attention to sexual issues for these purposes is not something unique to the Catholic Church, or even to religious bodies. Greeks and Romans sought a greater self-control through discipline in sexual matters, which can be compared with the emphasis that self-control is essential to human dignity which one finds in the writings of John Paul II. Islam has well-known rules concerning sexual matters, and sexual taboos are common in so-called primitive religions.

What is significant for our purposes is the restriction to *papal* attention of issues dealing with celibacy and conjugal morality in recent years. This was especially evident at Vatican II, when Paul VI restricted to himself (and excluded from consideration by the other council members) questions relating to birth control and clerical celibacy. These were clear claims of a papal monopoly to decide the issues; while a consultative process was used in coming to decisions on them, the decisions themselves were explicitly exercises of papal authority.[35]

What have been the effects of the exercise of papal power, authority and leadership in these issues? For some the position on birth control has been a major source of disaffection from the church, reflected in the United States by an observable sudden decline in mass attendance.[36]

More significantly, it has led to the development of an attitude of selectivity in regard to church teaching. This selectivity was already present in regard to some church teaching, particularly in matters related to social justice.[37] What is significant is that this same selectivity was now applied by many practicing Catholics to issues which confessors and penitents alike formerly considered exempt from it. This attitude appears to continue despite repeated papal rejections of it.[38]

The issue is indeed complex, as evidenced by the variety and degree of nuance in the statements of episcopal conferences following the publication of *Humanae vitae*.[39] These were part of the reason Paul VI called the first extraordinary meeting of the synod of bishops in 1969 to discuss mutual relations between the papacy and the bishops.

The celibacy norm reaffirmed by recent popes appears to be a significant factor in the decline in the numbers of active clergy and religious, and a factor in the decline in vocations experienced in the last fifteen to twenty years.[40] While this decline in the United States has not yet had the impact that the shortage of clergy has had in other parts of the world, by the year 2000 it will be a much more serious situation.[41]

This is not just a practical problem of finding sufficient clergy to staff parishes and those diocesan offices which require a priest; it also raises more deeply theological issues. Church teaching considers the eucharist central to Catholic life, and the participation in the celebration of the eucharist as specific to being a Catholic. But already in some parts of the world, and increasingly in the United States, this may not be possible on a regular basis. In some areas, Catholic communities are perforce becoming churches of the word rather than of the eucharist. Is this appropriate in the long run?

The commitment to serve still exists among Catholics in the United States, as is evident by the numbers actively involved in parish life, movements, and volunteer service overseas.[42] But this only serves to highlight problems with permanent commitment, and especially permanent commitment to celibacy.

The decision of the apostolic see to admit married men to the priesthood may be an opening to a more flexible response to the current situation. But the circumstances for this in the United States do not seem to be concerned with the pastoral situation of Catholic communities, but more with specific needs of individual converts. This is true, for example, in the case of married priests of the Episcopal Church who have sought full communion with the Catholic Church.[43] It should be noted that these men are considered married lay men despite their ordination in the Episcopal Church, for the apostolic see has ordered that they be ordained unconditionally (i.e. as if they had never been ordained). It may be still too soon to evaluate the impact of this practice on pastoral life or celibate vocations.

In reflecting on this exercise of papal power, authority and leadership, it appears that sexual issues have been a clear attempt to exercise specifically papal prerogatives. The manner of exercise as well as the content of what has been decided has led to the disaffection of some, and to an increased attitude of selectivity toward church positions by a notable number of Catholics. The long-range impact of papal decisions in this area are a cause of concern to many. It is difficult to see how this has not also led to an erosion of the credibility of the apostolic see in this country.

3. Truth Issues

Attention to orthodoxy is a traditional source for papal power, authority and leadership. In the early church, sees founded by the apostles were the guarantors of the "apostolic faith." Rome, as the place of ultimate witness by Peter and Paul, exercised a special function of witnessing to this faith.

That role was especially one of judge. When matters were not resolved locally or within a province, the judgment of the apostolic see was sought. Even when a more pro-active stance was adopted, early interventions on behalf of orthodoxy had to do with judgment, not with creating new teaching.

This role continues today. However, it is being exercised in a manner which reflects the worldview, the *epistome,* of the nineteenth century. This can be illustrated by three of the elements involved. First, the manner of exercising the apostolic see's role is still marked by the post-French revolution restoration of the church in Europe and a felt need to counteract Kantian philosophy and "scientism."[44] Second, it relies heavily on the development of the non-infallible (hence, "fallible"?) magisterium as a special form of authoritative teaching calling for *obsequium* (c. 752).[45] Finally, there is an underlying "classicist" approach to truth, as contrasted to twentieth century "historical mindedness."[46]

How, in fact, is this papal role being exercised today? It would not be possible in the limited space of this article to review or even cite the many instances in which it has been invoked, even in regard to the

United States. Moreover, many of these are confidential and could not be reported at this time.[47] But it is possible to sketch some of the major trends.

Negative restrictions have appeared, based on a limited theological system, in regard to contemporary truth issues. Thus issues of christology, "liberation theology," biomedical research, etc., have been addressed from a fairly narrow theological framework, at times accused of lacking a "catholic" sensitivity in judging these matters.[48] The rejection of any type of "dissent" from non-infallible positions has been severe, despite the exception made for many years in the case of Archbishop Lefebvre.[49]

There has been an on-going harassment of theologians, without an apparent consistent purpose, which often appears as an attempt to appease influential minorities. This judgment without consistent vision is evident in interventions in regard to the appointment of teachers, frequent letters to bishops about theologians in their dioceses, interventions in regard to permissions to publish books, etc.

Finally, the procedures which are to be followed in judging truth issues seem to reject basic church principles of fair treatment. This is done under the guise of claiming they are "pastoral" rather than "judicial," but the net effect is to deny basic procedural safeguards long admitted in church courts and administrative practice, and which the church calls on secular society to provide its members.[50]

In reflecting on this exercise of papal power, authority and leadership, it is clear that truth issues are an accepted area of competence for the apostolic see. But the manner in which the papal role is being exercised raises questions as to whether it is being consistently directed toward promotion of church teaching or even effective judgment on behalf of truth.[51] At times it has the appearance of a defensive effort to exercise centralized control—defensive against the "evil" world in contrast to the Second Vatican Council's view, or even a view of the world as the setting for evangelization; defensive against militant, influential groups (particularly of the so-called far right) who may attempt to seize control of doctrinal orthodoxy, especially through their use of the public media; defensive of a very limited school of theology.

Could it be that the net effect of the manner in which this function is exercised has also led to an erosion of the credibility of the apostolic see?

4. Justice Issues

The apostolic see has not claimed a unique competence in regard to justice issues, but since the time of Leo XIII the popes have exercised a very public role here. The exercise of papal power, authority and leadership has been twofold: teaching, through encyclicals and other usual means,[52] and diplomatic, especially through the papal diplomatic corps.[53]

The impact has been notable. In regard to teaching, the world in general appears to value papal leadership in this area to the extent that it represents a moral voice on the international scene.

Within the church there has been a mixed response. For some it has provided encouragement, and they readily support, study and attempt to teach the papal message. There have, however, been some difficulties in putting this teaching into practice. The implications of, for example, John Paul II's encyclical *Laborem exercens* for church employment practices have yet to be thoroughly explored.[54] Moreover, for other Catholics the teaching has not been received, and some even question the right of the church (including the pope) to teach authoritatively on such issues. It is one of the first examples of recent public selectivity in accepting papal teaching on the part of practicing Catholics in the United States, and remains so today.[55]

On the diplomatic front, in some parts of the world the apostolic see exercises a crucial role on behalf of peace and justice. It has at times encouraged bishops to act on behalf of the oppressed and the poor. But at other times the apostolic see gives the impression of being compromised through its diplomatic dealings with unjust regimes, and of chilling attempts of local bishops to address situations of injustice in their countries. It was for diplomatic reasons, for example, that the apostolic see forced the cancellation of the Brazilian initiative to have bishops discuss and meet to share their views on violence in the world.[56]

If one stops to reflect on the effect of this exercise of papal power, authority and leadership, it appears as an accepted area of competence but not as an exclusive one for the apostolic see. It has received a mixed response; for some Catholics in the United States it has been the occasion for selectivity in accepting papal teaching, while for others it has been well received. Its effect on the credibility of the apostolic see seems to be mixed.

C. PURPOSE: EMPOWERMENT AND CONTROL

Authority and leadership address the use of power for two major purposes within a group. One is empowerment: to enable the various members of the group to work together to achieve the group's purposes.[57] This applies to small groups, but also to large organizations and institutions such as the Catholic Church. A second purpose is control: to gain information on how the system is working, and to establish the speed and direction the system will take.[58]

The purpose for the church is primarily spiritual: to build communion with God and one another, and to carry out the mission of spreading the gospel. People today, however, have religious experiences outside institutional church structures and come to those structures to articulate and celebrate that religious experience.[59] The church does not have an institutional monopoly on religious experience, even for Catholics.[60]

Papal power, authority and leadership are directed toward the church's unity. As indicated above, this is the rationale given by Vatican I and repeated by Vatican II (LG 23) for the pope's special role. This unity is primarily a spiritual unity but it is expressed in the communion of churches (LG 13, 23). While the credibility of papal power, authority and leadership has been weakened, as discussed above, it remains. For the sake of the church's unity, it needs to be perceived as identifiably spiritual. This can be done if it relates more effectively to the experience and expectations of the faithful—building credibility and practical legitimation for the papal role, and relating most directly to the unity function within the church, itself a faith reality. It can also be aided by relating more explicitly to the fundamentally spiritual meaning of power, authority and leadership in the church as church. This may require revising some accepted manners of expressing papal prerogatives, seeking more genuinely religious ways of articulating the role of the apostolic see.

IV. Some Concluding Observations

1. The role of the pope is significant in the life of the church. He exercises real power, authority and leadership. The foregoing analysis has addressed some of the tension points in order to seek some understanding of how papal power and its related authority and leadership are exercised today, and some of their impact on the church in the United States. There are many other areas where the papal role is influential; it has not been possible to address all of these.

2. We live in a time of changing paradigms, or a changing framework for understanding power—and, hence, authority and leadership. These changes are part of our world and of our worldview. Various attempts have been made to explain this shift, such as Lonergan's reference to "historical mindedness." Secular philosophers seek to overcome the individualism of the nineteenth century even as they recognize the importance of the person within society. But power is not perceived as a function of the group rather than an individual: leaders need followers. These changing paradigms will affect how we approach "power," even if we are not consciously aware of this.[61]

3. It is important that papal power, authority and leadership relate effectively to the church community. The function of unity is increasingly necessary in a worldwide church: the credibility of the proclamation of the gospel is at stake, as well as the church's function of service to humankind. But it is also necessary that the manner of exercising this function become more credible. The effort to do this is not new to our day, but is part of the "continuing renewal" to which the church is always called. Moreover it will never be complete or perfect, given both the analogical meaning of power, authority and leadership in the church, and the fact that it participates in but does not replace the essential role of Christ and the Spirit in the life of the church.

4. We have examined this topic primarily from the perspective of the *papal* exercise of power, authority and leadership. In closing, it may be appropriate in the present context to offer two modest suggestions.

The first is that a correct understanding of the papal role cannot prescind from the local churches involved in the communion of the church. The present study, for example, cannot prescind from the United States context where this role is experienced in the life of Catholic people. A more complete analysis of papal power, authority and leadership would require a more detailed examination not only of its impact on the religious practice of Catholics in the United States, but also of its impact on the ability of the bishops to pastor their churches appropriately within their specific pastoral situations.

A second suggestion is the possibility that the relationship is more than a one-way street. If an improvement in the effectiveness of the papal role of unity is desirable, might not the way to achieve that be helped by considering the experience of bishops and their conferences in exercising leadership within their own churches? For example, the bishops in the United States have adopted a much more consultative approach in the exercise of their teaching authority; while the long-term results are yet to be evaluated in terms of credibility and effectiveness, the process itself is worthy of attention as an alternative for other teaching instances in the church, including the apostolic see.

Notes

1. In addition to the historical studies in the present volume, see Gerald P. Fogarty, *The Vatican and the American Hierarchy from 1870 to 1965* (Wilmington, DE: Michael Glazier, 1985).

2. See John P. Boyle, "The Ordinary Magisterium: Towards a History of the Concept," *The Heythrop Journal* 20 (1979) 380–398; 21

(1980) 14–29; Francis A. Sullivan, *Magisterium: Teaching Authority in the Catholic Church* (New York: Paulist, 1983).

3. See Vatican I, constitution *Pastor aeternus,* July 18, 1870: *Conciliorum Oecumenicorum Decreta,* ed. Josepho Alberigo et al. (Bologna: Istituto per le Scienze Religiose, 3rd ed. 1973), pp. 811–816.

4. That is, whether there are two subjects or one subject of power, depending on how one relates the pope and the college of bishops. See brief overview in James H. Provost. "The Hierarchical Constitution of the Church," in *The Code of Canon Law: A Text and Commentary,* ed. James A. Coriden et al. (New York/Mahwah, NJ: Paulist Press, 1985), pp. 263–264.

5. See George P. Klubertanz, *St. Thomas Aquinas on Analogy: A Textual Analysis and Systematic Synthesis* (Chicago: Loyola University Press, 1960) for a careful treatment of analogy; on the other hand, see the critique of Thomism's reliance on analogy by John S. Morreall, *Analogy and Talking about God: A Critique of the Thomistic Approach* (Washington: University Press of America, 1979).

6. In pre-Vatican II treatises on the church's constitutional law (*ius publicum ecclesiasticum*) the church was presented *as* a monarchy, not analogous to or similar to a monarchy. See Alaphredus Ottaviani, *Institutiones Iuris Publici Ecclesiastici* (Vatican City: Typis Polyglottis Vaticanis, 4th ed. 1958), 1: 347–357. More recently the applicability to the church of democratic concepts has been debated; for example, in favor of such an application in light of a sociological analysis of ecclesiastical power structures is Harry J.M. Hoefnagels, *Demokratisierung der kirchlichen Authorität* (Vienna: Herder, 1969), while opposed are Joseph Ratzinger and Hans Maier, *Demokratie in der Kirche: Möglichkeiten, Grenzen, Gefahren* (Limburg: Lahn-Verlag, 1970).

7. Michel Foucault observes, "Power exists only when it is put into action," so an analysis of power should look to "power relations and not power itself." See "Afterword: The Subject and Power," in *Michel Foucault: Beyond Structuralism and Hermeneutics,* by Hubert L. Dreyfus and Paul Rabinow, second edition with an afterword by and an interview with Michel Foucault (Chicago: University of Chicago Press, 1983), p. 219.

8. For a general overview see Stanley I. Benn, s.v. "Power," *The Encyclopedia of Philosophy* 6: 424–427. A critical overview of theories about power is provided by Stewart Clegg, *The Theory of Power and Organization* (London: Routledge and Kegan Paul, 1979). See also the collected articles of major theoreticians (including Russell, Weber, Arendt, Foucault, Galbraith, Simmel, etc.) in *Power,* ed. Steven Lukas (New York: New York University Press, 1986); studies of power in various

fields are presented in *Power in Organizations* (Nashville: Vanderbilt University Press, 1970). See also studies on power viewed from various specializations: Sik Hung Ng, *The Social Psychology of Power* (London: Academic Press, 1980); David W. Bell, *Power, Influence, and Authority: An Essay in Political Linguistics* (New York: Oxford University Press, 1975); Geoffrey Debnam, *The Analysis of Power: A Realist Approach* ["community power" debate] (London: Macmillan Press, 1984); Ingmar Pörn, *The Logic of Power* [symbolic logic analysis] (Oxford: Blackwell, 1970); Felix Hammer, *Macht: Wesen-Formen-Grenzen* [interrelationship of theology, philosophy and social sciences] (Königstein/Ts: Hanstein, 1979).

For an overview on leadership, see James MacGregor Burns, *Leadership* (New York: Harper & Row, 1978). Various views about leadership are studied in *Changing Conceptions of Leadership*, ed. Carl F. Graumann and Serge Moscovici (New York: Springer-Verlag, 1986). See also the insightful study by Robert K. Greenleaf, *Servant Leadership* (New York: Paulist Press, 1977).

9. See 1983 code, Book II, Part II, Section I: "Supreme Church Authority"; ibid., Section II, Title I: "Particular Churches and the Authority Established in Them."

10. This is a simplification of the more detailed analysis of power suggested by Foucault in "Afterword: The Subject and Power," pp. 222–224. However, such a complete analysis is beyond the possibilities of this limited paper.

11. On power, authority and leadership in the church generally, see the still fresh studies of the 1961 symposium, *Problems of Authority*, ed. John M. Todd (Baltimore: Helicon, 1962); the 1981 colloquium, *Authority in the Church*, ed. Piet F. Fransen (Leuven: Peeters, 1983); Gérard Defais et al., *Le pouvoir dans l'Eglise: Analyse institutionelle, historique et théologique de la pratique contemporaine* (Paris: Cerf, 1973); Christian Duquoc et al., *Autorité et liberté dans l'Eglise* (Paris: Epi Editeurs, 1971); *Power and the Word of God*, ed. Franz Böckle and Jacques-Marie Pohier, Concilium 90 (New York: Herder and Herder, 1973); *Power in the Church*, ed. James Provost and Knut Walf, Concilium 197 (Edinburgh: T. & T. Clark, 1988). On specifically papal power see J.M.R. Tillard, *The Bishop of Rome* (Wilmington, DE: Michael Glazier, 1983); Patrick Granfield, *The Limits of the Papacy: Authority and Autonomy in the Church* (New York: Crossroad, 1987).

12. See Michele Maccarrone, *Vicarius Christi: Storia del titolo papale* (Rome: Pontificia Universitas Lateranense, 1953).

13. See Urban Navarrete, "Potestas Vicaria Ecclesiae: Evolutio historica conceptus atque observationes attenta doctrina concilii Vaticani II," *Periodica* 60 (1971) 414–486; Reinhold Schwarz, "De potestate

propria Ecclesiae," *Periodica* 63 (1974) 429–455; idem, *Die eigenbe-rechtige Gewalt der Kirche,* Analecta Gregoriana 196 (Rome: Pontificia Universitas Gregoriana, 1974).

14. John Paul II describes these as primary in the church, which its structure is to promote and ensure; they would also seem to be, there-fore, the purpose for hierarchical service in the church. See John Paul II, apostolic constitution *Sacrae disciplinae leges,* January 29, 1983: *AAS* 75/2 (1983) xi.

15. See prefatory note of explanation to chapter 3 of *Lumen gentium,* n. 1. The parallel between Peter and the other apostles, and the supreme pontiff and the bishops, "does not imply any transmission of the extraor-dinary power of the apostles to their successors."

16. See explanatory note of explanation to chapter 3 of *Lumen gentium,* n. 1; Yves Congar, "Le problème ecclésiologique de la papauté après Vatican II," in *Ministères et communion ecclésiale* (Paris: Cerf, 1971), p. 181.

17. These are rich themes, much discussed today. See, for example, the two studies sponsored by the Canon Law Society of America, *The Church as Communion* and *The Church as Mission,* both edited by James H. Provost (Washington: CLSA, 1984).

18. Other issues might include the selection of bishops, operations of the Roman curia, finances in the church, oversight of diocesan opera-tions or the work of diocesan tribunals, and the religious witness of the diocese of Rome—an issue of significance even outside that diocese in light of the patristic emphasis on the importance of the *ecclesia* of the apostolic sees.

19. For an overview of the dilemmas, successes and failures of the liturgical reform in the United States see Mark Searle, "Reflections on Liturgical Reform," *Worship* 56 (1982) 411–430. See also the earlier reflections by George Devine, *Liturgical Renewal: An Agonizing Reap-praisal* (New York: Alba House, 1973). It should be noted that these studies are by persons favoring the liturgical renewal, not those who reject the renewal itself.

20. S. Congregation of Rites, instruction *Inter Oecumenici,* Septem-ber 25, 1964, n. 57; *Documents on the Liturgy 1963–1979* [*DOL*] (Col-legeville, MN: Liturgical Press, 1982), pp. 101–102.

21. Paul VI first permitted this experimentally in a concession dated January 31, 1967 (*DOL,* pp. 278–279); see also the letter of Cardinal Lecaro to presidents of episcopal conferences, "Dans sa récente allo-cution," June 21, 1967, n. 7: *DOL,* p. 146.

22. Paul VI, motu proprio *Sacram Liturgiam,* January 25, 1964: *AAS* 56 (1964) 139–144.

23. Paul VI, apostolic constitution *Sacra Rituum Congregatio,* May 8, 1969: *AAS* 61 (1969) 297–305.

24. Paul VI, apostolic constitution *Constans nobis,* July 11, 1975: *AAS* 67 (1975) 417–420. The new dicastery was termed the Sacred Congregation for Sacraments and Divine Worship.

25. For a detailed analysis of the shifts in policy over communion from the cup, see John M. Huels, "Communion Under Both Kinds on Sundays: Is It Legal?" *The Jurist* 42 (1982) 70–106.

26. Marcel Lefebvre was born in France in 1905, was ordained a priest of the Congregation of the Holy Ghost, and eventually became archbishop of Dakar, Senegal, Africa, in 1955. He resigned the see to become superior general of the Congregation of the Holy Ghost, and participated in the four sessions of Vatican II. His term as superior general concluded in 1968. He then began actively to oppose the reforms of the Second Vatican Council, especially in liturgical and ecumenical questions, and founded his own organization for priests, the Fraternité Sacerdotale Saint-Pie-X, with its own seminary in Econe, Switzerland. The fraternity was given canonical approval on November 1, 1970, but this was withdrawn on May 6, 1975 after Lefebvre's refusal to obey Pope Paul VI. Lefebvre was suspended for unauthorized ordinations to the priesthood in June 1977. After repeated efforts by Paul VI and John Paul II to effect a reconciliation, a special visitation was conducted on behalf of the Vatican by Cardinal Gagnon. See the review of the Holy See's actions in the statement released by the Vatican, "Breakdown of Negotiations with Archbishop Lefebvre," *Origins* 18/7 (June 30, 1988) 97, 99–101.

27. See list of documentary sources in *Canon Law Digest* 8: 936–937.

28. Congregation for Bishops, decree of July 1, 1988: *L'Osservatore Romano* [English edition], July 11, 1988, p. 1. See also John Paul II, apostolic letter *Ecclesia Dei,* July 2, 1988; ibid.

29. Letter from the secretary of the Sacred Congregation for Catholic Education, August 11, 1980, Prot. N. 589/80. The decision to do this was made by Pope John Paul II. However, for the reconciliation of priests ordained by Lefebvre who wish to return to full communion with the Catholic Church, each case must be referred to the apostolic see; see *Roman Replies and CLSA Advisory Opinions 1987* (Washington: CLSA, 1987), p. 36.

30. See c. 1248 §1, although c. 923 indicates that receiving communion at any celebration is governed by the norm of c. 844.

31. See "Breakdown of Negotiations with Archbishop Lefebvre," p. 99, for the contents of the May 5, 1988 protocol.

32. See John E. Lynch, "Marriage and Celibacy of the Clergy, the Discipline of the Western Church: An Historico-Canonical Synopsis,"

The Jurist 32 (1982) 14–38, 189–212; Roger Gryson, *Les origins du célibat ecclésiastique première au septième siècle* (Gembloux: J. Duculot, 1970); idem, "Dix ans de recherches sur les origins du célibat ecclésiastique," *Revue théologique de Louvain* 11 (1980) 157–185.

33. See history of this issue in Karl Heinz Kleber, *De parvitate materiae in sexto: ein Beitrag zur Geschichte der katholischen Moraltheologie* (Regensburg: Pustet, 1971). Clement VIII (1592–1605) and Paul V (1605–1621) are generally credited with imposing this position, but there are no documentary records of this; see also the response of the Holy Office, February 11, 1661 (DS 2013).

34. See remarks by John Paul II to the American bishops in Los Angeles, September 16, 1987: *Origins* 17/16 (October 1, 1987) 261.

35. See Paul VI, encyclical *Sacerdotalis coelibatus,* June 24, 1967: *AAS* 59 (1967) 657–697; idem, encyclical *Humanae vitae,* July 25, 1968: *AAS* 60 (1968) 481–503.

36. After analyzing various surveys and data bases, Andrew Greeley concluded that "*the birth control issue alone* seems to be the occasion for the substantial decline in religious behavior which has occurred among American Catholics since the early 1960s" (emphasis in original)— Andrew M. Greeley, *Crisis in the Church: A Study of Religion in America* (Chicago: Thomas More Press, 1979), p. 227.

37. See the reaction to John XXIII's encyclical, *Mater et Magistra* (May 16, 1961) by William Buckley in editorial comment, *National Review* 11/4 (July 29, 1961) 38, and his rejoinder to criticism in "The Strange Behavior of *America,*" *National Review* 11/8 (August 26, 1961) 114–115. The phrase "*Mater si, magistra no*" as expressing the views of conservatives was first reported in *National Review* 11/6 (August 12, 1961) 77.

38. The extent of selectivity is addressed by Terence E. Tanner, "Crisis of Credibility in the Church," *The Month* 242 (1981) 130–132. See also the impact on "core Catholics" in the United States as reported by James Castelli and Joseph Gremillion, *The Emerging Parish: The Notre Dame Study of Catholic Life Since Vatican II* (San Francisco: Harper & Row, 1987), p. 75. For a recent papal call to end this situation see John Paul II, address to the American bishops in Los Angeles, September 16, 1987: *Origins* 17/16 (October 1, 1987) 261.

39. See Joseph A. Komonchak, "*Humanae Vitae* and Its Reception," *Theological Studies* 39 (1978) 221–257; see various texts in *Pour relire Humanae Vitae,* with commentary by Philippe Delhaye, Jan Grootaers and Gustave Thils (Gembloux: J. Duculot, 1970); a survey of responses by bishops and their conferences, and by theologians and others, is provided by William H. Shannon, *The Lively Debate: Response to Humanae Vitae* (New York: Sheed & Ward, 1979).

40. See Dean R. Hoge et al., *Research in Men's Vocations to the Priesthood and the Religious Life* (Washington: USCC, 1984), p. 67.

41. See Richard A. Schoenherr and Annemette Sorensen, "Social Change in Religious Organizations: Consequences of Clergy Decline in the U.S. Catholic Church," *Sociological Analysis* 43 (Spring 1982) 23–52; Dean R. Hoge, *The Future of Catholic Leadership: Responses to the Priest Shortage* (Kansas City, MO: Sheed & Ward, 1987), pp. 3–36.

42. See Hoge, *Research in Men's Vocations*, pp. 59–61.

43. See statements by Archbishop Quinn, August 20, 1980: *Origins* 10/12 (September 4, 1980) 178; formal approval by the Congregation for the Doctrine of the Faith, March 31, 1981: *Origins* 10/43 (April 9, 1981) 674; progress report by then-Bishop Law, January 12, 1982: *Origins* 11/33 (January 28, 1982) 517, 519.

44. See, for example, the general distrust of modern behavioral sciences in reactions to such disparate issues in the United States as first penance, and the judgments of marriage tribunals. On the former, see S. Congregations for Sacraments and Divine Worship and for the Clergy, letter *In quibusdam Ecclesiae partibus*, March 31, 1977: *DOL*, p. 989. On the latter, see the remarks by the Secretary of the Apostolic Signatura, Zenon Grocholewski, "The Ecclesiastical Judge and the Findings of Psychiatric and Psychological Experts," *The Jurist* 47 (1977) 449–470.

45. See, for example, the letter of Cardinal Ratzinger to Charles Curran in *Origins* 16/11 (August 28, 1986) 201, 203.

46. See the analysis by Bernard Lonergan, "The Transition from a Classicist World-View to Historical Mindedness," in *A Second Collection* (Philadelphia: Westminster Press, 1974), pp. 1–10.

47. One case which has become public involves Professor Charles Curran of The Catholic University of America; for a discussion of underlying issues in this case, from a variety of points of view, see *Vatican Authority and American Catholic Dissent: The Curran Case and Its Consequences,* ed. William W. May (New York: Crossroad, 1987).

48. See the various documents issued by the Congregation for the Doctrine of the Faith, such as "Declaration Regarding the Safeguarding of Faith in the Mysteries of the Incarnation and of the Most Blessed Trinity from Some Recent Errors," February 21, 1972: *Origins* 1/40 (March 23, 1972) 665, 667–668; "Instruction on Certain Aspects of the 'Theology of Liberation,' " August 6, 1984: *Origins* 14/13 (September 13, 1984); "Instruction on Christian Freedom and Liberation," March 22, 1986: *Origins* 15/44 (April 17, 1986) 713, 715–728; "Declaration on Certain Questions Concerning Sexual Ethics," December 29, 1975: *Origins* 5/31 (January 22, 1976) 485, 487–494; "Instruction on Respect for

Human Life in Its Origins and on the Dignity of Procreation," February 22, 1987: *Origins* 16/40 (March 19, 1987) 697, 699–711.

49. See Richard A. McCormick, "The Search for Truth in the Catholic Context," *America* 155 (November 8, 1986) 276–281.

50. The norms followed in examining questions of doctrine have been published; see Congregation for the Doctrine of the Faith, "Nova agendi ratio in doctrinarum examine," January 15, 1971: *CLD* 7: 181–184. See also *The Right To Dissent,* ed. Hans Küng and Jürgen Moltmann, Concilium 158 (New York: Seabury, 1982), especially pp. 3–18, 95–107.

51. See the studies in *Authority in the Church,* ed. Piet F. Fransen.

52. See Joseph Gremillion, ed., *The Gospel of Peace and Justice: Catholic Social Teaching Since Pope John* (Maryknoll: Orbis, 1976) for more recent statements.

53. The current organization of the papal diplomatic corps is found in Paul VI, motu proprio *Sollicitudo omnium Ecclesiarum,* June 24, 1969: *CLD* 7: 277–284. For a discussion of recent experiences see the various articles on pp. 56–88 in *The Roman Curia and the Communion of Churches,* ed. Peter Huizing and Knut Walf, Concilium 127 (New York: Seabury, 1979).

54. However, see National Association of Church Personnel Administrators, *Just Treatment for Those Who Work for the Church* (Cincinnati, OH: NACPA, 1986); Canon Law Society of America, *Canonical Standards in Labor-Management Relations: A Report* (Washington: CLSA, 1987).

55. See the critique of the 1988 encyclical of John Paul II on social matters in Tom Bethell, "Mea Maxima Culpa?" *National Review* 40/7 (April 15, 1988) 34–36.

56. See discussion in Jésus Hortal, "Relationships Among Episcopates," *The Jurist* 48 (1988).

57. See discussion, for example, in Henry Mintzberg, *Power in and around Organizations* (Englewood Cliffs, NJ: Prentice-Hall, 1983).

58. See Peter Drucker, *Management: Tasks, Responsibilities, Practices* (New York: Harper & Row, 1974), pp. 494–505.

59. The significance of "movements" within the church was highlighted at the 1987 synod of bishops on the laity; cf. "The Synod Propositions," nn. 14–17: *Origins* 17/29 (December 31, 1987) 503–504.

60. See the report developed by the Vatican Secretariats for Promoting Christian Unity, for Non-Christians, and for Non-Believers, and the Pontifical Council for Culture, "On Sects, Cults and New Religious Movements," *Origins* 16/1 (May 22, 1986) 1, 3–10.

61. See John K. Hempbill, *Situational Factors in Leadership* (Columbus, OH: Ohio State University, 1949).

Contributors

BRIAN TIERNEY is one of the world's foremost historians about the late middle ages. His studies of the Council of Constance and of the origins of the notion of infallibility have had a major impact on contemporary ecclesiology. Tierney is presently professor of history at Cornell University.

JAMES PROVOST, a priest of the Helena, Montana diocese, is a professor of canon law at Catholic University, Washington, D.C. For the past two decades he has been a moving spirit in the Canon Law Society as director of its permanent seminar. The sessions of that seminar have produced several volumes of ecclesiology in the spirit of Vatican II.

FRED MCMANUS, a priest of the Boston archdiocese, is professor of canon law at Catholic University, Washington, D.C. Monsignor McManus has been one of the pioneers of the liturgical renewal in the United States as well as a leading figure in the field of canon law and editor of *The Jurist*.

AGNES CUNNINGHAM, S.S.C.M. at present is professor of patristics at St. Mary of the Lake Seminary, Mundelein, Illinois. She did her M.A. in theology at Marquette University and obtained her doctorate in Lyons in France. For several years she was secretary of the Catholic Theological Society and in 1977 became the first woman president of that group.

GERALD FOGARTY, S.J. is a leading historian of the U.S. church whose *The Vatican and the Americanist Crisis* established him as an authority on the history of Vatican/U.S. Catholic relationships. He is now professor of theology and church history in the department of religious studies at the University of Virginia.

WILLIAM PORTIER is professor of church history at Mount St. Mary's College in Emmitsburg, Maryland. He has been one of the leaders in the College Theology Society, serving as its vice-president in 1986–88.

JAMES HENNESEY, S.J. is recognized as an authority on the origins of the U.S. Catholic Church as well as of Vatican I. He has taught church history at Fordham University and Boston College before his present position as professor of history at Canisius College in Buffalo.

JAMES HEFT, S.M. is professor of systematic theology and head of the department of religious studies at the University of Dayton. His area of special expertise has been the theology of ecclesiastical authority, with a particular focus on the history and nature of papal infallibility.

MARVIN O'CONNELL, a priest of the St. Paul diocese, is at present professor of American church history at the University of Notre Dame. In addition to his research on the counter-reformation and the Oxford movement he has had a special professional and personal interest in the great U.S. churchman, Archbishop John Ireland.